109-12

D1625325

The Psychology
of Religion

Joseph F. Byrnes

THE FREE PRESS
A Division of Macmillan, Inc.
NEW YORK

Collier Macmillan Publishers
LONDON

*To my mother
and the beloved memory
of my father*

Copyright © 1984 by The Free Press
A Division of Macmillan, Inc.

All rights reserved. No part of this book may be reproduced or transmitted
in any form or by any means, electronic or mechanical, including
photocopying, recording, or by any information storage and retrieval
system, without permission in writing from the Publisher.

The Free Press
A Division of Macmillan, Inc.
866 Third Avenue, New York, N. Y. 10022

Collier Macmillan Canada, Inc.

Printed in the United States of America

printing number

1 2 3 4 5 6 7 8 9 10

Library of Congress Cataloging in Publication Data

Byrnes, Joseph F.
  The psychology of religion.

  Bibliography: p.
  1. Psychology, Religious.   2. Experience (Religion)
3. Religion and sociology.   I. Title.
BL53.B97   1984   200'.1'9   84-47854
ISBN 0-02-903580-5

Credits

We wish to thank those publishers and individuals whose textual or illustrative materials have been reproduced herein. All sources have been cited in this volume. The following credits refer to certain specified excerpts from:

The Child's Conception of the World, by Jean Piaget. Used by permission of Routledge & Kegan Paul, and by Humanities Press Inc.

The Moral Judgment of the Child, by Jean Piaget. Used by permission of Routledge & Kegan Paul, and by The Free Press.

Stages of Faith: The Psychology of Human Development and the Quest for Meaning, by James W. Fowler, copyright © 1981 by James W. Fowler. Reprinted by permission of Harper & Row, Publishers, Inc.

The Confessions of St. Augustine, translated by Rex Warner, copyright © 1963 by Rex Warner. Reprinted by arrangement with New American Library, New York, NY.

Responses to Religion: Studies in the Social Psychology of Religious Belief, by Gary Maranell, copyright © 1974 by University Press of Kansas. Used by permission.

Journal for the Scientific Study of Religion (Princeton Theological Seminary). Used by permission of the publisher.

"Personal Religious Orientation and Prejudice," in *Journal of Personality and Social Psychology* 5 (1967): 430–43, by Gordon W. Allport and J. Michael Ross, copyright © 1967 by the American Psychological Association. Used by permission.

Contents

Preface

LIFE, our personalities, and our minds are as complex as the universe of the astronomers. Any single theory or line of research in psychology, in fact any single interpretation of human life or individual lives, offers a very limited understanding of the world. Yet whenever we take all perspectives of psychology together, we find a much less limited—and more genuinely satisfying—view. In this book I offer a full range of psychological interpretations of that rich, complex, and—for many people—vital area of human life, religion. I want to present the sweep and the grandeur of the psychological insights on religion from the end of the nineteenth century up to the research of the past few years. The book is both a history and a beginning synthesis presenting the accomplishments, the possibilities, and the limitations of psychology of religion. I have emphasized the origins of contemporary psychological interpretations of religion, dividing theories and research into their proper traditions. The primary principle of organization of the book, then, is psychological: The chapters are organized according to psychological themes. A secondary principle of organization is chronological: Within chapters I generally present viewpoints and interpretations as they have developed across the years. The book aptly could be subtitled "The Development of Modern Psychological Perspectives on Religion."

The Psychology of Religion is designed in general as a readable overview for anyone interested in the topic, and in particular as a textbook for colleges, universities, and seminaries. As a textbook, it provides a full introduction, but it can serve as well as a basic reference in those classes where professors choose to concentrate on one area of psychology or on selected classics or on particular lines of research—and so wish to send students to a basic manual for general background. My presentation is to all appearances eclectic, because I have not favored one personality theory over all the others, nor absolutized any research tradition, nor treated psychology of religion as a unified field in which there has been a cumulative growth of knowledge. I have approached psychological interpretations of religion as a historian who wishes to trace the development of ideas, and as a philosopher who is interested in the nature of the concepts and explanations offered.

The sections of this book cover the history of psychology and religious studies as disciplines and the development of a vocabulary in psychology of religion, theories of personality, schemata of cognitive and emotional development, social psychology, reports and evaluations of correlations and experiments, and approaches to therapy.

Part I shows how modern psychology and the historical/philosophical study of religion began and developed; it examines the early work of American psychologists—William James in particular—who analyzed religion for their own purposes with their own vocabulary. Old and new descriptions of ordinary and extraordinary states of religious consciousness are given.

Part II is a thorough examination of analytic, humanistic, and existential psychologies. The psychological meaning of belief and morality as explained by Sigmund Freud and Carl Jung, Gordon Allport, Abraham Maslow, and Rollo May is presented with quotes, anecdotes, and analyses from primary and secondary sources.

Part III relates the work of developmental and social psychologists to the information provided in the previous section. Children's emotional and cognitive development as established by the interviews and analyses of Erik Erikson and Jean Piaget is presented with the religion-oriented work of James Fowler—on faith stages, and of Lawrence Kohlberg—on moral development. The areas of social psychology that both complement developmental theory and have special application to religion are discussed: consistency theory, social interaction and small group theory, and attitude studies.

Part IV sorts out religious research and approaches to therapy, and again coordinates this information with previous chapters. Accordingly, research that derives from the hypotheses of Freud, Allport, and selected developmental and social psychologists is summarized as part of a report on the accomplishments of contemporary empirical psychology. Emphasis is on the development of traditions of research on God-image projections, conversion, integration of personality, prejudice, cognitive and emotional moral development, and the content of religious attitudes. This section also contains summaries of modern therapies and their applicability to religious problems, with clear illustrations from case histories. Means of classifying the therapies according to social components and context, and a history of the use of therapies in specifically religious situations are given.

In Part V, the conclusion, all preceding material is summarized and applied to the classic Western religious experience already previewed in the first chapter, the conversion of St. Augustine of Hippo. The full range of vocabulary and theories is used to interpret and order data about the personality and conversion experience of Augustine. The values and limitations of general vocabulary and theories for comprehending individual religious experiences are examined, and, to conclude, consideration is given to the built-in limitations of all research and researchers.

Of course, I have made some practical decisions indirectly connected with my historical and philosophical orientations. For example, I have put the discussion of attribution theory in the William James chapter instead of in the social psychology chapter, and the discussion of consistency theory in the social psychology chapter instead of the personality theory chapter. I have taken some liberties with texts discussed, expanding some of James's ideas in *The Varieties of Religious Experience* and paraphrasing research reports. In my discussion of research I have restricted myself to material published in the last fifteen years. When necessary, reasons for these and similar decisions are given in the appropriate chapters.

Ideally, the study of psychology of religion should be an organized presentation of a number of psycholog*ies* of a number of religion*s*. We should have a knowledge of the principle modern European-American psychologies, and of the varieties of beliefs and behaviors found in the lives of Jews, Christians, Muslims, Hindus, and Buddhists. We are, however, limited by the work done thus far in the study of psychology and religion. European and American psychologists most often take "religion" to be the Judeo–Christian tradition, and most of the work so far has been done by psychologists who have not sorted out the variations in religious experience that result from membership in different world religions. Also, there is disagreement among psychologists about the meaning and value of the Judeo–Christian tradition. In this study we examine the roles assumed for Western Christian religious experiences in the basic modern Western psychologies. Where it is appropriate we remind readers of the limitations imposed by a Judeo–Christian focus and Western psychological perspectives: We cannot assume that our information applies equally to other world religions.

What I present here, when all is said and done, is my own way of understanding the role of religion in the lives of human beings. But I wish to acknowledge all those who have influenced and helped me in the formation of this book. Colleagues and mentors who read and commented upon individual chapters—those included and those now excluded—as the book went through various stages of development must be thanked first of all: for help with the psychological materials—Don Capps, Donald Fiske, Peter Homans, Don Browning, Bernard Spilka, Gary Alexander, William Rambo, Vicky Green, and Durhane Wong-Rieger; for help with materials in history of religions—Wendy Doniger O'Flaherty, Kenneth Dollarhide, Fazlur Rahman, and Bernard McGinn. I am further grateful for extended conversions with Stephen Toulmin, Salvatore Maddi, James Gustafson, Martin Marty, Jerald Brauer, Jonathan Z. Smith, Joseph Kitagawa, and Frank Reynolds during a recent semester of research at my alma mater, the University of Chicago.

While a research fellow at the University of Texas Medical

Branch I benefited from the advice of Chester Burns, Harold Vanderpool, Harold Levine, Edmund Erde, and Rose Yunker. This study was in part supported by two fellowships. I wish to thank the Hogg Foundation of Austin, Texas for a four-month grant that enabled me to spend the summers of 1980–81 at the Institute for the Medical Humanities, University of Texas Medical Branch, Galveston.

I am grateful to the Divinity School of the University of Chicago for receiving me as a Research Fellow at the Institute for the Advanced Study of Religion for the academic year 1981–82. The Dean's Office, School of Arts and Sciences, Oklahoma State University, provided typing services. My wife, Susan McCarthy, a literary critic possessing intelligence, love of beauty, and a rich humanity, gave me many helpful suggestions for clarifying my presentation and making it more attractive. I am also indebted to Ron Chambers, formerly of Free Press, for first encouraging me to expand my goals for this book. To Free Press editors George Rowland and Kitty Moore go my thanks for helping me realize these goals.

Finally, this book is dedicated with special gratitude to my parents, Cecelia Phelan Byrnes and Joseph F. Byrnes, who so cherished me that I never doubted the value of life nor my ability to properly communicate this value to others.

PART I

The Psychological Study of the Religious Experience

Whatever our religious beliefs, and whatever our personalities, a full effort to understand and explain religious experiences must involve the study of both religion and the human personality. The best way to study religious experiences and the effects they have upon the personality is to learn as much as one can about the history of religious beliefs and practices—religious studies—and to learn as much as one can about the psychological components of the personality—psychology. Religious experience depends upon the way people see their gods and their founder figures. It depends upon what people feel their behavior should be, the world of thoughts and images they grow up with, and the society that surrounds them. All these factors are dealt with in religious studies. Furthermore, religious experience depends upon the shape and elements of their own personalities, in other words, their individual psychologies. Formal research into the meaning of human life, as well as everyday self-understanding, is the province of the modern European and American science of psychology. To understand the role of religion in the personality, we almost automatically use psychological categories.

Chapter 1 examines the main lines of the development of modern psychology and religious studies as fields of study and research. Emphasis is on the psychologists' interests in the religious experience across the decades. The phenomenon of religious conversion is presented as a basic example of how psychology, informed by religious studies, can be used to interpret the religious experience. St. Augustine's conversion is examined from the psychological perspectives that are to be presented in later chapters. Chapter 2 presents a basic vocabulary, psychological descriptions, and psychological explanations of the religious experience, as developed by William James and a number of other past and present psychologists. They have discussed ordinary and extraordinary religious experiences without relying on personality theory as a context for the discussion.

General Psychology
and the
Psychology of Religion

the person is the medium of

the exper (b)

"THERE ARE AS MANY VARIETIES of religious experience as there are religiously inclined mortals upon the earth" (Allport, 1950, p. 50). The psychologist who said this, Gordon Allport, was not discounting the value of a systematic psychology of religious experiences, but he was aware of the challenges to psychologists who study religion. In psychology of religion there is no set arrangement of subject matter and methods such as one finds in each of the broad divisions of academic psychology (e.g. social psychology). In this field, there is no focus on a single activity, such as one finds in medical psychology, the psychology of organization, or psychobiology. Even if there were one psychological way of understanding religion there would still be the problem of the large number of different religions to comprehend. Although we use the word "religion" to cover them all, Judaism, Christianity, Islam, Hinduism, Buddhism, and tribal religions are quite different from one another, sometimes radically different. And if we are studying these religions, we need different approaches and techniques to begin to understand them.

Look at the varieties of basic religious experiences that are possible even when we generalize about the experiences of members of different world religions. For example, in all probability, a Jew, a Christian, and a Muslim will view God as One, all-powerful, who totally determines the wellbeing of the individual. But at the same time they will realize that no adequate mental image of such a God can be formed. To be sure, there are the varying notions of Moses as mediator of the covenant relationship between God and man, Jesus as Divine Savior, or Muhammad as the greatest of the prophets. Monotheists— Jews, Christians, Muslims—believe that they are created by God and destined to be fulfilled in him. They will be reared in such a way as to achieve some form of self-perfection according to the Divine plan, or at least feel guilty about not trying. Christians and Muslims especially have the expectation of a final reward or punishment to be granted after a once-only passing through the human-life stage of existence, a time in which one's actions will completely determine the state of the individual soul afterward. Hindus worship Shiva, Vishnu (often in the form of the appealing young hero, Krishna), or other, minor gods and goddesses. They will see themselves as indestructible souls going through a series of reincarnations and will be reared and guided in such a way as to preserve and develop their images and thoughts toward four ends in life: moral goodness, prosperity, pleasure, and liberation. They will be surrounded by an elaborate social system of castes that fixes them on a very constricted level of society all their lives.

Other religions do not have the same conception of divine personality. Buddhists, for example, see the Buddha as a teacher who had the supreme insight to show people the way to liberation from suffering. They will be reared in a conceptual world that is the result of centuries of guided meditation developed for the achievement of enlightenment. Finally, they will live in a society where pursuit of individuality is most often considered counterproductive. Some African tribes see their gods as creators of the universe who are now quite remote from it, while other gods are seen to be involved with human fortunes in love, work, and warfare. For these tribes the human personality is really the universe of gods and spirits in miniature, for within the personality the destiny of individuals is determined by the relationship of their thinking patterns to the power of their ancestors.

Instead of referring to different psycholog*ies* or religion*s,* we might better speak of "types of psychology" and "types of religion." Psychology has developed as a distinct discipline without insisting that any one approach to psychology is *the* psychology. Nor does it hold that some common denominator of cognitive–emotional experience is religion. So psychology of religion can be a study of different psychological approaches to different religions and the infinite variety of experiences possible within any given religion, though in practice it has not been that extensive. As fields of study psychology and religious studies have their own histories. Obviously they have made significant advances separately from each other. We examine the present state and earlier development of psychology and religious studies in order to clarify what was accomplished on those occasions when psychology and religion were studied together. Emphasis, of course, is on the psychological perspectives.

Here a basic example of the results attainable by bringing together religious studies and psychological analysis will be the conversion of St. Augustine. Conversion has been a basic interest, perhaps even the basic concern, of psychologists across the decades. St. Augustine's conversion in particular has been often referred to—sometimes intensely studied—in the psychology of religion literature.

The Contribution of Psychology to the Study of Religion

The chapters of an introductory psychology textbook appear to follow a logical sequence, starting with the anatomy of the brain, moving through philosophy and zoology, and finishing with appendixes on ink-blot tests and statistics. But it is all too neat: Today's psychology is a wide-ranging and widely varying assortment of interests and activities. Important areas of study and research in psychology have developed in our century, but the concerns involve quite different areas of expertise, everything from testing animal reflexes to coordinating quite abstract views.

Look at the general areas in psychology: biological foundations (brain and nervous system), perception, learning and memory, cognitive processes, consciousness, personality, social psychology, psychopathology, and therapy. In some areas religion is studied directly, and in others indirectly. For example, personality theory has been the concern not only of modern psychologists but of philosophers and historians of religion as well. Since there is no generally accepted definition of personality (Maddi, 1972), psychologists' theorizing about personality is based on assumptions about the totality of a person's qualities and attributes: the way one "generally is," one's general behavior patterns, role in life, or outward appearance. The role assumed for religion in the personality is based on assumptions about the personality in general. Hypotheses about personality and the religion within it may be modified and discarded, but original assumptions are necessary to begin asking questions, examining, and testing. For example, psychologists may ask: How do personality qualities develop? Does the existence of the quality predict anything about the likelihood that the person will have other qualities? What role do other people play in the development of an individual's personality? When and why do different persons behave similarly and some individuals behave inconsistently? How do genetic and physiological factors influence personality? Questions about religious thoughts and feelings are posed as part of these broader questions.

Theories of personality are devised to explain the commonalities among people and to identify and classify the differences among them. At issue is behavior that shows continuity in time and not so much isolated moments of activity. Developmental psychology deals primarily with the formation of the child's personality and serves as a support for the psychologist interested in the adult personality. Social psychology deals with the influence of various *others*, individuals or groups, upon the adult personality. In turn, both the developmental and social psychologists often base their theories or center their research upon motivation and emotion, cognitive processes, or learning and memory. Personality studies need the support of developmental and social psychology theory and research, and vice versa. Personality study itself is often centered upon motivation and emotion, cognitive processes, memory, and learning. These areas of psychology are not only interrelated but related to religious studies as well. The usefulness of each area of psychology for the interpretation of the religious experience is examined in the following chapters.

The direct ancestor of today's psychology is the scientific psychology that begins with Wilhelm Wundt (1832–1920). Wundt is considered the first experimental psychologist and the man who established that discipline as a scientific pursuit in its own right (Boring, 1950). He established the first laboratory specially designed and equipped to study psychological problems and trained the first generation of students for the Leipzig doctorate in psychology. His work falls into two main categories: systematic thinking about scope and methods, and experimental research (Thomson, 1968).

In his systematic psychology Wundt sought to clarify the scope, methods, and basic principles of the scientific study of the human person. He said that the subject matter of psychology was immediate experience, and the elements out of which experience is built were sensations. We can examine our bodies physiologically to understand how we come to have particular sensations, but the description and analysis of immediate experience are the task of psychology. Sensations may be classified according to the senses through which they are experienced, their duration, and their specificity. Images in the mind are derived from sensations and are the result of similar brain cell activity. Feelings, however, are not derived from sensations. They are, rather, combinations of sensations that have what Wundt called a "feeling-tone." He classified feelings in these categories: pleasant–unpleasant; tense–relaxed; excited–depressed. Emotions are sequences of feelings. Acts of the will begin as sequences of feelings with identical contents, but connect with reflexes in such a way as to produce adaptive actions.

Wundt went on to synthesize these elements in a process he called "apperception." In this process certain elements are focused and made dominant in consciousness. Apperception involves a creative synthesis; it organizes elementary experiences into a whole with new properties, just as two chemicals combine to form a third substance that possess new properties (Peters, 1965).

Wundt was trying to discover the nature of the mind's activities by analyzing the elements and structures of human consciousness. His system is more a set of classifications than a system of functional relations between elements classified or the structures described. Of Wundt's principal study, *Physiologiche Psychologie,* E. G. Boring, historian of experimental psychology, writes: "Wundt's lectures on physiological psychology, begun in 1867, were to become a book, the most important book in the history of modern psychology. . . . Wundt did not write another, more mature system of psychology: he modified, improved, and expanded the original. It was called a 'physiological psychology,' and it was his great argument for an experimental psychology" (Boring, 1950, p. 322).

In the laboratory that he established, Wundt and his students applied techniques from physiology and psychophysics to concepts and definitions from philosophy and physiological research. The research could be classified under four headings: vision and hearing experiments (color discrimination and tonal fusion), reaction experiments (varieties of responses and stimuli under different conditions), psychophysical experiences (comparison of stimuli in terms of feelings aroused), and association experiments (e.g. word association).

Because of the work of Wundt and others of his period, we see the importance of classifying data or at least establishing functional categories in psychology. We see the importance of working with these categories in a laboratory situation the better to understand the components of human mental activity: the structures of the mind and the behavior that results from these structures. In later chapters we shall deal with the development, by William James and others, of simple psychological categories of religion—a vocabulary if you will—and ways of doing research, laboratory and "field research," on psychological data.

Long before Wundt there were attempts to study and control mental illness, and from that work, the study of psychopathology, came more full-blown theories of the human mind and personality. Needless to say, the most important figure here was Sigmund Freud (1856–1939). As a result of his dealings with patients and his own self-analysis, Freud developed the theory and method of psychoanalysis. He arrived at the notion that unconscious wishes and present personality problems have their origins in infantile experiences. When certain situations in childhood are not properly resolved, the mechanisms of adult mental problems can be set in motion.

Freud described the elements of the mind in two ways (Jones, 1961; Ellenberger, 1970). For some years he spoke of the elements of the mind as conscious, preconscious, and unconscious, taking the most interest in the unconscious, the region where the locked-up thoughts and feelings of the past build up their dynamism. According to Freud, ideas that are not operative at a given moment exist on the level of the preconscious; conscious ideas are, of course, active at a given moment. Since Freud was so much interested in the dynamism of the unconscious, he constructed a more subtle description of the mind, speaking of the id, ego, and superego. Id was the basic reservoir of mental energy; ego, a controlling mechanism, similar to what we in everyday language call "reason"; and superego, the commands and ideas put in minds by parents and teachers.

Along these same lines the important disciples of Freud, Alfred Adler and Carl Jung, both of whom later broke with him, developed theories that described the inner workings of the mind in terms of mechanisms and images.

During the later part of the nineteenth century, the science of psychology was developing into a new discipline and breaking away from philosophy and medicine (Thomson, 1968). Although the physiological psychology of Wundt was clearly the most important, the British had begun the study of animal behavior—which led to a theory of behaviorism. Work had begun in child and developmental psychology, and Freud's psychoanalytic movement had just started. By 1910 there were considerable disagreements between groups derived from Wundt, those who emphasized structure and those who emphasized function. Freud's views had been formulated and published and had aroused controversy, not merely between him and Adler but between supporters of psychoanalysis and its critics, who opposed the unmitigated emphasis on sexuality.

Between the two world wars it became apparent that there would be no victory for any of the rival schools and philosophies contending for predominance. By 1940 it was fairly clear that the goal of making psychology *the* science of human nature was unattainable. Psychology could only be one of a number of studies dealing with human behavior, its motives and causes. Philosophy, history, law, economics, social science, and physical science all played a part. By 1950 the Oxford philosopher Gilbert Ryle was describing psychology as a "partly fortuitous federation of inquiries and techniques" (Ryle, 1949, p. 323). This led some psychologists to base their work on a general philosophy of human existence derived from the German thinkers Jaspers and Heidegger, and it led others to develop an optimistic view of human nature into a psychology and a style of counseling that simply encouraged the unfolding of an optimistically viewed human potential. Later chapters will discuss many of these efforts to deal with the inner workings of the mind and the dynamics of the personality, because they are full-fledged efforts to describe the meaning of human life and the role of religion in people's lives.

Most of these psychologists, in choosing their terminology and fashioning their theories, drew on religious data or reflected on their meaning. They almost always focused on one element or activity within the range of religious beliefs and behaviors and called that one element "religion." Fortunately, a wide variety of religious beliefs and behaviors have been focused upon, and by reviewing the approaches of a number of psychologists from the beginning of the present century, we can develop our own general perspective.

The Development of Religious Studies

Psychologists in the past have not often had occasion to encounter or make inquiry into religious experiences that differ sharply from the modern European or American types (Taylor, 1978). More recently, a number of psychologists have studied the work done in specifically religious studies (Murphy and Murphy, 1968)—appropriately so, if the words of the historian of religions Wilfred Cantwell Smith are to be believed: "The study of religion is the study of persons" (Smith, 1959, p. 54). The terms "history of religions," "comparative religion," and "phenomenology of religion," suggest different things about the study of the subject. To some they suggest a tour of the world religions, a description of events and experiences and an explanation of texts. To others these terms suggest a search for an essence of religion that underlies various individual religions, hence a philosophical analysis. Some think of a historical discipline wherein one studies important people and events in the history of other religions in the manner of Christian church history. A term that does not seem to favor any given approach and is more often used as a label for the proper departments in American universities is "religious studies." In any case religious studies develops out of a discussion among members of and students of the great world religions.

In nineteenth-century Germany the word *Religionsgewis-senschaft,* best translated as "general science of religion," came into use. An important translator of Eastern religion texts, Max Müller (1823–1900), first used the term in 1867. He argued that truth could be found in religion as a universal essence and not in particular manifestations of religion. He hoped that he could arrive at the essence of religion scientifically by studying the development of languages. To indicate that this supposedly scientific study was not under the control of theology or the philosophy of religion, he called his enterprise "general science of religion" (Kitagawa, 1959, p. 16). At its beginnings, then, the study of religion was rationalistic. Its exponents believed that a notion of deity, and hence of the general meaning of religion, could be arrived at by reason, and they rejected the authority of revelation.

A variety of supposedly impartial viewpoints came into prominence in the years following the work of Müller. Specific religious manifestations were considered to be symbols of primordial revelation; later, historians of religion had definite philosophical assumptions about religion and science. One of the more influential historians of religion in our century, Joachim Wach, promoted the view that studies of religion should be carried out not "philosophically" or "scientifically" but "religio-scientifically," that is to say, with methods that recognize the uniqueness of religion (Kitagawa, 1959, p. 18). Because religion is not a datum of philosophy or science, its varieties must be the data of a field of study uniquely designed to interpret and explain them. This field of study, whatever it is called (history of religions, comparative religion, phenomenology of religion, general science of religion, or religious studies), would have to gather a variety of other approaches—philosophy, history, sociology, psychology—into a unique set of data and range of methods.

Methodology is still being debated, as it has been from the outset, but there have been extensive efforts to assimilate, organize, and analyze facts about religions. One important attempt was the thirteen-volume *Encyclopedia of Religion and Ethics,* published from 1908 through 1921. The great American universities had courses, subsections of departments, or even departments of comparative religion by the end of the nineteenth century, and throughout our own century many Christian theology courses have dealt with philosophical religion or the other world religions without making unfavorable comparisons, which is to say that these religions have been dealt with on their own terms for the most part.

Today both historians of religion and social scientists generally describe five or six dimensions of religion (Glock and Stark, 1965; Smart, 1976). In one widely used introductory textbook of world religions, the author deals separately with the dimensions of ritual (gestures and words of worship), myth (the basic stories), doctrine (philosophical interpretations of the basic stories), ethics (required behavior), society (relation to surrounding culture and society), and experience (effect upon the personality of the individual). In dealing with real-life religion the dimensions cannot be isolated from one another, so when we are studying the experimental dimension, looking at the psychological components of belief and behavior, we must take seriously into consideration the myths and ethics that shape people's lives. When we study religious experience, we are studying beliefs (images and ideas that are part of the mythic and doctrinal dimensions of religion) and behavior motivation (ethical norms and ritual/social experiences). In other words, we are studying all the dimensions of religion insofar as they affect the final, experiential, dimension. Then, this final experience is explained in psychological terms.

Integrating Psychology and Religious Studies

At the turn of the century a number of American psychologists were carrying on the work begun by Wilhelm Wundt, attempting to classify data rather than create a system. Those scholars and researchers were developing a vocabulary to describe the individual aspects of the personality and, accordingly, of elements of the religious experience. William James, whose *The Varieties of Religious Experience* has continued to be the classic work in the psychology of religion, called religion "the feelings, acts, and experiences of individual men in their solitude, so far as they apprehend themselves to stand in relation to whatever they may consider the divine" (1979, p. 42).

The descriptions and explanations of religion found in *Varieties* and in other works of the period were the first important attempts to present a psychology of religion. About the same time, G. S. Hall and his pupils, James H. Leuba and Edwin D. Starbuck, as well as Edward S. Ames and George A. Coe, tried to explain the psychological features of the religious experience. Robert Thouless and, much later, Paul Pruyser made significant contributions in maintaining a tradition of categorization. A contemporary social psychologist sums up the psychology of religion interests of this period:

> The pioneers of the empirical–experimental approach to human behavior saw religion as a subject fit to study, and eagerly wanted to prove that even this area of study can be studied "scientifically." Great advances were being made in the sociology of religion and in anthropology. Studies of primitive religion by Frazer and Tyler aroused much interest and theorizing. Given this background, the pioneers in the movement felt that the time was right for a positivistic approach to religion in psychology. Another important factor was the basic positive attitude to religion. . . . Together with faith in the scientific spirit, there was also a profound respect for religion as a human and social enterprise. [Beit-Hallahmi, 1977, p. 20]

G. S. Hall had more influence than James on the American academic scene in the early decades of this century, mostly through his encouragement of empirical studies. As the founder of the Clark University school of religious psychology, Hall was the guiding influence in this area. Early in the 1880s he began lecturing and writing on the "moral and religious training of children and adolescents" as part of his general interest in developmental problems. The publication of his article on that subject in 1883 marked the beginning of the new movement. His students, Starbuck and Leuba, published their studies before James's *Varieties* appeared.

Edwin Starbuck published the first systematic work in the field, entitled *The Psychology of Religion*, in 1899. Although there was opposition to the types of questions he posed on religious experiences, he did much to popularize the questionnaire method as such. Starbuck was influenced by Max Müller's work on the scientific study of religion and presented a paper on Müller in 1870. In 1893 he published two questionnaires (then called "circulars"), one on conversion and the other on "gradual growth," apparently with the aim of mediating the feud between science and religion. He believed that a person was motivated by egotistic as well as idealistic considerations. Fear, a sense of sin, and the related phenomena of depression are the prominent characteristics of the preconversion state. In the conversion, personal will is surrendered for greater harmony to be achieved.

Born in Switzerland, James Leuba went to Bryn Mawr college and became head of the psychology department there. His widely discussed books (1912, 1926) and his articles in the *Psychological Bulletin* established his leadership in the movement as long as it existed. Leuba saw conversion as an attempt to deal with significant obstacles to the unification of the person.

Edward Ames constructed an anthropological and sociological theory of the origin, growth, and significance of religious behavior. His *The Psychology of the Religious Experience* (1910) was an attempt to describe the origins of religion in the human race and the rise of religion in the individual, as well as a general description of the place of religion in the contemporary experience of the individual and society. Ames moved from considering religion as part of the overall machinery of the individual to a discussion of religious consciousness in relation to democracy and science. George Coe, in various chapters of *The Psychology of Religion* (1916), dealt with intensities of religious thought and feeling. Religion could be made an object of psychological study but was "something more." The idea of God derived from functions, desires, and other ideas but included the element of awe and fascination that anthropologists called *mana*. Religious experience is not an event in the unconscious as much as it is personalistic, conscious self-realization in a social context. Because of this view, Coe concentrated on religious education. A particular contribution of his was a study that identified various religious experiences as a function of the individual's temperament. He constructed a list of questions to reflect the personality of the respondent. Subjects were interviewed to clear up doubtful points and acquire new facts; friends and acquaintances were also interviewed. Finally, the reports of independent observers were collated and checked off against one another.

In the 1920s Robert H. Thouless wrote his text *Introduction to the Psychology of Religion* (1956), basing it on a much broader range of human experiences, beginning with a section on "elements"—traditional, natural, moral, affective, and rational. The book also contained a section on the conscious and subconscious mind and the instincts and a final section on worship, conversion, and mysticism.

James, Starbuck, Leuba, Ames, Coe, and Thouless had specialized religious interests: conversion first of all, then religious development, origins of religion, instincts and unconscious motivations. James himself wanted to set religion in the context of the broader human experience (Browning, 1975, 1980), and his explanations were certainly more philosophical than psychological, so he did not need to make much use of the terminology he developed in his *Principles of Psychology* (Alexander, 1979). Others after him seemed reluctant to develop any specialized psychological vocabulary or develop any extended explanation of psychological processes.

Toward the end of the 1920s a rapid decline of interest in the psychology of religion was reflected in the disappearance of the annual reviews of the psychology of religion field published in the *Psychological Bulletin.* Such reviews were carried from 1904 to 1928. No reviews were published after that until 1933, when the review mainly contained material from French and German sources. Orlo Strunk attributed the decline to a number of factors: Theological interest in the new field had introduced speculative and apologetic tendencies that hampered its growth; psychoanalytic studies had attracted attention as a more promising approach to the study of religion; and the influence of behaviorism led to the neglect of complex human behaviors as the focus of attention in academic psychology (Beit-Hallahmi, 1977, p. 22). The rather short-lived field of psychology of religion as a subdivision of psychology broke up because theology, psychoanalysis, and behaviorism operated in different ways with different emphases (Homans, 1970). This is not to say that religion was no longer an object of study in psychology or that nothing said in behavioral circles had any connection with religion. We shall see how religion is discussed in these areas of psychology presently.

While not a subdivision of psychology at the moment, nor a distinct academic discipline, "psychology of religion" is definitely a subject of discussion and research. The current discussion on both sides of the Atlantic is not central to either psychology or religious studies. Although there is still a debate as to what might properly be called "psychology of religion" (Francis, 1978; Vine, 1978), there is no doubt that psychological interpretation of religion is taking place in many areas of psychology (Capps, Rambo, and Ransohoff, 1976), especially in social psychology, (Argyle and Beit-Hallahmi, 1975; Hunsberger, 1980). Humanistic psychology allowed for a new openness to religion and paved the way for dialogue between the two disciplines, psychology and religious studies. Orlo Strunk at Boston, James Dittes at Yale, and Paul Pruyser of the Menninger Clinic, among others, have tried to bring the two fields together. The program in religion and psychological studies at the University of Chicago is based on the presupposition that the two disciplines can be integrated for a variety of academic and professional purposes.

The Example of Conversion

Simply put, religious conversion is the way people become committed to a set of beliefs (Conn, 1978). In general, conversion is an event or a process in peoples' lives whereby they make a distinct move, or admit to having been moved, in some recognizable way. In most cases people move from having no religion to religiousness, from what they take to be an inferior religion to a superior one, or from a mild interest in religion to an intensification of their religious consciousness. Conversion is the religious experience that is the easiest to recognize or in some measure observe. While we can easily observe people "converting," going to church, or performing formally religious acts within their community, we cannot know everything about the performance, and so must begin to interpret (Lofland and Skonovd, 1981).

Conversion, then, makes an excellent first topic in the study of authentic, personally significant religious experiences. St. Augustine's conversion, for example, was a distinct event: He could describe it, and others could observe it, or at least could observe the hours and minutes before it. The first psychologists of religion moved easily from conversion to other experiences that could be called mystical experiences. William James considered the study of mysticism to be at the center of his psychology-of-religion work, because he took mystical experiences to be those that changed in a perceptible way an individual's sense of self.

Conversion has received considerable attention in recent decades as well, both from the general public and from students (Scroggs and Douglas, 1967). Conversion is at the center of the efforts of television preachers, who are an important social and political force in this country, and is the obvious goal of the often suspect efforts of the American new religions, the cults.

There is a striking change when indifference toward one's own religion turns into intense practice. Changes in religious belief and practice, as when a Jew converts to Christianity or a Christian to Islam, are also striking. When a Jew converts to Christianity, for example, accepting a new image of Jesus as divine and a serious reading of the documents of the historical church councils, a fundamental change of views and images is entailed, replacing one set of ideas with another.

In some religions of the world conversion is more properly called "enlightenment" or, perhaps, "release." When "everything comes together" in Hinduism and Buddhism, and one feels that one's life is changed, the image is not so much one of a turning from one thing to another, from one orthodoxy to another, but of an experience of unity or vision. The experience is different, because it is not so graphic and does not involve the rejection and acceptance of a range of ideas and formulations.

Conversion is a term we now use more often to describe the movement from outside a revelation religion (Judaism, Christianity, or Islam) into one, or from one revelation religion (or denomination within the revelation religion) to another. In any case we are talking about revelation religions. The conversion process in these religions is made up of changes that involve large areas of the personality, and these vary according to the religions themselves. It behooves us to know what religions are involved and how they are involved in any individual conversion. In the Christian tradition the best known conversions are those of Saul of Tarsus and Augustine of Hippo (354–430). In our own day the analysis of Saul's (St. Paul's) conversion from Judaism to Christianity has been the particular province of biblical scholars, but the conversion of Augustine from Neoplatonism (and vestige Manichaeism) to Christianity has attracted both historical and psychological analysis. St. Augustine heard a voice telling him to "take and read," then opened the Bible to read a passage that he must have seen many times before, which simply told him to do the things that he could not make himself do before.

The Conversion of St. Augustine

Here is the story, in Augustine's own words, of his conversion. We quote him at length and sum up his story (Van der Meer, 1965; Brown, 1969) as a point of reference in the discussion that follows afterward.

> I flung myself down on the ground somehow under a fig tree and gave free rein to my tears; they streamed and flooded from my eyes, an "acceptable sacrifice to Thee." And I kept saying to you, not perhaps in these words, but with this sense: "And Thou, O Lord, how long? How long, Lord; wilt Thou be angry forever? Remember not our former iniquities." For I felt that it was these which were holding me fast. And in my misery I would explain: "How long, how long this 'tomorrow and tomorrow'? Why not now? Why no finish this very hour with my uncleanness?"
>
> So I spoke, weeping in the bitter contrition of my heart. Suddenly a voice reaches my ears from a nearby house. It is the voice of a boy or a girl (I don't know which) and in a kind of singsong the words are constantly repeated: "Take it and read it. Take it and read it." At once my face changed, and I began to think carefully of whether the singing of words like these came into any kind of game which children play, and I could

not remember that I had ever heard anything like it before. I checked the force of my tears and rose to my feet, being quite certain that I must interpret this as a divine command to open the book and read the first passage which I should come upon. For I had heard this about Antony: he had happened to come in when the Gospel was being read, and as though the words read were spoken directly to himself, had received the admonition: "Go, sell all that thou hast, and give to the poor, and thou shalt have treasure in heaven, and come and follow me." And by such an oracle he had been immediately converted to you.

So I went eagerly back to the place where Alypius was sitting, since it was there that I had left the book of the Apostle when I rose to my feet. I snatched up the book, opened it, and read in silence the passage upon which my eyes first fell: "Not in rioting and drunkenness, not in chambering and wantonness, not in strife and envying: but put ye on the Lord Jesus Christ, and make not provision for the flesh in concupiscence." I had no wish to read further; there was no need to. For immediately I had reached the end of this sentence it was as though my heart was filled with a light of confidence and all the shadows of my doubt were swept away. [Warner, 1963, pp. 182–83]

A number of events in St Augustine's life led up to this incident. In his earliest years Augustine was much affected by his father's pagan casualness and his mother's Christian rigidity. Later in life he thought his mother too tolerant of the father's ways, but as a youth his judgments were different. Clearly exceptionally intelligent, his mind raced ahead of his general development: Youthful deeds that were normal in a free and easy society did not sit well with him, and he later judged his boyhood pranks and his teenage sex life harshly. Both personally and intellectually the problem of evil came to be central, but we do not have enough evidence from his earliest years (his *Confessions* were written much later) to see whether his personal negative reactions to his passions and behavior tendencies caused his intellectual preoccupation with the power of evil, or vice versa.

As a young intellectual he became interested in, and for nine years a number of, a sect called the Manichees, a small renegade group with a bad reputation in both Christian and pagan circles. They believed in a Principal of Evil that was virtually the equal of the Principle of Good. To free oneself from the weight of evil in the world required the individual to make extraordinary efforts. The "illumination" of Manichees was attained by hearing the writings of the founder Mani—who based his teachings on the earlier Persian religion, Zoroastrianism—in order to realize the foulness of the world and the corruption of the body. An enlightened member of the group could then begin the fight that would lead him or her to a state of light and purity.

Augustine eventually rejected Manichaeism but remained a Neoplatonic philosopher, believing that an interior journey to some higher place within the mind would bring him to truth. If life was a falling away from truth and beauty because of degrading external preoccupation, then the goal of the philosopher was to ascend to truth once again. The views of the most famous Neoplatonic philosopher, Plotinus, can be summed up in this way:

> Plotinus' universe was a continuous, active whole, which could admit no brutal cleavage and no violent irruptions. Each being in it drew strength and meaning from its dependence on this living continuum. Evil, therefore, was only a turning away into separateness; its very existence assumed the existence of an order, which was flouted while remaining no less real and meaningful. It was the self-willed part that was diminished, by losing contact with something bigger and more vital than itself. [Brown, 1969, p. 99]

If the Neoplatonic universe seemed beautiful, Augustine's life did not. Christian teachings on the evil of human beings and the possibility of their salvation were very appealing, but the simplicity of the Christian scriptures, the crudeness of the Father God, and the folly of Jesus' cross remained serious obstacles to Augustine. He himself could be simplistic in his philosophical conceptions of God, though, and he thought of God as physically extended in space, somehow physically present everywhere instead of being present by his power. The intellectual and personal influence of Ambrose, the Bishop of Milan, and the presence of Augustine's beloved mother, a reminder of many infantile and adolescent conflicts, moved him toward a life that promised to resolve his intellectual and personal problems. But for all his thinking and praying, he could not resolve the tensions within him until the day of his conversion.

Psychological Explanations of Conversion and St. Augustine

From the psychological perspective, we must be able to talk at least in a general way about the type of mental processes involved and types of personality qualities involved in a conversion (Rambo, 1982). We can say that one's intellectual and emotional interests move back and forth between different personal/moral choices, until one eventually centers one's energy. Sometimes, instead of moving between widely disparate choices (from sexual rigidity to hedonism, or from freethinking to fundamentalist faith), converts simply add certain ideas and experiences to their personality repertoire and subtract others (a Catholic may add the experience of revelation in Bible reading and subtract the authority of the Pope in converting to Protestantism). In the case of St. Augustine, we see his movement back and forth between a conviction that somehow behavior could be directed in accordance with God's will and a fearful "I-am-going-to-lose" attitude in the face of sexual drives he did not want to give in to. At a moment of seeming helplessness, when he gave up and let everything go as it were, his mental and emotional energies focused where he really wanted them to in the first place, in the area of belief and restraint.

Although conversions often happen because people wish it that way, they more often happen because part of their personality not directly under active control seems to take over. There will be more to say about this in the chapter on thoughts and feelings.

If we refer to personality theory to explain conversion, we might use several approaches. I introduce these approaches here, but they will be more fully explained in the chapters that follow and applied to Augustine's particular case in the last chapter. If we were to use a conflict interpretation, following Freud and Jung, we would emphasize that there are a variety of images that operate in the unconscious; they interact and suddenly one particular viewpoint with its behavior set surfaces: The playboy becomes a saint or the atheist becomes a believer, or a non-Christian comes to accept Christian views. What we have already said about Augustine is a general interpretation of this sort: What finally surfaced was believing and sexually continent living (Dittes, 1965; Daly, 1978). In a fulfillment interpretation, following Allport and Maslow, we would say that there has been an integration of viewpoints and values, that mental unity has been forged out of discordant impulses and aspirations (Fredericksen, 1978). For Augustine, it is obvious, things finally came together. Beyond the seemingly arbitrary resolution of conflict, a number of viewpoints and problems were integrated and resolved. There was a fit between his problems and new-found abilities to reach his goals as he saw them. What was needed was the ecstatic moment, the peak experience, the sense of communication from God (some call this an existential experience of God). Taking a conditioning (Skinnerian) approach, we would say that the convert has been randomly reinforced into a particular type of religious behavior. What really had no meaning suddenly appeared to be important. A moment of chance belief was found to be rewarding, and so the belief is continued, or an activity was reinforced by the approval of others, and so the activity is continued (Lofland and Skonovd, 1981). There will be more to say about this in the chapters on the role of religion within the context of personality.

In the development and education of the personality a person passes from the small universe of childhood to the wider intellectual and spiritual life of maturity. What was once taken literally is taken symbolically or is logically defended as literal truth. Today the cognitive (Piaget) and emotional (Erikson) study of children is focused on the ways children comprehend realities around them and grow emotionally through experiences and interactions with others. Augustine's development of a spiritualized view of God was tied to intellectual development involving increasingly abstract concepts of divinity. His earlier notion that God was a presence physically extended in space prevented him from formulating the concepts of sins and sinlessness that seemed to be the condition of his conversion. And he had to resolve the problems of identity diffusion that had existed since his adolescent confusion of the pagan and Christian values represented by two respected parents (Burrell, 1970).

To understand the encouragement and support of Augustine's social circles, we must explore the social correlates of conversion. On the one hand, if society dominates a person in a certain way and the person needs an outlet, a conversion to a renegade or disapproved religious group may provide a real outlet for the individual. On the other hand, belief in the invisible can make eminent good sense if the whole society encourages it, or a particular intensity of experience can be engendered if small group dynamics virtually cause it. The various conversion experiences within groups, such as those encouraged within Methodist Christianity or Pentecostalism, are heavily dependent upon the particular type of expectations the group engenders and the encouragement and approbation it gives. For Augustine, the influence of the Neoplatonist intellectuals at Cassiciacum and the Christian community at Milan supported and directed his intellectual and emotional tendencies (Brown, 1969).

In this book we explore much more fully the psychological and religious information useful in interpreting conversion and other religious phenomena: basic thoughts and feelings in different states of consciousness; the role of religion in personalities dominated by conflict, fulfillment search, or conditioning; features of development; social interaction involved in the growth and stabilization of the religious factor in the personality; current research; and clinical approaches. We return to the basic example of conversion in our conclusion, but there is much else to explore now.

RECEIVED
JUN 2 9 92
CENTER FOR THE ARTS

JUN 2 9 92

JUN 2 9 92

RECEIVED
JUN 2 9 92
CENTER FOR THE ARTS

2

Describing Religious Thoughts and Feelings: William James to the Present

How ARE WE TO UNDERSTAND the way ideas and states of consciousness determine the nature of religious experience? How are we to explain how joyful or depressed feelings interact with the belief and behavior requirements of a tradition. Even to begin to describe religious experiences, our own and others, we must have a vocabulary.

Although we have not inherited an agreed upon basic, or "ordinary," psychological vocabulary to describe the religious experience, a number of psychologists, beginning with William James, have described religious experiences with an ordinary vocabulary based on common sense. By ordinary language I mean everyday ways of speaking and writing in contrast to "specifically contrived notations, displays and terminologies," and by common sense I mean an understanding of personality and experience that is "intelligent and informed, but not necessarily technical, professional, or scientific" (Bromley, 1977, p. ix). In more recent decades philosophers have been interested in analysis of "ordinary language" as a way of describing different areas of life, psychology included (Austin, 1970; Toulmin, 1969; 1972). This study may involve simple reflection, the use of a dictionary, or the compilation of a list of psychological traits (Allport and Odbert, 1936). It may involve a developmental study of the way people—children especially, of course— describe the personalities and behaviors of others (Livesley and Bromley, 1973). To date no fully developed effort has been made to work up a vocabulary for description of religious experience in ordinary language. The work of James and a few others across the decades of this century is all we have on hand. In the shorter version of his general treatise on psychology, William James says that the data of psychology are "thoughts," "feelings," and "knowledge," all of which he calls "states of consciousness." His definition of psychology, though borrowed, is "description and explanation of states of consciousness as such" (1962, pp. 15–16).

Through the years the studies of James have influenced or served as a point of reference for many others. Interests have gone in a number of directions, but two have been most conspicuous. The first has been a more specific interest in altered states of consciousness. Examples would be the relationship of chemical changes in the body with religious awareness and the effect of meditation on brain waves or hallucination. The second direction has been a general concern to study all psychological data that might be considered religious: simple mental images of God and the saints, an ordinary sense of prayers, or the linguistic peculiarities of liturgical forms of worship. These two orientations will be examined in the last part of this chapter.

It would be stretching a point to say that all of this work is in ordinary language based on common sense, but one thing unites all such efforts: They are not geared toward the construction of a full-blown theory of personality and development. Those whose theories of personality and development are discussed in the following chapters give us a vocabulary, but the vocabulary is so tied up with the theory that we must examine the theory, and the role assumed for religion in the theory, in order to understand the use of the word. Think of Freud's notion of morality as the activity of the superego. You must know his theory of personality in order to understand how the superego functions.

When James began to describe and explain varieties of religious experience, he emphasized thought and feelings that were especially intense. He turned to the topic of conversion and from there to a broader range of intense religious experiences, all of which might be grouped under the heading mystical. He said that the religion most worth studying is authentic, "firsthand" religious feelings, acts, and experiences. Derived, "secondhand" religion is the more automatic, unthinking, social type of activity that characterizes most people who practice religion simply because everyone in their society or with their background does it. James studied the inner dispositions of those for whom religion formed a center of interest. The mystics, those whose consciousness of life is altered by their apprehensions of the divine, are the central personalities of James's work, while others whose thoughts and emotions are influenced by their religion are also of some interest. He did not think that philosophical considerations were religion at all, even though he himself was preoccupied with such considerations. At the end of his study he urged an impartial, nontheological, comparative approach to religious studies, which he called the "science of religions," as the best way to understand religion (1961).

James's contribution to the study of psychology of religion was not exactly the application of the views stated in the general treatises on the principles of psychology. Though not renouncing anything in these works, he dropped much of his psychological terminology and moved into a more broadly based description. James "shifted from what was primarily a formal discussion and description of the attributes and functions of the stream of consciousness in the *Principles* to an examination of the meaning of a particular mode of human experience, and the shift entails a more comprehensive method in inquiry than does that of his earlier psychological text" (Alexander, 1979, p. 424). In fact, he moved immediately into a discussion of the broadest possible human orientations before he discussed conversions. Those orientations are, of course, optimism and pessimism: He spoke of healthy, sick, and twice-born personalities, with conversion as his example of the core experience and saintliness as a general state of religious intensity. In other words he examined what happens to people psychologically when the setting is conversion or the constant background qualities are those of saintliness.

Personal Orientations: Healthy-Minded, Sick-Soul, and Twice-Born Types

If we reflect now on the types of religious people that we are or that we know, we would probably admit that fundamental pessimism and optimism, or a bouncing back and forth between the two, very strongly affects religious thoughts and feelings.

For healthy-minded types happiness seems impossible to hold back. They rejoice in everybody and everything and feel "grateful admiration for the gift of so happy an existence." Since the whole world, all of nature, is good, their enthusiasm and sense of freedom become what might be called a "cosmic emotion." They refuse to feel unhappiness, as if it were something demeaning. James calls such people "once-born," following the categories of one of his authors. Such people make their way innocently, happily, unreflectingly through life. In James's day individuals such as Walt Whitman and groups such as the Mind-Cure Movement were good examples of "cosmic emotion" (1961, pp. 78–113). The happiness types feel that trouble and grief can be pushed away.

The sick souls maximize evil because of their "persuasion that the evil aspects of our life are of its very essence, and that the world's meaning most comes home to us when we lay them most to heart" (p. 116). There are different levels to this morbidity. For some, evil means only a maladjustment in things, a lack of adjustment to the environment, but for others evil is something more radical and general, a wrongness essential to human nature that no simple remedy can cure, but requiring supernatural intervention. Such types have a very low pain threshold. Sensitivity and awareness of pain predominate. James uses both the Stoics and Epicurians of the ancient Greek world as examples of sick souls, because both proposed ways of escaping from a gloomy existence. This sense of life as gloomy and painful may at times be only a viewpoint, but it can cause a pathological melancholy in some people, which the French psychologist Théodule Ribot called *anhedonia:* joylessness and dreariness, discouragement, dejection, lack of taste, zest, and spring (pp. 114–142).

For the sufferers, the sick souls of history, the experience of melancholy (or, more dramatically, "failure" or "the sepulchre") varied considerably. For the Russian novelist Leo Tolstoy, the overall mood at one period in his life was one of melancholy, because the sense that life had any meaning whatever was for a time wholly absent:

> An invincible force impelled me to get rid of my existence, on one way or another. It cannot be said exactly that I *wished* to kill myself, for the force which drew me away from life was fuller, more powerful, more general than any desire. It was a force like my old aspiration to live, only it impelled me in the opposite direction. It was an aspiration of my whole being to get out of life. [p. 133]

John Bunyan, the famous Puritan divine of the seventeenth century, expressed his own melancholy attitude in the title he chose for his autobiography: *Grace Abounding to the Chief of Sinners*. The worst kind of melancholy, however, takes the form of panic fear. James quotes an anonymous Frenchman (in fact he was referring to himself): After seeing someone in a mental asylum, "the universe was changed for me altogether. I awoke morning after morning with a horrible dread at the pit of my stomach, and with a sense of the insecurity of life that I never knew before, and that I have never felt since" (p. 138).

All these types must be twice-born in order to be happy. Peace cannot be revealed by the simple addition of pluses and elimination of minuses from life. Natural living and natural goodness are not really enough. Rather, what is natural must be put aside and salvation must be sought in some self-transcending spiritual realm. The most complete religions are probably those that give a sense of deliverance to those who see things in this way.

The sick souls—unless locked in the most negative and unchangeable condition—often admit the possibility of another realm, almost always spiritual, in their universe: "There are two lives, the natural and the spiritual, and we must lose the one before we can participate in the other" (p. 143). Typical of those who lean in the negative direction is a certain discord in basic temperament, an incompletely unified moral and intellectual constitution. Such a situation leads to a great suffering, because, although a certain amount of inconsistency does not make much difference in a personality, a strong degree of discord may cause havoc. "There are persons whose existence is a little more than a series of zig-zags as one tendency and now another gets the upper hand" (p. 145).

Augustine's description of the period before his conversion is a perfect portrait of the divided self where, as James puts it, "the higher wishes lack just that last acuteness, that touch of explosive intensity . . . that enables them to burst their shell, and make irruption efficaciously into life and quell the lower tendencies forever" (p. 148). This dividedness is overcome in conversion with the resultant rejoicing, the centering and balancing of energies that resolve the dividedness of the personality. When the dividedness is overcome, it is not as if it had never been there, but it is overcome, and the individual has the sense of being whole, converted, reborn.

By conversion a divided self is saved. People direct their energies in different directions, but in the case of the divided self energies are aimed first in one direction (e.g. luxurious living) and then in the opposite (e.g. self-chastisement). These energies are not fully explainable: We cannot be sure how an experience of family celebration, a church service, or a sexual attraction causes us to change energy directions. The best examples of divided selves who are fit subjects for conversion are adolescents. James cites Starbuck's presentation of adolescent characteristics: brooding, depression, morbid introspection, sense of sin, anxiety about present doubts and later punishments, and so on. Suddenly, by adjusting to a wider outlook, the adolescent passes from the child's small universe to a mature intellectual life.

Conversion can be willed by some people. Gradually building up new ideas and discarding old ones, checking their feelings and putting them into place, they develop a firm new set of religious ways. There are really no surprises, just a series of rational and gratifying steps. For others, the reason and subconscious energies are directed in a way that the conscious personality does not understand. The person has to cease striving on the conscious level as did Augustine when he was trying hard to understand and put an end to his own evil living. When striving ceases the subconscious energies achieve their stability of direction. James refers to these as volitional and self-surrender types of conversion.

There are different ways of describing self-surrender (we will explore Freud's and Jung's complex, theory-bound analyses of subconscious religious behavior in the next chapter), but James uses a vocabulary that is built around the words "field of consciousness." This is a space metaphor, of course: The mind is pictured as a territory or a series of regions of some sort. Although James knew of Freud's presentation of the subconscious and was positively disposed toward it, he favored the description of the mind as "field," that is, a "wave of consciousness" or "field of objects" (p. 190). He said that it was impossible to outline this field with any definiteness, and that mental fields succeed one another, some of them being open and wide so that we can see and understand many things together, and others narrow so that we understand little and are turned in on ourselves. Memories, thoughts, and feelings that are outside of our primary fields of consciousness are called "extra-marginal," "ultra-marginal," and sometimes subconscious (in latin "extra" means outside, "ultra" means beyond, and "sub" means beneath). Self-surrender enables the inner changes to come into the primary field of consciousness:

> The most important consequence of having a strongly developed ultra-marginal life of this sort is that one's ordinary fields of consciousness are liable to incursions from it of which the subject does not guess the source, and which, therefore, take for him the form of unaccountable impulses to act, or inhibitions of action, of obsessive ideas, or even of hallucinations of sight or hearing. [p. 192]

This is a simple way of describing self-surrender or sudden conversion that has been central to the discussion over the years.

Incursions from outside the field of consciousness often result in a faith state or, better, a state of assurance that has pleasing, integrating results. Converts feel as if they are perceiving truths not known before, and the world seems to undergo an objective change to the extent that minor hallucinations may take place. Most important, the genuine convert feels very happy, an ecstasy is produced. If this happiness produces benefits in the lives of converts and those around them, James suggests, we must then judge the conversion positively (pp. 197–208).

Types of Saintliness: Asceticism, Strength of Soul, Purity, and Charity

"Saintliness" is the optimal developmental outcome possible for all personality types. It is hardly a psychological term, but

James chose to discuss it and to build a vocabulary around it in order to show its psychological value. Saintliness is set as a goal against the extremes of light-headedness and depression that can be found in the healthy-minded, the sick souls, and the divided souls who never overcome the radical divisions of their personality to become twice-born.

For all types there are inner traits of saintliness that might be described as (1) a feeling of a wider life than that of the material world, with the conviction that an ideal power exists; (2) a sense of the continuity of this power with one's own life and self-surrender to it; (3) a feeling of elation and freedom as selfishness dissolves, (4) a steering of the emotional center toward very positive, loving, and harmonious affections. These inner traits have certain practical consequences that can sometimes be carried to extremes, although they are good in themselves. Asceticism, strength of soul, purity, and charity are the outward manifestations of these traits (pp. 220–60).

Asceticism is a mortification of sense pleasure and a turning away from mundane happiness; it derives from preoccupation with a wider life and an ideal power. But it may simply be a touchiness, a hardness in people who find something weak, even disgusting, in a life of ease. From one of James's correspondents we have the following remarks: "Often at night in my warm bed I would feel ashamed to depend so on the warmth, and whenever the thought would come over me I would have to get up, no matter what time of night it was, and stand for a minute in the cold, just so as to prove my manhood" (p. 241).

Strength of soul enables the person to attain new heights of patience and fortitude, to relegate personal motives and inhibitions to utter insignificance. It derives from a sense of continuity with the ideal power and self-surrender to it. A Huguenot persecuted under Louis XIV wrote of her inspiration to endurance and strength:

> They brought a cord with which they tied me to a beam in the kitchen. They drew the cord with all their strength and asked me, "Does it hurt you?" and then they discharged their fury upon me, exclaiming as they struck me, "Pray now to your God." It was the Roulette woman who held this language. But at this moment I received the greatest consolation that I can ever receive in my life, since I had the honor of being whipped for the name of Christ, and in addition of being crowned with his mercy and his consolation. [pp. 232–33]

Purity enables a person to get rid of brutish and sensual elements that derive from selfishness and are incompatible with feelings of elation and freedom. But, in fact, a certain brutality can be turned against oneself. Purity of spirit sometimes takes a very severe turn, and weaknesses of the flesh are treated with real harshness. A more balanced purity of spirit seems to be at the basis of efforts made by William Ellery Channing, a Unitarian minister. The following excerpt is a description of him when he started his ministry:

> He was now more simple than ever, and seemed to have become incapable of any form of self-indulgence. He took the smallest room in the house for his study, though he might easily have commanded one more light, airy, and in every way more suitable; and chose for his sleeping chamber an attic which he shared with younger brother. . . . In sickness only would he change for the time his apartment and accept a few comforts. The dress too that he habitually adopted was of a most inferior quality; and garments were constantly worn which the world would call mean, though an almost feminine neatness preserved him from the least appearance of neglect. [pp. 241–42]

Charity is a kind of loving awareness of fellow creatures. It arises from the turning of the emotions toward positive and harmonious affections. James describes this important aspect of the Christian life:

> Religious rapture, moral enthusiasm, ontological wonder, and cosmic emotion are all unifying states of mind, in which the sand and grit of selfhood incline to disappear, and tenderness to rule. The best thing is to describe the condition integrally as characteristic affection to which our nature is liable, a region in which we find ourselves at home, a sea in which we swim; but not to pretend to explain its part by deriving them too cleverly from one another. [p. 225]

This notion of love is not confined, James says, to the revelation religions that promote worship of a personal, lovable God, because he believes it can be found in Stoicism, Hinduism, and Buddhism. Such affections flourish whenever there is a dependence of people on general causes, whenever there is that sense of a wider self.

In general, all these virtues can be turned around by pessimistic views of the self and a negative view of God as someone merely to be appeased. In psychopathic persons, the negative motivation becomes genuinely irrational, an obsession, something that exists on its own. Positive, saintly qualities are transformed by the mystical experience.

The Mystical Experience

The center of James's presentation of the religious experience is his chapter on mysticism: "Personal religious experience has its root and center in mystical states of consciousness; so for us, who in these lectures are treating personal experience as the exclusive subject of our study, such states of consciousness ought to form the vital chapter from which all other chapters get their light" (p. 299).

There is a range of experience that can be called mystical, and at least four basic qualities can be pointed out.

INEFFABILITY. The experience cannot be described. The religious experience is such that it defies expression, and no adequate report of its contents can be given. The one who has the experience has the feeling that he or she cannot make clear its content to others unless they, too, have had the feeling. James gives the example of Alphonse Ratisbonne, who said this: "Heavens, how can I speak of it? Oh no! human words cannot attain to expressing the inexpressible. Any description, however sublime it might be, could be but a profanation of the unspeakable truth" (pp. 185–86).

TRANSIENCY. These mystical states are brief, pass quickly. Otherwise they would cease to be distinct from the regular emotions of life, thereby losing their power. They are so powerful that they cannot be sustained for long; it is not a question of people themselves deciding to keep these states brief in order to maintain their distinctness from everyday life. James cites the example of David Brainerd:

> My soul was so captivated and delighted with the excellency of God that I was even swallowed up in him; at least to that degree that I had no thought about my own salvation, and scarce reflected that there was such a creature as myself. I continued in this state of inward joy, peace, and astonishing, till near dark without any sensible abatement; and then began to think and examine what I had seen; and felt sweetly composed in my mind all the evening following. [p. 178]

PASSIVITY.   The state seems to come on of its own accord. It cannot be *caused* in any absolute way or hurried. It can be facilitated by preliminary operations such as fixing the attention or going through certain bodily performances. Yet mystics have a sense of the powerlessness of their wills to cause anything. James cited this case:

> I cannot express it in any other way than to say that I did "lie down in the stream of life and let it flow over me." I gave up all fear of any impending disease; I was perfectly willing and obedient. There was no intellectual effort, or train of thought. My dominant idea was: "Behold the handmaid of the Lord: be it unto me even as thou wilt," and a perfect confidence that all would be well, that all *was* well. The creative life was flowing into me every instant, and I felt myself allied with the Infinite, in harmony, and full of the peace that passeth understanding. There was no place in my mind for a jarring body. I had no consciousness of time or space or persons; but only of love and happiness and faith. [p. 109]

These mystical qualities can be found in a wide range of experiences, not all of them religious or connected with the special virtues of saintliness. Poetic moments inspired by sights, thoughts, and feelings, or by the actual reading of beautiful literature, are the basic examples. There are dreamy states, a kind of vague nostalgia or spirit or reminiscence. Drug- or alcohol-induced states, whatever their ethical implications, can be included here. And the most generalized state is what the Canadian psychiatrist Dr. R. M. Bucke, generations ago, called "cosmic consciousness," similar to the Hindu realization that one is part of an eternal, infinite process. Bucke explained his own experience of the cosmic consciousness in this way:

> For an instant I thought of fire, an immense conflagration somewhere close by in that great city; the next, I knew that the fire was within myself. Directly afterward there came upon me a sense of exultation, of immense joyousness accompanied or immediately followed by an intellectual illumination impossible to describe. Among other things, I did not merely come to believe, but I saw that the universe is not composed of dead matter, but is, on the contrary, a living Presence; I became conscious in myself of eternal life. It was not a conviction that I would have eternal life, but a consciousness that I possessed eternal life then; I saw that all men are immortal;

that the cosmic order is such that without any peradventure all things work together for the good of each and all; that the foundation principle of the world, of all the worlds, is what we call love, and that the happiness of each and all is in the long run absolutely certain. [p. 314]

There can be a methodical cultivation of these experiences. The methods used by Hindus, Buddhists, Muslims, and Christians, though in many ways different, have common elements. James' sources are quite limited, but he briefly explains the yoga tradition of Hinduism, the higher states of contemplation in Buddhism, and the experience of divine union of the Sufi, Al-Ghazzali. He commends the systematic methods of meditation developed in Catholic Christianity while lamenting that Protestantism has often left any methodical cultivation of prayer to the mind-curer type. St. Theresa of Avila, St. Ignatius Loyola, and St. Margaret Mary Alacoque are among the best-known Catholic mystics since the Reformation. However, all the methods are used to arrive at a goal far less easy to explain than the steps along the way: the mystical state. "We pass into mystical states from an out of ordinary consciousness as from a less into a more, as from a smallness into a vastness, and at the same time as from an unrest to a rest. We feel them as reconciling, unifying states. They appeal to the yes-function more than to the no-function in us" (p. 326).

Other Forms of Experience: Devotional and Philosophical Religion

Devotional Experience

When James speaks of prayer plain and simple, he is speaking of ordinary, devotional religion. It is "consciousness which individuals have of an intercourse between themselves and higher powers with which they feel themselves to be related"; it is a "more habitual and so to speak chronic sense of God's presence." The basic requirement is that people believe that something is being transacted between themselves and a higher power when they pray. He cites one example, taken from Starbuck's research, as something that probably could have been written by "thousands of unpretending Christians" (p. 72). This can give rise to the more intense mystical experience but is not itself so intense. It is the ordinary experience of communicating with God, which is done in simple belief and within an ordinary range of emotion. One simply believes that there is a personal God to whom one can talk. This is the ordinary prayer experience of most monotheists and Hindus, as well as a large number of Buddhists, but it is not common to all forms of religion.

Although James mixes his examples of mystical and devotional religion together, we can clarify issues by a paraphrase of what he had to say about mystical experience, and use some of his examples.

DESCRIBABLE.   The devotional experience can be recounted to other people. It can be described, because the personal relationship between the devotee and God is perceived in very human ways: "I told God this," "I saw that He wants that." Different thoughts and emotions, the process involved in going from one to another, all this is quite describable, because everything has its parallel in human relationships. Just as a regular hour's discussion with comments and reactions can be described, so an hour of prayer to and thoughts about God can be described.

NOETIC.   In the devotional experience, people know what they are doing. They are not transformed by some force outside of themselves over which they feel no control.

The following quote shows how the person experiencing the devotional life is perfectly capable of analyzing the mental and emotional contents of his experience; this kind of experience is, then, describable and noetic:

> I remembered the promise of the Holy Ghost; and what the positive declarations of the Gospel had never succeeded in bringing home to me, I learned at last from necessity, and believed, for the first time in my life, in this promise, in the only sense in which it answered the needs of my soul, in that, namely, of a real external supernatural action, capable of giving me thoughts, and taking them away from me, and exerted on me by a God as truly master of my heart as he is of the rest of nature. Renouncing then all merit, all strength, abandoning all my personal resources, and acknowledging no other title to his mercy than my own utter misery, I went home and threw myself on my knees, and prayed as I never yet prayed in my life. From this day onwards a new interior life began for me:

not that my melancholy had disappeared, but it had lost its sting. Hope had entered into my heart, and once I entered on the path, the God of Jesus Christ, to whom I then had learned to give myself up, little by little did the rest. [pp. 199–200]

LONG-TERM OR FREQUENT. The experience is continual rather than brief and evanescent. There is no intense experience involved in the mental picturing of scriptural scenes or in imagining a simple conversation with a heavenly listener. Instead of the passing, indescribable sense of presence or union, the believer's imagination simply creates the situation or the conversation that he or she believes in. Those who pray almost constantly, or very frequently, have an experience that is not different from their awareness of everything that goes on during a morning of work, study, or recreation.

ACTIVE. In all devotional activity, people have a sense of simply setting themselves to pray. The initiative is their own. There is nothing they have to wait for, they have no sense of being "taken over." Since they are habitual believers, there is something more than the mental activity involved in picturing something that is not there, the way one might have a memory of an event of the year before or picture a family member who is geographically distant.

We can note that the judgment and prayer activity of the following witness are long-term and active. He describes what goes on from day to day, the ordinary conversation of a simple believer who can analyze what is happening to him.

God is more real to me than any thought or thing or person. I feel his presence positively, and the more as I live in closer harmony with his laws as written in the body and mind. I feel him in the sunshine or rain; and awe mingled with delicious restfulness most nearly describes my feelings. I talk to him as a companion in prayer and praise, and our communion is delightful. He answers me again and again, often in words so clearly spoken that it seems my outer ear must have carried the tone, but generally in strong mental impressions. Usually a text of Scripture, unfolding some new view of him and his love for me, and care for my safety. I could give hundreds of instances in school matters, social problems, financial difficulties, etc. That he is mine and I am his never leaves me, it is an abiding joy. Without it life would be a blank, a desert, a shoreless, trackless waste. [p. 72]

The range of experience varies, going from the simplest mental pictures up to and perhaps including the mystical experience. Possibilities for prayer are best conveyed through family and official religion by means of the rituals and stories of the tradition. But the conversations or exchanges with a personal God or with a teaching–redeeming founder figure run the gamut from the calm sense that one is being listened to to the sense that one is being responded to. Obviously, the belief that a God exists somewhere who is similar to the image in the mind, and who listens, is the basic belief. Beyond that there is a sense of a God responding, in a somewhat vague way telling the devotee what to do; and beyond that still is a sense of a very clear message. The ultimate is the experience of specific relation with the message to preach it. In those latter stages, though, the experiences have the extraordinary quality that we have classified as mystical.

The methodical cultivation of the prayerful imagination is the essence of devotional prayer. James cites several times the use of the Spiritual Exercises of St. Ignatius Loyola, which involve imagining gospel scenes and a process of methodically examining the different physical and supposed personal elements of the scene. On these occasions James was speaking of the mystical experience, because those who undergo mystical experiences often begin with graphic imaginings of religious scenes and personalities (p. 319). But even if we agree that "sensorial images" play an important part in inducing the mystical experience, there is no need for us to deny that the simple working of the imagination is basic to all ordinary religious experience. Even St. Ignatius Loyola, whom James refers to when speaking of the mystical experience, thought so.

Philosophical Religion

Philosophical religion is not religion in the direct, full-experience sense. It is, in the eyes of James, simply reflection upon religion, and he uses the term "philosophy of religion" to describe it. If it is religion at all, it is religion after the fact. Yet philosophical religion is drawn into the ambit of religious experience in several ways. Philosophy is touched with emotion "if it represents living thought for both formulator and reader." In other words, the philosophical reflection on religion represents beauty for some, solutions to problems for others. Philosophical religion serves a valuable purpose, because it enables people to deal with one another, to understand one another, and so creates a certain species of unity (pp. 337–56).

It is, obviously, describable, noetic, continuing, and active, with rational, intellectual activity predominating. One studies, one reflects, one uses logic, whereas feelings and altered states of consciousness are not as operative. The activity of interpretation and explanation is central to the philosophical task. Still and all, personality orientation and more feeling forms of religion are joined to philosophical speculation; otherwise there would be no motivation to speculate about religion and its subject matter. Intellectual work is not divorced from inner unhappiness, with its need for deliverance, or from mystical elation.

James says that with the use of philosophy one can construct a critical science of religion, suggesting that philosophy abandon "metaphysics and deduction for criticism and induction, and frankly transform herself from theology into science of religions" (p. 355). Many values can result from this: dialogues between different types of believers, so that some kind of consensus can be arrived at; distinction of common and essential elements from the individual and local elements of religious beliefs; removal of historical incrustations and scientifically absurd or incongruous ideals; and the discovery of better means of testing hypotheses. James says it can "offer mediation between believers, and help to bring about consensus of opinion."

Theology, a believers' enterprise, is useful, but it is not the same thing. James for one would prefer that it evolve to his science of religions, because any attempt to come up with universally valid concepts or principles must convince people universally. If one looks at the collection of arguments for the existence of God, one sees that a philosophical theology of this sort is probably doomed to failure. There have been centuries of unbelieving criticism of such arguments, though they have never been wholly discredited for believers. Believers are convinced by the arguments, while atheists are not. "The bare fact that all idealists since Kant have felt entitled either to scout or to neglect" the arguments for God's existence, James says, "shows that they are not solid enough to serve as religion's all sufficient foundation." The pragmatic approach would look to see if there are any related ideas or teachings that are effective and important in human life, and that are genuine rules for action. James paraphrases Charles Sanders Peirce, who used the term *pragmatism* to describe his own views, "To develop a thought's meaning we need therefore only determine what conduct it is fitted to produce; that conduct is for us its sole significance; and the tangible fact at the root of all our thought-distinctions is that there is no one of them so fine as to consist in anything but a possible difference of practice." Accordingly, any discussion of the attributes or qualities of God must have some effect on people if they are to be of any use (pp. 347–49).

While James considers theological reflections on God's unity and eternity to be of no real human value and reflections on God's moral attributes, such as goodness and omniscience, to be of very limited value, he recognizes that such reflections are useful to a certain type of mind. He notes that the abstract beauty of concepts and formulations has value for the likes of Cardinal Newman ("intoning [theological formulations] as he would a cathedral service"), and the discussion of God's existence and attributes does represent a solution to the intellectual problems of some theological types (p. 357).

Additional Features of Mystical, Devotional, and Philosophical Religion

Simple descriptions of the religious experience—and appropriate vocabulary—can, of course, be found in other psychologists whose work paralleled or developed James's *Varieties*.

Predispositions, feelings, and the importance of overall control concerned psychologists who analyzed the *mystical* experience. Their discussions expand James's vocabulary on personal orientations, the elements of mysticism, and the valuable practical results of the good mystical experience.

Whether a reaction to fear (Leuba, 1912) or not, the herd and sex instincts are the predispositions of every human experience (Thouless, 1956). They may be especially potent in the mystical experience because of the predominance of subconscious mental activity and the intensity of emotion or affect. For example, in conversion experiences the problems caused by adolescent sexual intensity and the heightened enthusiasm of religious gatherings cause the two instincts to surface with great force. The most obvious religious result of the herd instinct and the sex instinct is a keen sense of the presence of the divinity.

In the distinctively religious range of feeling, the self-surrender associated with conversion is the most important. Since there is a real sense of transformation, the conversion experience is often a mystical experience. According to E. D. Starbuck, an image or an idea occurs to the person, the will power focuses attention on this ideal, but it cannot move the person through to the experience or goal; there is great unrest and distress, as in the case of Augustine, and finally, unexpectedly, the experience or goal is achieved. Emphasis here is on the centrality of self-surrender, not only in conversion, but in all striving for the higher life. It is as if the experience, or goal, itself must become central rather than the individual's own striving. "The act of yielding, in this point of view, is giving one-self over to the new life, making it the center of a new personality, and living, from within, the truth of it which had before been viewed objectively" (Starbuck, 1899, pp. 116–17).

There are a number of human feelings, plain and simple, that are connected with self-surrender (pp. 325–27): joy ("I experienced joy almost to weeping"), bodily lightness ("I felt as if a load were lifted from my body, and I was very happy"), weeping and shouting ("I wept and laughed alternately"), peace and happiness ("I felt as if I had gained greater peace and happiness than I have ever expected to experience"), relief and oneness with God ("There followed a delightful feeling of oneness with God and love for Him"); and so on to feelings of being calm, subdued, perhaps a bit disappointed. In the subsequent religious moments that occur regularly after these emotional heights, people have a sense of personal independence and freedom, joy and ecstasy, and spiritual exaltation. There is a sense of a larger world outside the self, resulting in awe, sense of mystery, reverence, love, and aesthetic appreciation. There are two forms of this feeling of an outside life depending upon whether the life "outside" is more vivid, impressive, and awe-inspiring, or one's own life is satisfying. From a sense of outside greatness or majesty arise feelings of dependence, humility, and resignation ("I have no confidence in myself or anything but God; I have completely submitted to God's way"). If one's own life is more satisfying, then the resulting feeling is oneness with God or divine companionship ("My soul feels itself alone with God and resolved to listen to His voice in the depths of Spirit. My soul and God seek each other. The sublime presence comes over me").

Among the valuable practical results of these experiences are the organization of the higher mental activities and the pleasure received from exercising them. The nervous system itself is coordinated in such a way that the personality becomes identified with association centers of the brain. People need personalities large enough and strong enough to safeguard this coordination, but they cannot regulate it a great deal (Ames, 1910). As we have already seen, mystical personalities are themselves regulated by automatic, subconscious movements, even going so far as self-hypnosis.

Because *devotional* religion is describable and active, people can organize their emotions and thoughts for the performance of good ends; because such religion is long-term and noetic, an emotional–intellectual appreciation and a simple, conscious awareness of reality grow over the years. Prayer enables individuals to organize their desires into a system of desires recognized as superior and then made into their own (Coe, 1916). By living a prayer life over the years, people seem to work themselves to an independent point of view whereby they do not simply view religion objectively but come to appreciate it (Starbuck, 1899). In a sense, the devotional experience is the way people join the world of intense religious experience to that of purely secular reality; it enables them to "experience" religion and at the same time develop the attitudes of mind that are the basis of democratic societies.

The obvious features of *philosophical* religion are centrality of ideas, systematic organization, and analysis. In one of his chapters, "Ideas and Religious Experience," Ames (1910) assigned an important role to the intellect and rational thinking. Starbuck (1899) argued that a rational system of ideas and beliefs is a basic component of religion. Thouless (1956) said that rational elements are not an extremely strong element of people's religious lives, inasmuch as pure rationality leads to skepticism when it does not have the support of emotional elements. But he pointed out that the religious experiences of individuals are better if such individuals have in mind their own traditions and their own personalities. Somehow people have to pay rational attention to their tradition in order to have it enter more fully into their lives. And a healthy religious consciousness is really objective introspection into one's own religious personality. Leuba says, "The control of the psychical forces is the practical aim of psychology—of the psychology of religious life as well as any other branch of the science" (1912, p. 269).

Modern Studies of Mystical and Ordinary Religion

Efforts to describe and label the thoughts and emotions involved in the religious experience and to place them in categories have continued in one way or another to the present day. But few psychologists have been willing to call themselves psychologists of religion since the 1920s. There were certain individual psychologists who did study religion extensively, but since their vocabulary was closely tied to their theories we discuss it elsewhere. There have been important studies of the relationship between psychology and religion by psychologists with church concerns or religious scholarship as their primary focus—Dittes, Clark, Hiltner, Johnson, and Strunk—but non–theory-bound efforts to describe and label were few and far between. Nonetheless, there has been a return to analysis and research that revives or expands simple descriptive vocabulary to pose one or two questions or to solve one issue at a time.

Two areas of study are modern-day counterparts of the projects and vocabularly development just reviewed. Since these areas correspond roughly to the studies of mystical and ordinary states, leading researchers in them refer or at least bow their heads to William James, although James himself probably would not welcome their attentions. A contemporary psychologist of religion put it this way:

> Some of the battles James was fighting would be viewed by contemporary scientists as on their behalf; he can be quoted and proof-texted for his opposition to a monolithic, supernatural, reductionistic understanding of religious phenomena, a view that precludes psychological investigation. Because his philosophy insisted on taking religious phenomena seriously as *phenomena*, he fought battles that paved the way for scientific study. But because James was opposed to established, exclusivistic, monolithic reductionism of any kind, and not just *religiously* established monopolies, his philosophy can be

turned against much of contemporary science just as well. Because he insists on taking religious phenomena seriously, as *phenomena* with an authority and importance in themselves, he raised constant objection against attempts to capture these phenomena in the name of science. [Dittes, 1973, 295–96]

The problem is that James gave us psychological labels without any encouragement to use them for psychological research. In addition, he gave us philosophical understanding of psychological phenomena without creating a psychological theory.

But a majority of psychologists who wish to study religious experiences as unique phenomena described in some scientifically useful way and interpreted in some broadly philosophical manner, refer themselves back to William James. There is no unity to their work in the sense of the theory-bound psychologists of the chapters to come. The work of Starbuck, Leuba, Coe, Ames, and several others of the first decades of this century was done, for all practical purposes, in dialogue with James. None of them approached his philosophical acumen, but all shared his goal of understanding the psychological meaning of religious phenomena in their own right. The studies of religious thoughts and feelings to be presented now do not follow a James tradition, strictly speaking, because there is none. But they do try to delineate these religious thoughts and feelings psychologically: Psychologists of recent decades who purport in one way or another to carry on the work of James keep their labels clear but do not absolutize them; they try to understand the psychoreligious meaning of these human phenomena without assuming a role for religion within personality structure.

We look, then, at modern studies of altered states of consciousness and clinical psychology-of-religion studies. Because attribution theory emphasizes so much the ordinary-language labeling of psychological and religious data, it provides an overall setting for these studies. Contemporary studies of "attribution theory" attempt to describe the conditions under which meaning can be attributed to experiences, religious or otherwise. People interpret diffuse physiological arousal in the light of the context in which they find themselves: The same kind of arousal could be interpreted as anger or as joy. Today researchers try to discover the conditions under which attributions are made.

The roots of attribution theory are found in William James, and research on the theory can illuminate some data described in James (Proudfoot and Shaver, 1975). The theory deals with individuals' interpretations of their own experiences and behavior, an important issue in psychological study of religion. It is a specific religious interpretation of a given insight or feeling that makes it religious. Religious experiences are more than naturalistic processes (Havens, 1963).

There is no formal, unified "theory" here, but really a collection of findings and interpretations. One set of findings indicated that arousal of the sympathetic nervous system caused by physical activities, drugs, or hormones could receive all different types of labels from the most rewarding to the most distressful (Schacter and Singer, 1962). Given these results, it is plausible to say that at least some religious experiences are due to diffuse emotional states that are given a religious interpretation. Another set of findings indicated that people who are not sure of their original motivations for behavior interpret it and form self-concepts in light of the context in which they find themselves (Bem, 1972): People may not be right about themselves, but their self-evaluations are the ones that most powerfully affect their future behavior. Research on high and low achievers is especially clear on the issue of interpretation of behavior, because high achievers and low achievers when given a pill that was supposed to interfere with psychomotor coordination reversed their usual ways. High achievers, believing that the superior energies attributed to themselves would no longer carry them to success, did not achieve as much as high achievers in the no-pill group. On the other hand, low achievers, believing their accomplishments no longer impeded by their self-attributed inferior abilities, achieved significantly more than low achievers without the pill.

These results have been applied to two specific instances of religious experience, a classic case of conversion recounted in William James's *Varieties,* and an American Nichiren Buddhist group, Nichiren Shoshu (Proudfoot and Shaver, 1975). In James's report a certain Stephen Bradley notices a suddenly increased heartbeat. Since he has just returned from a revival meeting, he attributes this to the Holy Spirit and finds a scriptural quote that he believes perfectly describes his situation. Members of the Nichiren group constantly recite "Glory to the wonderful truth of the Lotus Sutra," because they are told it will change their lives. By relaxing and attributing everything to an external cause, members are able to accept even changes for the worse in their lives as something better. More recently, attribution theory has been able to reveal the likelihood that people will attribute religious significance to events that are personal, important, negative, and medical (Spilka and Schmidt, 1983).

Mystical Religion: Altered States of Consciousness

An altered state of consciousness does not automatically imply a religious experience. Those whose consciousness is altered must start out in some kind of religiously significant context or have a religious interpretation put to them afterward (the attribution of meaning to processes, functions, and relationships at the very moment they are operative is proper only to ordinary states of consciousness). Especially with altered states of consciousness it may seem more likely that there will be a religious attribution, but it is not necessary. While people may normally associate anything that is a change or a release from the normal with religion, they may also associate it with sex or medicine (Butts, 1978). We can say, though, that states of consciousness quite different from the ordinary are more likely to be interpreted as religious in many cultures. In fact, some cultures assume an altered state for the basic religious experiences. Take the example of "light," used as a metaphor for the divine presence in Western Christian culture but understood literally in several widely varying Eastern traditions. The figurative interpretation, promoted in the guided affective imagery of the *Spiritual Exercises* of St. Ignatius Loyola, is appropriate to the daily routine of meditation and living. But forms of meditation taught by some Buddhist, Islamic, and Greek Orthodox writers promote an experience of a literal pure, white light (Fischer, 1977–78a). This interpretation is appropriate to the extremes of ecstasy and meditative quiet described below.

In the contemporary lay literature regarding "altered states of consciousness," mysticism, and meditation, the words seldom have standardized meanings: We have too much vocabulary. Meditation, the most general term, suggests a step-by-step set of procedures for religious prayer. But it is more the development of a "way of being somewhere," a "mode of presence" (Maupin, 1969; Naranjo and Ornstein, 1971). As Ornstein says, "No matter the object of meditation or how superficial the practice of meditation, the exercises seem to be attempts to restrict awareness to a single, unchanging source of stimulation for a definite period of time" (p. 145). Mysticism is a meditative or reflective experience of a special intensity. So many different kinds of "intense" artistic, religious, and relational experiences have been called mystical (Laski, 1961; Maslow, 1970; Greeley, 1974) that mysticism cannot be sharply defined. Until recently there was no real attempt to give a psychological working definition to mysticism or to scale the intensities of the mystical experience to permit the researcher to examine distinctive differences in the experience, and some think that the concept of mysticism has not been clarified by research done thus far (Thomas and Cooper, 1978). Ultimately only slight nuances have been added to the descriptions of mysticism given by James and his contemporaries. The components of the mystical experience are still taken to be awareness of God or divine power; a sense of new knowledge and spiritual enlightenment; feelings of unity and oneness, joy, peace, and happiness; a variety of strong emotions and physical reactions; and sometimes extreme sensory stimulation and hallucinations. This list might be summarized in a fourfold classification of religious experiences: transcendental, vertigo (disorientation), life change, and visionary (Margolis and Elifson, 1979).

Research has indicated that those reporting mystical experiences of whatever kind were more religiously committed and possessed more psychological strength and openness (Hood, 1973, 1975). Attempts to "account for" mystical experiences emphasize the incongruities between low-stress anticipation and stressful activity, and between a low-stress setting and a stressful experience (Hood, 1978a). Mysticism, then, is many things:

> The available scientific evidence tends to support the view that the mystic experience is one of internal perception, an experience that can be ecstatic, profound, or therapeutic for purely internal reasons. Yet for psychological science, the

problem of understanding such internal processes is hardly less complex than the theological problem of understanding God. [Deikman, 1969, pp. 45–46]

The research that has the more precisely developed description and vocabulary is on the type of mysticism that involves altered states of consciousness.

We call some states of consciousness "altered" because they are altered from the ordinary consciousness of a given culture (Tart, 1975b) and can partially or totally restrict the interpreting activity of the brain. Raw sensory experience (called subcortical activity) cannot be made the object of organization, understanding, and reasoning (all called cortical activity). However, altered states of consciousness take place in settings that engender a religious awareness before the experience and a religious interpretation afterward. The extremes, or "heights," of mystical experience are such that attribution of religious meaning cannot be made in the midst of the experience, but only before or afterward: The alteration of consciousness is so extreme that images no longer work.

So, to understand the ecstatic and mystical states, researchers today—Fischer, Ornstein, Tart, West—analyze what happens to the brain and nervous system as people move from ordinary perception of life around them to ecstasy at one end of the spectrum, and from ordinary perception to profound meditation at the other.

Roland Fischer (1971, 1975) used the term (hardly ordinary language!) ergotropic arousal to describe the activity of the sympathetic nervous system—that part of the nervous system that engenders energy. "Ergotropic" simply means "turning toward energy." With ever increasing arousal, people can progressively pass through sensitivity, creativity, anxiety, even acute schizophrenic and catatonic states, to ecstatic and mystical rapture. Fischer calls the movement toward inactivity and calm trophotropic arousal, which is an integration of the parasympathetic nervous system—the part that causes calmness—with the body's motor activities. This includes behavioral patterns that conserve and restore energy and decrease people's sensitivity to external stimuli and sedation. People pass from ordinary perception through a tranquil and hypoaroused (underaroused) state to ultimate zen and yoga meditation (Anand, Chhina, and Singh, 1969; Karamatsu and Hirae, 1969). Those going in either

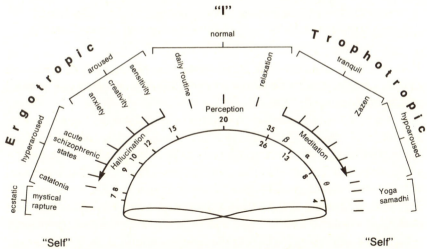

Figure 2-1. Varieties of conscious states mapped on a perception–hallucination continuum of increasing ergotropic arousal (*left*) and on a perception–meditation continuum of increasing trophotropic arousal (*right*). These levels of hyper- and hypoarousal are interpreted by man as normal, creative, psychotic, and ecstatic states (*left*) and Zazen and samadhi (*right*). The loop connecting ecstasy and samadhi represents the rebound from ecstasy to samadhi, which is observed in response to intense ergotropic excitation. The numbers 35 to 7 on the perception–hallucination continuum are Goldstein's coefficient of variation, specifying the increase in variability of the EEG amplitude with increasing ergotropic arousal. The numbers 26 to 4 on the perception–meditation continuum, on the other hand, refer to those beta, alpha, and theta EEG waves (measured in hertz) that predominate during, but are not specific to, these states. *Reproduced with permission from Roland Fischer, "A Cartography of the Ecstatic and Meditative States," Science 174 (1971): 897–904. Copyright © 1971 by the American Association for the Advancement of Science. Used by permission of the AAAS and the author.*

of these directions experience alterations of space and time perception. They report a depersonalized type of self-awareness.

A number of related brain functions are analyzed by researchers trying to understand altered states. They study brain waves, eye movements, the relation of sensory to motor (S/M) ratio, apposition to proposition (A/P) ratio, right hemisphere to left hemisphere brain activity, and the relationship of cortical to subcortical activity. These terms overlap, because some of them are very specific terms and some very general. They are not theory-bound, however, so we need only see what they apply to.

Though analysis of brain waves cannot give us all the details of the mental imaging that goes on in ecstatic or meditation experiences, the states of ergotropic and trophotropic arousal are characterized by brain wave activities that can be interpreted as corresponding to one another (as measured on an elec-troencehpalogram). L. Goldstein worked out a mathematical pattern (a coefficient of variation) showing the decrease in variability of the brain wave (EEG) amplitude with increasing ergotropic arousal. These numbers parallel the beta, alpha, and theta brain waves (measured in hertz) that predominate during, but are not specific to, the meditative states (Fischer, 1971).

Frequency of eye movement also characterizes increased ergotropic arousal. If we remember that rapid scanning movements are regarded as a prerequisite for the fixation of an object in physical space-time, then we can be impressed by the fact that the frequency of eye movements is increased fivefold to eightfold in response to ergotropic arousal. Eye movements decrease proportionately to trophotropic arousal along the perception–meditation continuum.

Another concomitant is an increased ratio of sensory to motor activity, that is, experiences of intense sensations in-crease while the voluntary motor activity capable of verifying these experiences decreases. Fischer (1971) says that verifiable perceptions can be described as having low S/M ratios, while non-verifiable hallucinations and dreams can be characterized by increasing S/M ratios. He supports this statement with hand-writing and handwriting-pressure experiments. More general-ized notions that can be expressed in ratio measurements con-comitant to ergotropic and trophotropic arousal are "apposition" and "proposition." Appositions are generalized sensibilities, attitudes, or felt meanings, while propositions are distinct ideas, clear thoughts and expressed judgments. In-creased arousal means increased ratio of apposition expressions to proposition expressions (A/P ratio). Hyperaroused and hypoaroused meditative states bring an increased inhibition and, finally, blocking of the intentions and the capacity for verification through peripheral voluntary motor activity. Hallucinatory behavior occurs under conditions characterized by high S/M and high A/P ratios.

The two separate hemispheres of the brain can process infor-mation separately from one another. While the left—the analytic, verifying, and deciding portion of the brain—is operating, the other can rest, and when the right side is process-ing visuospatial forms and fields, metaphors, music, and imagery, the left side can be disengaged. With increased arousal, the ability to check out the ideations of the right hemisphere with the left hemisphere through the section of the brain called the *corpus callosum* is diminished. The subject "spends more time" in the right hemisphere than the left one. Hallucinogenic drug and sleep experiments (Goldstein, Stoltzfus, and Gardocki, 1972; Goldstein and Stoltzfus, 1973) have begun to establish that activity is shifted to the visuospatial, or right, hemisphere whenever a person moves toward the hallucination side or the meditative side of the spectrum.

In fact, one definition of an altered state of consciousness is "any state where the left hemisphere is in abeyance" (Gowan, 1978, p. 141). Right hemisphere function can then be described according to a given order. If the right hemisphere function is mediated by the left, it gives rise to intellectual creativity. If the right hemisphere alone functions, it gives rise to artistic creativity. If the right-hemisphere-alone function cannot be expressed at all, it must find some bodily outlet in trance or even in schizophrenia.

With the movement toward ecstasy or samadhi (deep meditation) the separateness of cortical from subcortical activity disappears, the self does not distinguish between subject and object, and symbols take the place of rational object and discourse. Subcortical activity is the sensory experience of observational relations, such as the image of an external stimulus configuration on the retina, a subcortical structure. Any subsequent interpretation of this is labeled cortical activity. With increasing hyperarousal or hypoarousal, the subject's capacity to verify gradually wanes, and the intense sensory experience becomes an event received internally that cannot be verified externally (Fischer, 1975). However, some interpreters insist that there must always be some type of intellectual control, distinguishing two fundamental strategies for meditation: concentration and insight (Goleman, 1978–79). Concentration is careful attention toward a single object or point of focus, while insight results from the maintenance of a specific perceptual cognitive attitude toward objects rising to consciousness. Concentration can result in visions on the perception–hallucination continuum or in absorptions on the perception–meditation continuum. Movement toward insight involves a training of attention that is at the beginning of the perception–hallucination continuum, or it involves an increasing sense of detachment from the objects contemplated on the perception–meditation continuum.

A positive interpretation of all this is that at the extremes of ecstasy and meditation people are most themselves. They move from the "I" of the physical world to the "self" of the mental dimension: "The 'Self' of exalted states is that which sees and knows, while the "I" is the interpretation, that which is seen and known in the physical space–time of the world 'out there'" (Fischer, 1971, p. 902). There is an alternation between the ecstasy and samadhi states. Life in general is an alteration between activity and repose, intensity and relaxation, so there is no reason why this alternation cannot take place on specialized levels of consciousness.

To the extent that we can describe what happens to the brain and the nervous system during an altered state of consciousness, we can describe the physiological phenomenon of the intense mystical experience. The work of Fischer and others is a worthy attempt to coordinate information and vocabulary. The meaning of the physiological phenomenon is what the experiencer attributes to it.

Ordinary Religious Attribution

For the most comprehensive list of the processes, functions, and relationships that can have a religious attribution we turn to the work of Paul Pruyser (1968). Pruyser places himself in the psychology of religion tradition that began with William James, but with his own clinical experience and his knowledge of the clinical experience of psychologists, psychiatrists, and chaplains he has been able to describe a range of religious experiences far more extensive than the purely mystical. He says that the basic question is, "Which data of experience are of religious significance?" (Pruyser, 1968, p. 12).

In every instance Pruyser labels a literal physical and/or psychological datum and a symbolic, metaphorical derivative that then affects the original activity. For example, the faculty of hearing is brought into play in most religious gatherings: Physiologically there are sounds received by the ear, and mentally there is the shaping of those sounds into some kind of meaning. In Christian circles the metaphor of *hearing* the Word of God has developed to represent the notion that people receive communications from God. When the Bible is read, then, the sense of hearing is brought into play in a way that is specific to the religious context. So the physiopsychological and the symbolic together form a religious attribution. Let us look at some of these processes in order.

PERCEPTUAL PROCESSES (Pruyser, 1968, Chapter 2). Having used hearing as an example, we move on to vision. Ordinary visual processes take in the light, color, and space variations that provide the context for a religious act, be it formal, ritual, or simple meditation in natural surroundings. Metaphors of light and of sacred space about here: sun and moon divinities, wars between light and darkness, underworlds, and spheres of infinite distance. Hence religious believers often feel they are seeing something different when witnessing a religious act or meditating upon the meaning of nature. Touch: laying on of hands, changing of clothes, use of touchable sacred vessels. Some touches are suggested for the sake of healing; others are forbidden as causes of defilement. Positioning (kinesthesis): yoga and prayer promotes and symbolizes variants of restfulness, peace, and attention. Smell and taste: sacramental meals and the "odor of sacrifice," incense, candles, and flowers, expressing delight, pleasure, and gratification, as well as loathing and nausea, are smell and taste metaphors transferred to prayer experience and morality. Pain: penance and mortification are involved in a variety of religious activities both within and outside the actual rites of worship. Suffering and endurance are seen as ways of sharing in or commemorating the painful and self-giving activities of divinity figures and heroes.

INTELLECTUAL PROCESSES (1968, Chapters 3 and 4). The content of religious thought and intellectual exchange ranges from straight "God talk" to stirring secular ideas. Memory conserves the collective experiences of a religious tradition and the important religious moments of an individual life. The range of acceptable information goes from openness toward a wide variety of world views to the narrowest forms of fanaticism. Imagination, or image-making if you will, is central to all but the most rationalistic religious activity. The religious believer imagines activity going on in other worlds, events that have taken place or are going to take place. Sometimes the image-making operates in such a way that gods, heroes, stunning nature changes (dancings of the sun, rivers of blood) are perceived and understood to be as real and logical as everyday nature. Sometimes the believers guide their imagination through an array of religious fantasies and ideas, knowing full well that they are simply recalling, picturing, thinking about these things. Contradictory images can be brought together (as they are in dreams) to express the paradoxes and mysteries of the religious tradition. Plain, simple stories can be told.

EMOTIONAL PROCESSES (1968, Chapter 6).   The emotions of the believer are often responses to the emotions that are attributed to the divinities or cosmic powers of a given tradition. Thus, the deity's power, mystery, wrath, majesty, energy, admirability, and otherness are responded to by the believer's creatureliness, awe, dread, humility, commitment to acts, bliss, and nothingness. Most religious traditions demand a selectivity in emotions, a negative way of sensory deprivation (mortification, abstinence, asceticism, withdrawal, denial, repression, supression, isolation) and a positive way of selective ambitions and passions (relative to the feelings allowed toward deities and toward other people). Rituals facilitate everything from boundless ecstasy to quiet; there is the whole range, from whirling dances to heads bowed in prayer. One can hate evil spirits; one can love the good God.

LINGUISTIC FUNCTIONS (1968, Chapter 5).   Words are signs and symbols that represent the mental operations and viewpoints of their users, hence myths and rituals are considered expressive of the mental faculties of the people who create them. Religious language often has special qualities; there are dialects or holdovers of older ways of speaking, or special scripts and alphabets that in one way or another set religious speech apart from day-to-day expression. Religious language accomplishes specific tasks, such as philosophical demonstration, admonition, erotic or aggressive expression, and pious, ecstatic, or fanatical sentiment. There are sacred words, sacred names, and even the establishing of a sacred atmosphere by speaking in tongues.

MOTOR-SYSTEM FUNCTIONS (1968, Chapter 7).   The motor system has to do with the generation and concentration of energy. There is an interaction between the concept of divine or cosmic power and the physical—perhaps we could say psychomotor—energy that exists at an active level in the person. If the person has a sense of transaction with the holy, there may be an increase in psychomotor energy. Energy can be controlled through rituals and interiorized norms. There is a further interaction with other processes and functions: between motor and verbal cognitive activity and symbolic gestures, between energy generated in ritual activity and social concerns that become operative as a result. Finally, the activity that takes place in sleep, such as physical refreshment and dream activities, can be both an impetus for and a tangible result of intellectual and emotional religious activity.

In religious experience these processes and functions are combined into larger units of mental activity—relationships that are expressed in attitudes. The physiological, the emotional, and the intellectual all combine into attitudes toward others, things, and ideas, and into the self-attitudes that are sometimes obviously religious in theme and sometimes not.

RELATIONAL ATTITUDES TOWARD OTHERS (1968, Chapter 8). The individual is integrated into a group by common experience, which usually takes the form of celebration or social morality. The scope of human relationships is regulated by religious norms that sometimes restrict, sometimes broaden the scope, depending on the role of a religious individual within the community. Patterns of childbearing, family size, and parental roles are regulated within religious traditions. As a young person grows, responsibility to and for the believing community beyond the family is well regulated. Regulation is most obvious in the personal attachments formed at various points in the individual's life and the relationship of these attachments to the individual's role. The role of the hermit who completely withdraws from society is important in several of the great world religions, as is that of the monk who withdraws into a small group. At the other end of the scale is the missionary who goes outside of his or her own normal area of activity, presumably because of a concern for other people. Between these two one finds the basic family and community roles, and they are regulated by religious norms regarding sexuality, openness, and balance of work and celebration.

All these relationships are often thought to be in imitation of, parallel to, or a preparation for the communal existence of

another world. The life experience of any group of people influences their beliefs in the communal meaning of religion and in
some species of heavenly community.

RELATIONAL ATTITUDES TOWARD THINGS AND IDEAS (1968,
Chapter 9). Possessions are vital to most people, so the way
they are defended, on one hand, and shared, on the other, is central to religious development and goals. Naturally, they are often
the objects of moral regulations or even faith attitudes.
Psychological sense of time and of space can certainly determine
religious concepts, as is evident from attitudes of people of
vastly different sociocultural backgrounds and even more evident from an examination of the psychologies of people of different historical periods: Modern knowledge of galaxies and in-
terstellar space makes modern people different from their
ancestors, who thought that the earth was the center of the
whole universe. A sense of the world evolving over millions of
years is different from a sense of a five-to-six-thousand-year-old
world. Concepts of the powers of the universe and the personalities that people them can be vastly different.

Views of nature and views of art also strongly influence
religious sensibilities. Is nature fearsome, or is it suffused with
the creative presence of the deity? Does art represent divine inspiration in the human personality, or must the individual expression be neutralized to certain church-acceptable norms?
Does art represent the divine world or compete with it?

RELATIONAL ATTITUDES TOWARD THE SELF (1968, Chapter 10).
Consciousness of body, consciousness of a unified self, and consciousness of some kind of extended self are involved in attitudes toward the self. The importance of directing bodily functions and of controlling the body is underlined in both legal and
religious codes of behavior. Sometimes control is simple, and at
other times it involves coping, which for the religious person
means praying as part of official worship and as part of personal
fantasy formation. Attitudes toward the body—amiable,
despicable, or in between—are probably the primary determinants of attitudes toward the entire personality: but there can
often be a split whereby individuals despise their physical bodies
to the great favor of some imagined distinct, spiritual self.
Religious traditions can either place a high value on the body
and emphasis on its transforming functions or denigrate the
body as the personality's principal enemy or hindrance to prog-

ress. On the other hand, when the various facts of the personality are considered to be part of a unity, in other words, when the body–soul dichotomy is bypassed, there is still the major problem of accepting, or at least working with, the whole of one's personality. Religious traditions often cause individuals to internalize admonitions and prohibitions, so that people find themselves tyrranized by scruples or see no sense of obligation at all. The balance is to make various forms of self-control lead to recognized self-fulfillment. This can lead individuals to a consciousness of an ideal self, either derived from the image of divinity or savior or derived from a communal idea.

Pruyser's listings for exploring fundamental religious attributions have scarcely been explored, but there is no more complete or suggestive list than his. Almost all psychological faculties that have been interpreted as functioning religiously in ordinary human experience are listed here.

If we take stock of what we have accomplished in this chapter, we see that a miscellaneous collection of words relatively useful to describe mystical and ordinary religious experiences has been gathered. This has been a simple report, not a systematic attempt to create a basic vocabulary for psychology of religion.

Since the beginning of this century psychologists have analyzed the thought and feeling components of a number of religious phenomena. The vocabulary used by William James in his discussion of religious experience was used as the point of departure. He used the terms healthy-minded, sick-soul, and twice-born to discuss personality orientations and discussed general qualities of asceticism, strength of soul, purity of heart, and love. With this as a background to his analysis of conversion and mysticism, he developed a discussion of "fields of consciousness" to understand conversion. He also analyzed the ineffable, noetic, transient, and passive qualities of the mystical experience. Along with other psychologists he listed the perceptual factors (awareness) involved in the range of emotions possible in mystical experiences, ordinary prayer, and philosophical reflection. In the last decade or so discussion and research have resulted in the development of more detailed descriptions of perceptual factors and the range of emotions. Roland Fischer and others speak of the changes involved (brain waves, S/M and A/P ratios, relationships of right to left brain hemispheral activity and cortical to subcortical activity); Paul Pruyser gives a long list of religious attribution examples (processes, functions, and relational attitudes). This is not necessarily the best vocabulary possible, but it is what has developed in the course of the sporadic psychology of religion study in this country in this century, drawn from much observation and some research.

Ways of talking about religious psychological experiences that have been fashioned as part of a theory may describe and explain more. Theories both resolve and create problems in the psychology of religion, as we shall see in the next two chapters.

PART II

Religion Within the Context of Personality

Explanation of the role of religion in the personality has been part of a more broadly based effort to explain the personality as a unity and in all its parts (Maddi, 1972). This is an obvious step beyond categorizing religious thoughts and feelings or the development of vocabulary for ad hoc considerations. Explanations of religion are part of explanations of the overall direction of living with its basic instincts, ideals, and goals. In the conflict version, of which theories of Freud and Jung are examples, the person is seen as shaped by powerful and opposing forces, either the individual and society (Freud) or forces within the individual. The fulfillment version, of which the theories of Gordon Allport and Abraham Maslow are examples, sees the person as shaped by only one great force, either a drive toward ideas and goals (Allport) or a genetic blueprint that determines the person's capabilities. In the conditioning version, of which the theory of Skinner is the best-known example, an individual is shaped by an environment that reinforces certain types of behavior.

The role of religion in each version is different, of course, and more or less coordinates with the theory as a whole. In turn, the theory has its setting in the life of the psychologist who developed it. When Freud, Jung, or any of the other psychologists speak of instincts, forces, images, dispositions, peak experiences, or crises of the will, they are necessarily relying on their own experiences of life and the world. Their theories are related to their personal lives.

In Part II ways of discussing the personality are presented as if they go together in balanced fashion, as if the psychologists who created them or support them get along perfectly, complementing (and complimenting) one another. This is not the case: Freud and Jung had a serious disagreement; Allport did not work with large areas of psychoanalysis; Maslow's and Rollo May's concerns were far from identical. This is not necessarily a problem for psychologists today, however, because few of them are willing to adopt a given theory as *the* way of describing people's personalities and the details of mental functioning. Psychologists now tend to choose ways of explaining mental activity from a repertoire of procedures and concepts fashioned in various circumstances by theorists of the past. It is possible today to make use of a number of psychological terms, ideas, and modes of explanation without committing oneself to the whole of a theory of becoming part of a controversy (Garfield, 1980).

How should we divide up personality theories and decide which ones have the most interesting assumptions about religion? One may divide them into conflict theory (Freud, Jung et al.), fulfillment theory (Allport, Maslow, and existentialist psychologists) and consistency theory (Kelley, Festinger et al.) (Maddi, 1972). Or one may choose divisions into analytic, humanistic, and behavioral psychologies (Homans, 1970; Nye, 1981). Some handbooks simply discuss personality theories as products of individual psychologists (Hall and Lindzey, 1970).

I have chosen to discuss two approaches to personality here, the analytic and the humanistic. Accordingly, one chapter is devoted to Freud and Jung and another to All-port, Maslow, and Rollo May. Consistency theory is dis-cussed in the chapter on social psychology. Behavioral psy-cology receives no chapter of its own, because, in spite of the reflections of B. F. Skinner on religion, behaviorists usually do not concern themselves with the meaning of reli-gion or the basic causes of religious behavior. They are less interested in theorizing than in experimenting and estab-lishing patterns of control, and religion has received no sig-nificant attention in the development of their theories.

Religion Out of Depth Conflict: Freud and Jung

FREUD TOLD OF AN EXCHANGE of correspondence with a young doctor who had a religious experience resulting in conversion to active Christianity. The young doctor wrote to Freud:

> I am writing now to tell you of an experience that I had in the year I graduated at the University of X. One afternoon while I was passing through the dissecting-room my attention was attracted to a sweet-faced dear old woman who was being carried to a dissecting-table. This sweet-faced woman made such an impression on me that a thought flashed up in my mind, "There is no God: if there were a God he would not have allowed this dear old woman to be brought into the dissecting room."
>
> When I got home that afternoon the feeling I had had at the sight in the dissecting-room had determined me to discontinue going to church. The doctrines of Christianity had before this been the subject of doubts in my mind.
>
> While I was meditating on this matter a voice spoke to my soul that "I should consider the step I was about to take." My

spirit replied to this inner voice by saying, "If I knew of a certainty that Christianity was truth and the Bible was the Word of God, then I would accept it."

In the course of the next few days God made it clear to my soul that the Bible was his Word, that the teachings about Jesus Christ were true, and that Jesus was our only hope. After such a clear revelation I accepted the Bible as God's Word and Jesus Christ as my personal Savior. Since then God has revealed himself to me by many infallible proofs. [Freud, 1959b, pp. 243-44]

The man had seen the body of the old woman ready for dissection, and he wanted to deny the existence of a God who could allow this final degradation to such a sweet old thing. This antireligious feeling persisted until, after rereading some biblical sources, the young doctor "gave in to a notion of God as allpowerful and all righteous." This is easy to understand, says Freud: It is just the projection into mental images of a conflict that happened in the man's life when he was a youngster. The results are the same in the new conflict as in the original one, the man gives in. He submits to an image of God that is the representation of his own father.

Jung's analysis of one of his patient's dreams is not unlike Freud's analysis of the doctor's religious experience, but his conclusions are different. The dream: "I am in a lofty cathedral filled with mysterious twilight. They tell me that it is the cathedral at Lourdes. In the centre there is a deep dark well, into which I have to descend" (Jung, 1972, p. 103). The patient connects the dream with a description, given by his mother when he was a child, of Cologne cathedral. This description and his mother's connection with it haunted him. As a child the patient wanted to be a priest in such a cathedral, so Jung believes that the symbol of Cologne cathedral, mutated in the dream, of course, is related to the need to find a substitute for the mother. The well is a baptismal font, which in fact is conceptualized as a womb in some church literature. "The Church represents a higher spiritual substitute for the purely natural, or 'carnal' tie to the parents" (Jung, 1972, p. 105). It thus has a freeing function. For Jung the role of religion is as varied as the different figures that appear in the conscious or unconscious mind.

Both Freud and Jung constructed extremely complex theories of personality in their efforts to describe the depths of the unconscious mind and explain its workings. Their descriptions and explanations are intimately bound up with their personality theories, thus distinguishing them from the non–theory-bound descriptions in the last chapter. Because the theories do differ from one another, we examine separately their descriptions and explanations of religion, concentrating on what each of them had to say about religious belief and religious morality.

Freud's Interpretation of the Religious Experience

Sigmund Freud grew up in Catholic Vienna in the latter part of the nineteenth century. The abolition of the Jewish ghettos and the granting of a number of civil rights had profoundly affected Jewish home life, and young people often modified considerably or rejected the religious ways of their parents. Religion did not interest Freud much as he made his way through the early school years and medical studies. Though normally not concerned with his Jewish identity, he was still influenced by it (Bakan, 1958; Ellenberger, 1970).

Trained in medicine, Freud was a researcher and a professor, primarily concerned, of course, with psychological issues. His earliest studies were of cell tissue, but he quickly moved to the physiology of the brain, specializing in aphasia and cerebral palsy. By 1895 he had completed a draft study of neurology in which he attempted to account for complex psychological behavior.

In the following years Freud tried to arrive at a theory of neurosis that depended on brain physiology. After working with theories of hysteria, he published, in 1900, long studies of his own dreams and, in 1905, discussions of the oral, anal, and phallic stages of development that attracted strong criticism. When it appeared as if Freud's theoretical structures were just about complete, he began major alterations. Replacing his earlier notions of conscious, preconscious, and unconscious by id, ego, and superego in 1923, he emphasized analysis of the subtle dynamics of repressions by the controlling element of the mind (ego). Of course, from the turn of the century onward he had made periodic suggestions about the technique of psychoanalysis, with special emphasis on transference. In his later years Freud turned to speculation about the meaning of religion in general and the Judeo-Christian God in particular. We look at these studies in relation to the theory of personality that he developed.

In Freud's version of the personality, religious experience is seen as a projection of the father figure, which in turn is a result of the conflict between an individual and those closest to him in surrounding society, the parents. Such a view presupposes that the universe around the individual is mysterious and unconquerable. It is a fitting "screen" on which to project the results of personal strife: One "sees" in the heavens the results of the conflict with the father-figure that has been going on in one's own mind.

Freud was concerned with the two sides of religion, formation of beliefs and ethical behavior. Relative to beliefs, he tried to describe the images that form in people's minds (Rizzuto, 1979), and relative to conscience, he tried to describe how a proper understanding of oneself leads to moral behavior (Rieff, 1961). Conflict is at the center of both developments, but they are distinct or at least can be discussed separately.

God-Image Out of the Oedipus Complex

In several of his works Freud explains the conflict between father and little boy, and the projection of the mental images resulting from his conflict onto the boy's picture of the universe. The most important phase of the infant's development occurs when he loves the mother in such a way as to see his father as a rival for the attention and love of the mother. There is an infantile sexual element here involving the child's deepest drives, so the resolution of the conflict is vital. Here is Freud's description of the Oedipus complex in the little boy (he assumed something similar happened to the little girl):

> At a very early age the little boy develops an object-cathexis [a type of dependency love] for his mother . . . ; the boy deals with his father by identifying himself with him. For a time these two relationships proceed side by side, until the boy's sexual wishes in regard to his mother become more intense and his father is perceived as an obstacle to them; from this the Oedipus complex originates. His identification with his father then takes on a hostile coloring and changes into a wish to get rid of his father in order to take his place with his mother.

Henceforward his relation to his father is ambivalent; it seems as if the ambivalence inherent in the identification from the beginning had become manifest. An ambivalent attitude to his father and an object-relation of a solely affectionate kind to his mother make up the content of the simple positive Oedipus complex in a boy. [1960, pp. 21–22]

Freud earlier introduced a bit of supposed primitive history into his theorizing to show how people through the ages have made their father-figure sacred. Relying heavily on some of the anthropology of his day—Tylor, Long, Frazer, and others—he posited that people originally lived in hordes under the domination of a single powerful and violent father. One day, sons who had been driven away came and devoured their father. An animal image (called a *totem*) in effect was chosen to represent the father. The father was remembered at a ritual meal where the killing was commemorated by the eating of the totem. "The totem meal . . . would thus be a repetition and a commemoration of this memorable and criminal deed, which was the beginning of so many things—of social organization, of moral restrictions, and of religion" (1950b, p. 142). As societies further evolved the totem animal was gradually replaced by a god in a series of transitions, until power was given to a single god who tolerated no others. Freud thought that all of this left memory traces in the mind of modern human beings and combined with an individual's own father representation to form the mental imagery that became the individual's own representation of God.

With this profound experience of father, both personal and collective, humans must face the more general and fearsome otherness of the whole world about them. Beyond the awesomeness of the father, there is the awesomeness of all of life, time, and space; beyond the frustrations that come from the rivalry with the father is the frustration of failure in life, of underachieving, or even constant suffering. In *The Future of An Illusion* Freud says this:

When the growing individual finds that he is destined to remain a child for ever, that he can never do without protection against strange superior powers, he lends those powers the features belonging to the figure of his father; he creates for himself the gods whom he dreads, whom he seeks to propitiate, and whom he nevertheless entrusts with his own protection. Thus his longing for a father is a motive identical with his need for protection against the consequences of his human weakness. The defense against childish helplessness is what lends its characteristic features to the adult's reaction to the helplessness which *he* has to acknowledge—a reaction which is precisely the formation of religion. [1961, p. 24]

Varieties of fears and guilt feelings cause religious practices that we call compulsive. Decades before *The Future of an Illusion* Freud pointed out the close connection between the repetitions of religious ceremony and all other obsessive-compulsive acts; even then he was calling religion a "universal obsessional neurosis" [1959a, p. 34]. Religion, then, enables people to "make it," to put up with or perhaps even cope with ultimate frustrations, though at the cost of increased obsessiveness and surrender of personal freedom. Reverence and fear of the personal father and of the original human father, along with reverence and fear of the universe, lead to reverence and fear of a cosmic father figure, with appropriate accompanying religious practices.

Moses and Monotheism, written just before Freud's death in 1939, contains an outright discussion of the Western monotheistic "God," in contrast with Freud's earlier works, where he referred only to a religious force behind things or to some kind of group leader. Freud explains the Father-God of the Jews as a combination of the old Egyptian monotheism of Pharaoh Akhnaton brought by a certain "Moses," who actually was an Egyptian prince, with the tribal God Yahweh of the territory of Mambre. Moses chose one of the Hebrew tribes to propagate his religion and law, but the people were not capable of understanding the profoundity of his thought. During one of their rebellions against him they murdered him and, like the brothers in *Totem and Taboo,* never forgot their crime. In their remorse they idealized Mosaic law and submitted to a monotheistic God. For the Jews the memories of the primeval father murder and the Moses murder were repressed, so the unconscious guilt from these acts was projected onto a God-image. Freud makes some complicated comparisons between Moses and God as murdered authority images. He believed that the Christ image in Christianity was a means of assuaging guilt for father murder that the Jews never availed themselves of: Christ was a sort of resurrected Moses and the returned primeval father at the same time but was seen as a son in place of the father (Freud, 1967).

Freud saw great value in Mosaic religion, because "it allowed the people to share in the grandeur of a new conception of God, because it maintained that the people had been 'chosen' by this great God and was destined to enjoy the proofs of his special favour, and because it forced upon the people a progress in spirituality which, significant enough in itself, further opened the way to respect for intellectual work and to further instinctual renunciations" (1967, p. 158). Religion, then, can render a culture the service of encouraging the higher intellectual processes of memories, reflection, and deduction over direct sense perception. This evaluation of religion was the most positive thing Freud ever wrote on the topic.

The formation of the Oedipus complex, so important in the development of personal religion, is one of a series of stages familiar to those who know Freud's theory. The oral stage, occurring in the first year of life, is so named because the pleasure zone is the mouth and the basic activities are receiving, taking, and ways of handling the feeding process. In the anal stage (second year) the pleasure zone is the anus, and bowel training is the important area of conflict. In the phallic stage (third through fifth years) the genitals are the primary pleasure zone, and principal activities involve heterosexualizing action. Although development is by and large completed at this point, there are two further stages: the latency stage (sixth year through puberty) where sexuality lies dormant and the child learns skills that are directly related to sexuality, and the genital stage (from puberty on), characterized by mature sexuality that combines all that is learned in the pregenital stages and relies primarily on intercourse and orgasm. The person reaching genitality is fully able to love and work—*lieben und arbeiten* was Freud's theme (Erikson, 1964)—and to love and work with some small measure of success is the ultimate that the human being can hope for.

The three well-known elements of the personality, id, ego, and superego, become differentited in these stages of development, and last throughout life (1960). The id is the central reservoir of mental energy that furnishes all the power for the personality and is anything we can call mental or psychological that is inherited. The id's principle of operation is called the pleasure principle; it causes tension reduction, because the id cannot tolerate increases of energy that are experienced as uncomfortable states of tension. The fundamental activity of the id, called primary process, is the forming of a mental image that, if achieved in reality, will reduce the tension. An obvious example is hunger: The tension caused by being hungry can be reduced if the hunger is relieved. Thus primary-process thinking forms the image of food that, if attained, will actually reduce the tension.

The ego directs the energy by distinguishing first of all between things in the mind and things in the external world. The ego's principles of operation is called the reality principle, which asks whether a thing is true or false, whether it has external existence or not. This activity is called secondary process and is really nothing other than realistic thinking. The ego formulates a plan for the satisfaction of a need and then tests this plan to see whether or not it will work.

The superego is an internalized moral regulator of conduct that develops in response to rewards and punishments meted out by parents and others in authority. The superego is inclined to oppose both the ego and the id and to make the world over in its own image. As such, it has characteristics of the other two faculties even as it opposes them: somewhat nonrational like the id, and a kind of controlling function like the ego.

At the beginning of life infants simply want their needs fulfilled. They quickly discover that some needs cannot be fulfilled or that specific means must be taken to arrive at fulfillment. As they concentrate on oral, anal, and sexual pleasures, they seek means to satisfy the pleasures. If they cannot control pleasure by realistic reflection on what is good or bad for them, they are controlled by others and eventually internalize this control. In the formation of the Oedipus complex and the image of the powerful father they form an idea of a judging God. This is the result of the operation of the id, the ego, and the superego at the phallic stage. So Freud's young medical doctor in the example recounted above, driven by instinctual id to love his mother, controlled the id poorly with his ego, hence the internalized fear of his father came to control things. Years later this improper resolution of the oedipal conflict caused him to rebel against the image of God formed years before because of this lack of resolution, and once again he submitted to this image in a religious conversion. In effect, as children gradually develop a sense of themselves and surrounding reality, and especially a sense of parents in dealing with the oedipal conflict, they establish a basis for later religious (or antireligious) thoughts and feelings. For

Freud, proper exposure to secular thought and the resulting view of life will be rationalistic and nonreligious.

The clearest presentation of the development of the God-image is shown in Figure 3-1. Note that an evil image, the devil, also develops out of the racial and individual experience and comes to exist in the mind, and how that image then becomes an idea. Freud did not explain all these connections causally (Rizzuto, 1979, pp. 26–29). He held that one thing led to another —and that is all we have presented here.

We move on to another area of religious life that is necessarily related to the God-image and the personality structures that underlay it: good behavior—that is, moral behavior, ethical behavior, or whatever term is preferred. Freud believed that much of what came under the heading of moral or religious behavior was not good. What follows is an interpretation of Freud's variously expressed views on good behavior.

Sense of Self and Ethical Behavior

The ethical life as Freud understood it was a life dedicated to expansion of the ego's influence. One of the principal goals in life is the discovery of the contraints caused by the superego, that is, caused by the internalization of parents' and teachers' constraints from infancy on. People should live their lives aware of their own reality and the reality of the world around them, controlling their passions and the constraints of the past by means of the ego. They must discover and exorcise all those constraints built into the personality by others. Freud argued that reason (or, more broadly speaking, awareness of reality) could not make life very easy but could mitigate the cruelty of living. The way to a better life by recollecting the past and dealing with it by means of reason is not an easy task. But Freud was most demanding: Philip Rieff, the interpreter of Freud who is our guide here, considers Freud's theory to be the "message of a very severe moralist" (Rieff, 1961, p. xxii).

A number of connected issues are, in Freud's view, at the center of ethical living. Obviously, he did not create a philosophical or theological system, so we can only look at a set of random problems that derive from his concern with goals for the personality. Freud emphasized the role of the ego in honest self-

PRIMEVAL TIMES

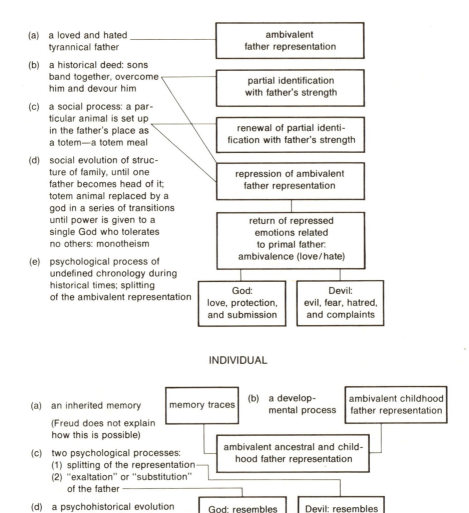

(a) a loved and hated
     tyrannical father

ambivalent
father representation

(b) a historical deed: sons
     band together, overcome
     him and devour him

partial identification
with father's strength

(c) a social process: a par-
     ticular animal is set up
     in the father's place as
     a totem—a totem meal

renewal of partial identification with father's strength

(d) social evolution of struc-
     ture of family, until one
     father becomes head of it;
     totem animal replaced by a
     god in a series of transitions
     until power is given to a
     single God who tolerates
     no others: monotheism

repression of ambivalent
father representation

return of repressed
emotions related
to primal father:
ambivalence (love/hate)

(e) psychological process of
     undefined chronology during
     historical times; splitting
     of the ambivalent representation

God:
love, protection,
and submission

Devil:
evil, fear, hatred,
and complaints

INDIVIDUAL

(a) an inherited memory

memory traces

(b) a develop-
     mental process

ambivalent childhood
father representation

     (Freud does not explain
     how this is possible)

(c) two psychological processes:
     (1) splitting of the representation
     (2) "exaltation" or "substitution"
         of the father

ambivalent ancestral and childhood father representation

(d) a psychohistorical evolution
     of the individual's relation to
     that representation and the
     actual object which provided it.

God: resembles
father in the flesh

Devil: resembles
father in the flesh

*The individual's "personal relation to God depends on
his relation to his father in the flesh and oscillates and
changes along with that relation" (Freud, 1913, p. 147).*

Figure 3-1. Development of community and individual God-images. *Reproduced, with permission, from Ana-Maria Rizzuto,* The Birth of the Living God *(Chicago: The University of Chicago Press, 1979), p. 24. Copyright © 1979 by The University of Chicago. Used by permission.*

discovery. This process involves the relationship of the bodily organs involved in physiological and psychological development to the broader areas of personal, ethical behavior, especially as regards relationship to the parents and the later love life. Behavior in society is taken into consideration in relation to the individual who must learn the proper way of living in society. Freud's writings on therapy clarify his views on ethics, in that he discusses how self-discovery can be achieved and how problems in earlier physiological and psychological development can be worked through relative to parents, adult loves, and the surrounding society.

The meaning of ethics can be stated in one word: honesty. To replace moral commitments that lead in useless or inhuman directions, Freud offered a standard that Rieff calls an "ethic of honesty." People should try to disengage themselves from and make better use of the reality around them. By means of honesty they get in touch with their emotional depths. The deviousness caused by the conscience or superego and by the id must be controlled by the ego in order to resolve problems. The ego may even take the offensive in achieving new integrity. Honest talk and painful working through of illusion in the therapeutic setting lead to a new personal integrity.

In assigning the ethical task to the ego Freud was sparing in his explicit references to morality, because he associated morality with the superego. The ego is responsible for whatever prudence, rationality, craftsmanship, and flexibility the person can muster. "In its task of mediating between the conflicting drives of the super-ego and id on the one hand, and the realistic prompting of the outer world on the other," Rieff says, "the conscious role of the ego becomes representative of the character values of prudence and rationality" (1961, pp. 64–65).

The series of stages that were important in the infant's and young child's development of the God-image are important in the development of honesty. Freud holds behavioral and moral development to be physically focused by pleasure experienced in various bodily organs—mouth, anus, phallus. To see the connection between the physical organ and the moral reality, reflect for a moment on the sex drives as connected with relationships. If development goes properly, sex drives are combined with respect and affection. Since there is a strong tendency for the elements to become divided, they must fuse for love to be normal. In adulthood normal sexuality is still a challenge, because later loves are only surrogates for the original love of the parent. Sexuality never seems fully satisfying, because it yearns for the original love object, the parent. Sexual excess can come from imperfect emancipation from the child's never satisfied need for authority figures. Ethical behavior, then, is focused by a bodily organ, and the way pleasure is experienced in it becomes a part of the personality.

Since the primary tasks are self-discovery and stabilization of sexuality, Freud did not have much to say about the broader range of social responsibilities. With his therapeutic concern for the individual, he had a low opinion of the state, the mass, or the crowd. But he does expect society to civilize the individual: The ego-oriented individual may be helped by the state, because the state represents the sum total of the needs of those surrounding the individual ego. Even the ego-controlled person would not know the type or amount of renunciation required of him or her for the maintenance of a stable civilization of many individuals, were it not for the state.

The relationship of non–ego-controlled individuals to the state is the same as that of the undeveloped child to the father. Freud was perfectly content to see the acquisition of rights by powerful leaders because of the anarchical tendencies, passivity, and weakness of the masses. He even had a messianic strain that caused him to admire resolute and ruthless minorities. In the back of Freud's head was the problem that, as Rieff puts it, "the love through which we become sociable signifies a willful self-defeat: the 'I' submerges itself in the group" (1961, p. 256).

Thus it is really a negative view of unresolved authority in the family that is translated into a negative view of social respect. Freud said that from the time of puberty onward individuals must devote themselves to the great task of self-liberation from their parents. He was especially severe in his appraisal of the depths of childishness and barbarism an individual might sink to under the compulsions of group life. The official morality preached by religion and the state—in other words, by the state —is harmful. Given his view of religion as authority, Freud seems quite sure that religion is not responsible ethics at all. Religion is just another political device representing the oppressive claims of the community over the individual. It panders to the emotional needs for authority and the childishness of the individual. Aggression and guilt are thus at the center of any religious behavior, of anything that is moral behavior in the religious sense. To resist the demands of such a religious conscience should be a mature act. Authenticity and freedom are found only within the individual whose instinct and intelligence are reconciled. They are not found in society or in political structures. The individual, strictly speaking, has no debts to society but only debts to self vis-à-vis society. One's only political obligation is the preservation of personal freedom.

The unresolved oedipal conflict and the need for authority are alleviated by the therapy session. Memory is ultimately focused on the Oedipus complex, that combination of sexual desire, repression, and identification with a parent-figure that all persons experience. Freud naturally assumed that there would be a level of reality underneath when all the outer layers had been stripped away, because he had no serious philosophical problems about the rational order of the universe or the trustworthiness of the senses. Rieff links Freud's belief in the continued existence of the past with the romantic poets "for whom the whole of experience, and especially childhood, survives in a mental underworld" (1961, p. 44). Infant and childhood experience of a family molds the individual, and traces of it in the memory do not change over the years, having been sealed off in some way by repression as individuals develop.

The dynamic of transference in the therapy session accomplishes a resolution of the parent problem. These varied passions of dependence are transferred to the therapist—that is, the emotions are brought to the surface and projected upon the therapist. It is the therapist's role, then, to be therapeutic authority figure, not a repeat of the original parental figure. He does not reciprocate love and does not become a full authority figure, as if he were a parent. He begins more or less with an imitation of an authority figure and then becomes a far more permissive person, giving the patient the freedom to react to him in ways the patient would have liked to react to the parent. Once these emotions have surfaced they can be defused and handled rationally.

Personal integrity cannot be achieved immediately, because the true self is hidden, and what is usually called conscience and morality—censorship really—gets in the way of its discovery. In therapy, by both encouraging the activity of the ego and preventing it from acting too soon, the analyst must keep patients from censoring themselves. Since dreams and random associations are the best revelations of the hidden self, there has to be a freedom and spontaneity about the self-examination, with reason—the ego activity—being the ultimate guide in sorting out values.

Freud's work has generated numerous interpretations since his death in 1939. During World War II the initial impact of his work gave rise to narrow, forceful interpretations and the establishment of training societies. After the war individual clinicians developed their own approaches: Karen Horney (actually beginning in the late 1930s), Erich Fromm, and Erik Erikson. In the 1950s the clinical work continued, but a new phase of reinterpretation was initiated by those not immediately connected to the psychoanalytic movement: The political theorist Herbert Marcuse, the sociologist Philip Rieff, the literary critic Norman O. Brown, and the philosopher Paul Ricoeur have attempted systematic explanations of Freud's significance for modern social and individual life.

Such has been the influence of Freud's thinking that it is almost impossible to function in modern academic or professional life without taking a stand vis-à-vis Freud's ideas. He has become a mythic figure, impossible to prove correct or to refute in his principal ideas (Sulloway, 1979), although some of his analysis of the less dramatic dynamics of mental life have been supported by recent research (Fisher and Greenberg, 1977). Empirical research on his theories about the production of the God-image is presented in Chapter 7.

Jung's Interpretation of the Religious Experience

Carl Jung was born in Switzerland and lived there his whole life. His parents would have undoubtedly remembered civil strife in the earlier part of the nineteenth century, but Jung's Switzerland passed unscathed through the wars and turmoil of the later nineteenth century and the twentieth. His home town of Basel, a center of culture since the Renaissance, represents a certain stereotype of the Swiss mentality, with its strict organization and orderliness. Jung was not unaffected by that mentality (Ellenberger, 1970). His father was a Lutheran clergyman, a modest country pastor who was interested in classical languages and Hebrew. But the grandfather was a man of oversized personality and figure, reputed to be an illegitimate son of Goethe. Grandfather Jung, one of the most sought-after doctors in Basel, was a rector of the University and Grandmaster of the Swiss Freemasons. Jung never knew his grandfather, but what he knew of the old man captured his imagination (Jung, 1961). Jung's mother was said to be somewhat homely and authoritarian, a difficult character in Jung's own judgment; small wonder that he was never attracted to Freud's views on the infant's love of the mother.

Jung was an obviously superior student with interests in theology and mysticism during the years of medical studies. In his 1902 dissertation he studied the trances of a young medium, his cousin Helene Preiswerk. During nine years at the Burgholzli mental hospital in Zurich he concentrated on complexes and word association tests. Between 1909 and 1913 he developed his ideas in close correspondence with Freud, but divergent viewpoints were never overcome. Early respect and friendship gave way to personal antagonism that led to a final split.

In the years before the 1920 publication of *Psychological Types,* virtually a new system of dynamic psychiatry, Jung made his own inner search by a method of active imagination and analysis of dreams similar to Freud's self-analysis. He would tell himself stories and, forcing himself to prolong them, would write down his thought associations. He also wrote out and drew his dreams each morning. Like all such experiments, these were somewhat dangerous, so Jung was careful to give serious attention to family and professional life.

After leaving the psychoanalytic movement he fully developed his ideas about the structure of the human psyche and *individuation,* a process that leads to the unification of the personality. Jung's ideas about the structure of the psyche and the process whereby individuals realize their full potential are naturally the basis for his views on religion. From the psyche come the archetypes, some of them determining people's God-images, and thus religious faith. Individuation, or realization, as explained by Jung, is really ideal, moral behavior. Following the pattern we established in the Freud discussion, we look at the faith and morality aspect of Jung's theory.

Religious Mental Images and the Structure of the Psyche

When Jung describes how the mind or personality is shaped, we must somehow picture what he is talking about in diagram form. Diagrams do not, of course, represent a cross-section of the brain or a cutaway view of the human body. Rather they represent mental functioning by attributing "levels" or "layers" to the mind, or psyche. Most of us are so used to this by now that we always picture the unconscious mind as something "lower" than the conscious, even though we know well that this represents truth no more than the notion of the sun setting "behind" the hills. Descriptions of the psyche, sometimes with accompanying diagrams, were at the center of the work of Jung's earliest followers. I have chosen one such method here but will later describe the changing work of Jungians across the decades. Jung's followers concentrated on unifying descriptions of the psyche culled from the master's diverse and, at times, virtually contradictory writings (Goldbrunner, 1966; Jacobi, 1973; Whitmont, 1969).

The outside of our personalities, the façade we present to other people, Jung called the *persona,* after the Greek word for mask. The conscious thinking and directing activity of the mind is called the ego, a notion not unlike Freud's. Jung took the personal unconscious seriously, though not as seriously as Freud; it contains the many forgotten or repressed elements of an individual's personal life. However, the foundation of the personality Jung called the collective unconcious or objective psyche, a basic level of the mind that is shared with all human beings (but not some kind of mysterious spiritual participation in other people's lives or thinking, as we shall see). In the objective psyche are the archetypes—instincts, attitudes, and mental mechanisms of a sort—that produce the images which enable people to understand objects in their world. The Self, a powerful and complex image, is the central archetype. The ego is one's own conscious self-image, and shadow is the negative image or dark side of the personality. The anima (or animus), is the image of the basic personality of the opposite sex.

To be true to the Jungian tradition—and before saying anything more complicated about the objective psyche and the archetypes—let us examine an illustration of his ideas in Figure 3-2.

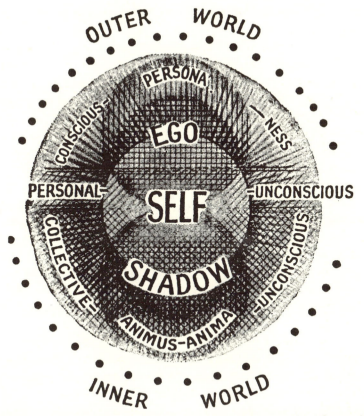

Figure 3-2. Jung's structure of the personality. *Reproduced, with permission, from Jolande Jacobi,* The Psychology of C. G. Jung *(New Haven: Yale University Press, 1973). Copyright © 1962, 1968, 1973 by Jolande Jacobi. Used by permission.*

There is more to say about the objective psyche, the total apparatus that generates ideas and images, religious and otherwise. Some may be more familiar with the term originally used by Jung, "collective unconscious," because the objective psyche is inherited and is shared with other people. This terminology is misleading, because it suggests some kind of mass psyche or a universally shared transmission of brain waves, uniting all peoples of all generations. Of course, nothing is shared in this sense. Rather, people share something when they have the same *kind* of organism or idea. All that Jung is saying is this: People have mental apparatus that operates in the brain just as they have a brain organism that is common, the same in everyone.

As the objective psyche operates, it produces two results

that together are called a complex. The complex is the basic product of the objective psyche and can best be pictured as a structure with a central core and an outer reaction pattern (Whitmont, 1969). Figure 3–2 does not enable us to picture the archetypal image as "surfacing" in the personality and being used by the person to understand something. This surfacing results in the formation of a network of personal reaction patterns around the archetype. Reaction patterns then become related to, or are taken over by, other elements of the individual's personality structure, but they are always ready to adhere to the archetype whenever it surfaces.

The core is called the archetype and is an idea or image (a religious image of Father-God would be an example), though more accurately the archetype should be defined as the basic attitude or tendency to react to a person or situation. When the attitude is imaged in idea, fantasy, or dream, then you might say that the archetype is "complete." We often speak as if the produced image were the archetype, but the notion of archetype must include the basic instinctual attitude or tendency that results in the actual image.

The "outer shell" of the complex is called a reaction pattern. Each reaction pattern is dependent upon the individual, personal network of the associations that group themselves around the archetype. It is what happens when the archetype surfaces or meets outside reality in the life of an individual person. For example, in the objective psyche an attitude or tendency to relate to father results in the image of father (independently of knowing one's own or anybody's actual father, because it is objective). When this image is used in the actual real-life experience of father, a reaction pattern is formed personal to each individual. Likewise, the archetype of Father-God surfaces and is further shaped in reaction to the image of Father-God presented by society. Jung, then, describes the generation of belief quite differently from Freud.

Jung said: "Only in the age of enlightenment did people discover that the gods did not really exist, but were simply projections. Thus the gods were disposed of. But the corresponding psychological function was by no means disposed of; it lapsed into the unconscious, and men were thereupon poisoned by the surplus of libido that had once been laid up in the cult of divine images" (1972, p. 94). It sounds as negative as anything Freud said, but Jung explains the "psychological function" of the "projections" in a positive way. The projections certainly exist, whereas the existence of the divinities and infinities beyond could neither be proved nor become the subject of Jung's research. According to Jung, when we understand that the projections in our minds cannot be identified with God but are only projections, we can deal directly with the role assumed for religion in the personality. Jung was as pro-psychological as Freud without being anti-religious. He said that the idea of God was an "absolutely necessary psychological function of an irrational nature" and that it had nothing to do with the existence or nonexistence of God, a question that human beings cannot answer (1972, p. 71).

Religions are also concerned with devils, saviors, criminals, and the collective nature of religion itself. These, too, must be understood as psychological functions or projections:

> In so far as through our unconscious we have a share in the historical collective psyche, we live naturally and unconsciously in a world of werewolves, demons, magicians, etc., for these are things which all previous ages have invested with tremendous affectivity. Equally we have a share of gods and devils, saviours and criminals; but it would be absurd to attribute these potentialities of the unconscious to ourselves personally.[1972, pp. 93–94]

The image of the Church, as a spiritual, otherworldly group and as a building, also has an important psychological function. Such images can enable people to sever their childish ties. Jung compares the role of projections of the Church to the role of the initiation ritual in tribal societies: It cuts people off from the world of childish family dependencies. Jung clarified what he meant through an explanation of two church dreams of one of his patients.

Recall the dream reported at the beginning of the chapter, and then consider the following dream in which the sexual imagery is more apparent.

> I am in a great Gothic cathedral. At the altar stands a priest. I stand before him with my friend, holding in my hand a little Japanese ivory figure, with the feeling that it is going to be baptized. Suddenly an elderly woman appears, takes the fraternity ring from my friend's finger, and puts it on her own.

My friend is afraid that this may bind him in some way. But at
the same moment there is a sound of wonderful organ music.
[1966, pp. 106–7]

The tiny figure connects the initiation imagery of baptism with
the initiating imagery of circumcision. The presence of the friend
and the fraternity ring is obvious to the dreamer, who explains to
Jung that he has had homosexual problems with the friend, who
belonged to the same fraternity. The elderly woman looks somewhat like his mother but is actually a friend of his mother. The
patient himself was very fond of the woman; she represented a
heterosexual friendship of a particular kind. For Jung, the circumcision imagery under the supervision of a priest represents
initiation into a life beyond infantile family life. The elderly
woman represents both a break with homosexuality and a step
beyond the mother toward a mature masculinity.

The archetypes of gods or godlike figures (Jung occasionally
calls them "mana personalities") and religious situations like
that in the dream content described by Jung's patient can be
harmful if not properly dealt with. Archetypes can take the form
of powerful, often sinister male and female figures that frighten
and control, especially when people think they have learned how
to handle the mental images of the opposite sex. Archetypes can
obsess the conscious personality, the ego, so that someone can
think he is a superman or people can think they are divine. Or
else the God-figure can stand on its own, forming such an image
of transcendent divinity personality. Jung comments on each
one of these possibilities.

The powerful male figure takes the various forms of hero,
chief, magician, medicine man, saint, the ruler of men and spirits,
and the friend of God, while the powerful female figure takes the
form of the Great Mother, the all-merciful, and the sorceress.
These are much more powerful versions of simple diffuse images
of members of the opposite sex (anima-animus). They occur in
dreams and affect people's interpretations of interaction with
others. In conscious and semiconscious thoughts, they can
haunt one's mental life (1972, pp. 227–28).

There is a way that these powerful images can take over entire personalities. When the conscious ego begins to draw on
these archetypes' power, a person attributes the power to
himself or herself. Various musings about power and victory

over one's opposites can cause people to attribute heroic power to themselves. This means that the ego, believing itself to be superpowerful, lays itself open to attack by those archetypes of power (1972, pp. 233, 234).

The archetypes create special problems when they are simply identified with a transcendent heavenly figure. Jung criticizes such an identification, even though it seems to be a basic dynamic of Judeo-Christian belief; but he is really opposing the absolutizing of one's mental images as if they were God. Noting that one would also tend to absolutize image of the devil, Jung says this:

> On psychological grounds, therefore, I would recommend that no God be constructed out of the archetype of the mana-personality. In other words, he must not be concretized, for only thus can I avoid projecting my values and non-values into God and the Devil, and only thus can I preserve my human dignity, my specific gravity, which I need so much if I am not to become the unresisting shuttlecock of unconscious forces. [1972, p. 236]

All divinity and power images should be brought into relationship with the central archetype of the personality. This is the central, indescribable "something," a self that is basic to the personality. It is us, and yet it is unknowable. It seems to make us kin to beasts and to God, to the tiniest and the greatest elements of nature. "I have called this centre the *self*," says Jung. Intellectually the self is not more than a psychological concept, a construct that serves to express an unknowable essence that we cannot grasp as such, since by definition it transcends our powers of comprehension. It might equally well be called the "God within us" (1972, p. 238). When conscious mind, this ego, realizes its relationship to the central archetypes, when the personal unconscious and the many other archetypes of the objective psyche are coordinated with this "self," then a person is said to have achieved a goal of human growth, individuation, or self-realization. Jung sums up: "Sensing the self as something irrational, as an indefinable existent, to which the ego is neither opposed nor subjected, but merely attached, and about which it revolves round the sun—thus we come to the goal of individuation" (1972, p. 240).

everyday consciousness = ego

The Process of Individuation

Although both personal unconscious life and the everyday consciousness (ego) of an individual are obvious elements of the individual's personality for Jung, they were not central to his interests. The ethical task, the significant "making real" of one's personality, takes place when the archetype of self is coordinated with all the other archetypes after having passed through enough important personal experiences. The realization of the full self obviously cannot take place without a person's individual faculties operating. The personal unconscious, though it involves a superficial consciousness of who one is, is part of the mental life of the individual. Certainly the more significant personality events would not take place without this day-to-day activity. But if the surface levels of the personality are not coordinated with the depth elements, they produce the persona only, a façade, a mask that is not a true personality, a realized self, at all. If the inner self is made real, then the exterior expresses it and the persona is not an artificial mask (Whitmont, 1969).

Self-realization takes time, however, and a continuous development thus goes on as an interaction between the ego's understanding of things at a given moment and potential wholeness centered in the self. Jung sees this interaction occurring in phases.

In childhood the original undeveloped unity of the personality comes apart, because the objective psyche with its archetypal potential is not sufficiently controlled. Images become random, forceful, and frightening. People and things are threatening powers, because the images in the psyche are uncontrolled and random. As the individual matures, the ego gains too much control and becomes estranged from the world of instinctual attitudes that, ideally, should be coordinated into a balanced self. The only power acknowledged is that of the ego: "Where there's a will, there's a way." In middle life, however, a fundamental change begins (hence forty is a more significant age for development than Freud's five). In the second half of life the now rational elements press for integration, and the ego is drawn into the reestablishment of relationship to the self in the form of conscious encounter. There is a moving toward individual wholeness and fulfilling of personality potential.

While this is going on in the individual, a personality type emerges and presses for balancing. Jung's division of basic personality types is straightforward: A person tends to be introversive or extroversive, and each of these types can be further subdivided into those who are thinking–feeling types, on one hand, and those who are sensing–intuiting types, on the other. Though it may seem strange, Jung does put thinking and feeling types together, because he believes that such types *actively* record what happens around them (1974).

Take the example of people who are introversive, feeling types. Their feeling is contained within the tendency to separate themselves from other people. The outside observer may think them unfeeling, because their feeling is so intensely held within that it is directed toward an external object or person only with great difficulty. Their tensions are all inward; consequently they may outwardly appear to be banal, childish, and often melancholic. They seem cold, remote, and difficult to approach, for they are primarily attentive to their own subjective reactions. Because of the intensity of their inner world and their sense of being overwhelmed by its power, they tend to shield themselves from outside contacts. They are likely to be shy and inarticulate, to find communication difficult. They hold others at arm's length, because what is evoked is no small matter to them. Occasionally the accumulation of inner intensity may erupt in seemingly heroic, dramatic, or drastic acts. Individuals of this type are naive in evaluations that require thinking and do not like to engage in it. What thinking they do is often projected in negative form, causing them to be oversusceptible to what others think about them. This can make them almost paranoid at times, but in any case they are frequently prone to scheming, rivalries, hysterics, and tendencies toward the "nothing but" kind of judging and dogmatism. All this is a description of an extreme, because such a pure introversive, actively recording, feeling type will be found only rarely, but in a number of personalities this type of functioning predominates.

There is a conflict within, then, as a person develops an ensemble of inner impulses (and their images), individualizing them by interactions with the world of outer objects. Through interaction, individuals integrate all the elements of inner life around a central self, and religious symbols convey the profoundest relationships of this self to the mysteries of life and the universe.

A look at successive interpretations of the archetypes can show us how successive "generations" of Jungians have reinterpreted Jung's original ideas (Goldenberg, 1979). The master himself sometimes associated the archetypes with the instincts: "unconscious images of the instincts," "patterns of instinctual behavior." At other times he used metaphors taken from chemistry or physics, like "the axial system of a crystal, which, as it were, preforms the crystalline structure in the mother liquid" (Jung, 1972, p. 155). His interpreters have emphasized one or another of these comparisons.

The theories of archetypes and of the four functions of thinking, feeling, sensation, and intuition were developed during World War I as part of Jung's own self-exploration. In fact, his experiences of fantasy figures produced by the archetypes were the origin of his ideas about the four functions. Out of these complex experiences and ideas arose his linkage of the self and God archetypes (linkages about which he issued warnings, remember). A contemporary commentator explains how this concept of self includes so many things:

> Whether the concept of self is used to refer to the total personality, to the totality of conscious ego plus personal unconscious plus collective unconscious, to the God image, or to compensatory, emergent symbols leading towards an expansion of interests or of awareness, there is a common element in Jung's usage of the word, a concept of something superordinate to the conscious "I" with some kind of power or organising force. Symbols of the self can lead us into the discovery of hitherto dark parts of ourselves, for example, the phallic God, or they can help to lead us to our true path, our true selves, for example the spherical jelly fish. They are ego-expanding, whether they lead us outwards or inwards, forwards or backwards in the way they point. [Redfearn, 1977, p. 135]

The self is a conceptual mechanism that brings together a variety of God-images into a balanced unity. But the shape and the limits of the Jungian self have never been fully defined and were never meant to be. So the accusation that Jung equated God and self is not right.

As the years passed, it became obvious that some kind of coherent account of Jung's many and varied writings was required. Interpreters concentrated on studies of specific archetypes—the Old Man, the Mother, the Child, the Spirit, the

Trickster, the Sun, and so on—and diagrams of archetypal theory such as we have reproduced in Figure 3-2. At the same time there was an attempt to base archetypal theory on some kind of empirical evidence, but this involved more goal-setting than goal realization. In general, interpreters wanted to demystify the archetype, urging the understanding and control of these mental images. Yolande Jacobi, Edward Whitmont, and June Singer are noted for their work here.

More recently there has been a reevaluation of the theory of archetypes, and they have been given a far more substantial role in human life. The term "soul" has been given new value in ways that Christian theologians and Platonists would find congenial. James Hillman (1972, 1975) is the foremost exponent of the new way of interpreting Jung. We are told to explore ultimate meaning and the foundations of self through images. Scientific facts and proofs are not the ultimate explanations in life; it is the fantasies behind them that count the most. Since there is no ultimate explanation in life, the path to follow is exploration of the soul through imagination. One simply follows the progression of the metaphors. Hillman says: "It is as if human existence, even at its basic vital level, is a metaphor" (quoted in Goldenberg, 1979, p. 213). If psychological behavior is metaphorical, then we must turn to the dominant metaphors of the psyche to understand its behavior. Therefore, we may learn as much about the psychology of instinct by occupation with the archetypal images as with physiological, animal, and experimental research. Even pathologies, then, are essential components of the human soul and are to be taken seriously: They can represent something natural and basic to the soul (Hillman, 1975). Authors have examined how Christ is a paradigm for the individuating ego (Edinger, 1973) and how the religious symbols represent a genuine religious logic (Mosier, 1968-69). A number of studies of religious symbols within a tradition suggest ways of dealing with a God-image where the good and evil elements are undifferentiated, either in the tradition itself (Dreifuss, 1972) or in the lives of individuals (Avens, 1977). This type of detailed study of the ways the complexes form in people's minds should help them or their therapists and counselors in resolving religious problems related to the complexes.

Personal Religious Goals: Allport, Maslow, and May

GOALS TAKE PEOPLE beyond themselves. They are oriented toward the future. While some may sound very explicit—"I want to be a surgeon"—most often people's goals are more vague and generalized. Gordon Allport and Abraham Maslow have chosen to describe personality by accenting the goals of the individual. They believe in the basic abilities of human beings to attain freedom and goodness, and to enjoy life at the same time. Their emphasis is on choice, will power, conceptual thought, imagination, introspection, self-criticism, and creativity (Maddi and Costa, 1972).

Although both Allport and Maslow can present a clear, reasoned argument in defense of their viewpoint, neither of them has tried actually to work out philosophical positions, whereas the "existentialist" psychologists—notably Ludwig Binswanger in Europe and Rollo May in the United States—have based their psychological work on the philosophy of the same name. Allport and Maslow both gratefully welcomed the influence of existentialist psychology, although they were critical sometimes of its needless complexity. We shall see in this chapter that Allport, Maslow, and May concern themselves seriously with the self-transcending possibilities of freely expressed individuality in a given environment. As I have said, they are interested in different aspects of the religious experience: faith and ethical behavior (Allport), self-transcending experience (Maslow), and the relationship of individual freedom to interpersonal communion (May). When they talk about personality, and about religion in the context of personality, they emphasize abstract ideals or individual personalities of high achievement.

Allport's Interpretation of the Religious Experience

Born into a hardworking and relatively well-off family in Indiana, Gordon Allport was taught the importance of learning in general and of searching for answers to the basic religious problems in life—an atmosphere of simple Protestant piety and hard work, Allport called it. Although feeling somewhat isolated from other youngsters, he gradually made friends, did well in high school, and went on to Harvard. In college he was interested in both psychology and social work, the latter because it gave him a feeling of competence and because, quite simply, he liked to help people. He was gradually replacing his earlier piety with a humanitarian religion.

Allport worked with Harvard psychologists during his Ph.D. years and later encountered some of the most noted German psychologists during a two-year fellowship in Germany. Brought back to Harvard by one of his former professors, he taught social ethics and psychology of personality. The personality course may have been the first in American higher education. Influenced by philosophers, sociologists, and experimental sociologists, Allport isolated a broad area of study that might be called "social relations." Eventually a Department of Social Relations, separate from but allied to the Department of Psychology, was started at Harvard. At different times, Allport was head of both departments. Across the years he was a journal editor and president of the American Psychological Association. We might sum up the relationship of his theorizing to his work in this way:

The key to Allport's formal theorizing is carried in the concept of functional autonomy, underlying as it does the distinction between propriate and opportunistic functioning. One may start life by performing on demand, for the rewards granted by others and to avoid punishment by them, but one does not end there, Allport feels. Even performing in this initially conventional way leads to changes in the direction of more personal, idiosyncratic commitments. The conventional or conformist conscience of childhood is replaced by the generic, personal set of values marking maturity. Performing to please others gives way to performing to please oneself. This emphasis on turning initially imposed values and commitments into personally satisfying versions comes rather directly out of a concern in Allport's own life. [Maddi and Costa, 1972, pp. 158–59]

Allport believed religion to be the highest form of human striving for a goal. He used the word "intention" to indicate faith's special dynamism and "conscience" to indicate the personal sensitivities needed to get to the goal. Religion is a drive toward the discovery of human goodness and anything, anyone, that serves as a model of human progress. The ultimate discovery of a transcendent God is not possible with human faculties, nor are techniques for producing perfect goodness going to be found. But Allport believes that the religious intention is the great unifying drive that makes people move beyond themselves: There is something about the power and forward thrust of dream or fancy that leads people to truth or to techniques for making something come true. Think of the number of science fiction creations that have come true.

Faith: The Religious Intention

According to Allport, faith is a strong positive mental movement toward a goal. It is based upon an indistinguishable blend of emotion and reason, which he calls a sentiment or disposition, of feeling and meaning. He defines the mature religious sentiment as "a disposition, built up through experience, to respond favorably, and in certain habitual ways, to conceptual objects and principles that the individual regards as of ultimate importance in his own life, and as having to do with what he regards as permanent or central in the nature of things" (Allport, 1950, p.

65). Instead of the word "disposition" we might equally well use the words "interest," "outlook," or "system." "System" in this sense can be more or less a habit such as riding a bicycle or a trait such as politeness or aggressiveness. But if it is an organization of feeling and thought directed toward some definable object of value such as a parent, an heirloom, or a fatherland, we can call the system a sentiment. And so the religious sentiment is directed toward objects and principles of ultimate importance.

Maturity of the religious sentiment is indicated by a number of qualities. The mature sentiment helps a person to make distinctions so that uncritical abandon can be avoided. It is dynamic in that it has its own power to move people on its own: Mature religious behavior cannot be explained by some other reason or cause, because it is functionally autonomous. It directs people even though their religious sentiment may not be orthodox (Allport regards most altruistic activity, whether inspired by a religious orthodoxy or not, as religious in some sense). It takes in all of life and has a homogeneous pattern. And it is a means of interpreting life rather than a final answer.

With this disposition in the background of the personality, there can be a move toward commitment, a subjective thrust of the mind, called a religious *intention*. The religious intention is Allport's expression for faith:

> So important is this forward thrust in all desires emanating from mature sentiments that I propose the term "intention" to depict the dynamic operation we are endeavoring to describe. Better than "desire" this term designates the presence of the rational and ideational component in all productive striving. Some sort of idea of the end is always bound into the act itself. It is this inseparability of the idea of the end from the course of the striving that we call faith. [1950, p. 149]

When Allport discusses faith, he is little concerned with images of gods in the imagination or how they got there. He is more interested in the committed acceptance of propositions about the nature of the universe and the divine force of personality that might rule it. To be more precise, he thinks acceptance of rational human ideals constitutes the essence of faith, whereas the particular way of conceptualizing divinity figures, and so on, is secondary:

> Faith is basically man's belief in the validity and attainability of some goal (value). The goal is set by desires. Desires, how-

ever, are not merely pushes from behind (drive ridden). They include such complex, future oriented states as longing for a better world, for one's own perfection, for a completely satisfying relation to the universe. [1950, p. 149]

Faith, or the religious intention, dominates individual activity in varying degrees (1950, 146–47). Using terminology developed in Christian theological circles, Allport says that faith is *actual* if it is kept in mind while the action is taking place: "If one intends to worship God and proceeds with his devotions to this end, his intention is actual." Faith is *virtual* when the previous religious act of faith or commitment is still a motive of an action but is not consciously referred to: "A person who has decided to order his life according to a religious pattern finds this decision influencing his daily conduct even at times when he is not aware that it does so." Faith is *habitual* when, though not active, it has never been rejected: A person who is no longer religious in any way but has not embraced an atheistic position is still a habitual believer.

Faith itself develops in stages (1950, pp. 114–15). Credulity, the stage at which one believes almost anything, comes first. When this original naive frame of mind is met by a variety of intellectual challenges, it gives way to doubts of many sorts. In spite of built-in problems, credulity can be quite simple and not necessarily narrow superstition. Doubts can be quite positive, the results of good, clear thinking, and not necessarily negativistic and self-interested. Although mature faith is the final goal, doubts have an important part to play in arriving at faith. Doubts that are negative or reactionary can be small, mean, and unproductive, but they most often do indicate some kind of deep feelings. The militant atheist exhibits a distinct concern about the topic of religion. Doubts can be caused by self-interest, by the obvious failures of organized religion, or by the challenges presented by psychological and scientific information. Some psychologies explain the origins of religious seeking in the personality, while science can give an explanation of many causes that have been heretofore cloaked in religious mystery. People who search for "evidence" of truth find that religion does not provide it for them.

Faith, then, is a mental act based upon a mature response to life, so that individuals are objective about themselves and can live with incompleteness even though having a unified philosophy of life. The person of mature faith can then mentally picture an ultimate goal and use religious practices to focus that goal.

Allport sees mature religious faith as a sensible cognitive operation (unlike Freud), because it rests on *probabilities.* If the context of faith conformed to sense perception, reason, and generally accepted beliefs of others, it would be "knowledge"; lacking all these supports it would be called "delusion." But it is in between, probably resting upon personal mystical experience and pragmatic argument. Emphasis, obviously, is on *future* rather than past experiences. The future is what concerns people most of all—past associations with father or other family members are not as operative. Freud also had the future in mind when he spoke of the vastness and unknowability of the universe as a field of religious projections, but Allport, true to his abstract way of analyzing, means future as something genuinely yet to come, not a present-day concept that simply causes fear. He says, a propos religion, "Most psychologists see behavior as pushed 'from behind' by goads that prod us out of our past. Yet is it not characteristic of maturely directed activity, arising from the sentiments that form personality, that it is always oriented toward the future?" (1950, p. 148).

Allport says that prayer and ritual are specifications of the activity of faith. Prayer focuses faith, sometimes in a very general way by self-reflection or concentration of inner energies, sometimes "as a means of reaching a God that dwells at the terminus of the intention." While rituals are the extensions and dramatizations of a variety of human activities, they are transformed by the religious intention toward the perfecting of these human activities. Ritual also draws people together, enabling them to integrate these intentions, to express much more than they would have otherwise expressed individually. Allport calls this the social facilitation of the religious intention, because it intermixes similar attitudes and sentiments of those taking part in the ritual (1950, p. 152).

Basic to Allport's explanation of the function of religion is the explanation of the two levels of human functioning. Opportunistic functioning is simply functioning in order to justify biological survival needs. Propriate functioning is functioning in a manner expressive of the unique human personality, which is called the *proprium* by Allport, hence the name. Each individual is unique, not a copy of anyone or anything else. But since we cannot describe uniqueness by making up new words, we must compare the unique person or thing with other similar persons or things. Allport tries to develop a vocabulary that allows a description of the unique human individual, the *proprium,* and the functioning that corresponds to that uniqueness.

Different aspects of the proprium are operative when the believer focuses on religion. In turn, they are modified by the effect of religion upon the personality. Bodily sense, self-identity, ego enhancement, ego extension, rational agency, self-image, propriate striving, and substantive knowing are the elements that go into the functioning proprium. The dynamic and expressive results of propriate functioning are called dispositions, such as emotional security, self-acceptance, and, of course, faith. These dispositions are unique to each individual and are more important than those surface traits that are the same in every individual, such as fearfulness, joy, love of food, and so on (Allport, 1955, pp. 41–56).

Bodily sense is the stream of sensations that arise within the organism—muscles, joints, interior organs, all regions of the body that have even the vaguest sensation-producing nerve ends. The sum of these feelings is the lifelong anchor of an individual's personal awareness. Bodily sense helps to determine the ways individuals are negative or positive toward themselves. If, for example, their religion is negative about bodily pleasures, they will be more or less negative relative to the official negativity of the religion. Self-identity grows gradually as one is clothed, named, and marked off from the surrounding environment. An awareness grows of being the same organism as the day before, and the ability to reflect on one's earlier thoughts makes one aware of self-identity. This more developed sense of one's whole personality creates a more individualized religious identity, because the day-to-day experiences of God or the world, of beauty or of sin are part of a self-identity, hence of a religious self-identity.

Ego enhancement is a polite term for pure self-seeking. Even our language, with its terms compounded of the word *self* or *ego,* emphasizes this aspect of the problem, with *selfish* and *egotistical* being the primary examples. People's religion and their particular religious experiences become part of them. They can become proud or defensive about it all—not only their socially shared religion but also the cumulative personal religious experience they have built up individually. Ego extension, however, is a more mature process. Individuals extend their indentities to objects of importance, to whatever they call "theirs." As time goes on, people identify with groups, neighborhoods, nations, as well as possessions, clothes, home. People often vehemently defend religious beliefs and practices that they as individuals may not be particularly good at following or fulfilling. Their religion is, properly speaking, very much "theirs," and an attack upon it is an attack upon them.

Rational agency or activity is another activity of the proprium. Traditional philosophies have considered the rational nature of a personality to be its distinctive property. For a more general and personal understanding of reasoning, we can simply say that it involves the synthesizing of inner need and outer reality. When people do philosophy in order to understand themselves, they are attempting more than the solution of abstract logical problems. Philosophical religion is very much the synthesizing of inner needs and outer reality. Everyone develops a personal way of thinking about a religious experience.

Self-image is the way people look at themselves. It is a combination of perception of present facts and projection of future goals. Present abilities, status, and roles are combined with aspirations. The proprium is guided by this image, whether it is correct or incorrect, attainable or unattainable. Here we can see how religious experience, based as it is upon a search for a fulfilling goal, contributes to a particularized image, a particularized set of reflections on the past and projections about the future.

Propriate striving is made up of special efforts beyond survival and satisfaction of bodily needs. It is the effort made to unify the personality, to pursue long-range goals, to follow through on humanistic and artistic plans. Here a person does not try to reduce tension but makes use of tension to move toward the future. The efforts an individual makes to achieve religious goals are at issue here. Think of the efforts to attain understanding, equilibrium, and charity in the different world religions. Proprium as knower is the final aspect of individuality. A person not only knows things but knows the specific features of his or her own proprium. Reflecting upon a personal collection of thoughts and even one's own propriate functioning, one experiences their essential togetherness and notes that they are somehow bound to the knowing function itself. Religious traditions demand that individuals "know themselves," often suggesting means for arriving at self-understanding. The proprium reflects upon the diverse elements of which he or she is composed and the diverse religious factors that are part of experience.

All these functions come together in varying ways as an individual develops. Often one of the functions predominates, and so concomitantly a particular aspect of the religious experience predominates.

Thus, in discovering themselves people grow beyond the functioning that satisfies bodily needs into something more: personal fulfillment, which, if subordinated to the fulfillment of a group, is even more productive of human good. To stay on the level of bodily functioning or to make one of the functions supreme is to leave potential for human personal goodness unfulfilled. The unsocialized infant must become an adult with structured loves, hates, loyalties, and interests, and with the capability of taking his or her place in a complexly ordered society. All the religious aspects of bodily sense, self-identity, ego enhancement, ego extension, rational agency, self-image, propriate striving, and knower contribute to this adult properly functioning in society.

People grow, of course, in a fashion that is somewhat, though obviously not completely, parallel to the whole race. In anthropology or natural history books we see a series of sketches, four or five manlike creatures representing different stages of development. The more animal-like stages are not more evil; they are simply inferior. Human beings have developed in different ways on the face of planet earth. We who stand at the end of hundreds of thousands of years of development look back and believe, quite confidently, that we have come a long way and that many improvements have been made during the years. A basic improvement, if one accepts evolutionary theory quite freely, is that we have gone from being animal-like to something better. Animals need to mate, sleep, eat, and eliminate waste; they have strong instincts to preserve themselves as a species. But there is nothing more than that, nothing to transcend the physiological needs of the individual.

One step up is the species or individual that can rise above this level, showing more perception or artistry relative to just one of these animal functions. Naturally, the bodily functions—

mating, eating, and so on—continue. In addition an organism can smoothly unite all the other functions, both satisfying them and diminishing their importance, so that any number of higher ideas may be striven for with choice, imagination, and creativity. To accomplish all of this integration however, the religious intention must be assisted by another faculty, religious conscience.

Integration of Personality: The Goal of Religious Behavior

Conscience is the sensibility that one is or is not attaining the sublime human goals one has set for oneself. Quite unlike Freud, Allport has an exalted view of the word "conscience." Instead of being a mechanism of unthinking obedience in the adult, the center of conscience is propriate striving. The conscience develops from the former into the latter as an individual matures. Allport says, "Conscience presupposes only a reflective ability to refer conflicts to the matrix of values that are felt to be one's own. I experience 'ought' whenever I pause to relate a choice which lays before me to my ideal self-image." Moral development depends upon the possession of long-range goals and an ideal self-image. In other words, adults who are said to follow their consciences have various value schemata that inspire their activity, even though they cannot fulfill these schemata entirely (Allport, 1950, pp. 101–102).

In the development of this conscience, important changes occur: external sanctions give way to internal; experiences of fear, "must," and inhibition give way to experiences of preference, self-respect, and "ought." A number of difficulties continue even after these good developments take place, because childishness, impulses, and revolts against one's own well-chosen ideals occur frequently. An overall integrity and an ongoing search to discover the unity of being are the behavioral correlates of a conscience. When an individual relents from the propriate striving that is essential to the maintenance and perfecting of the person he or she has become, conscience reacts; it is a reaction mechanism.

Allport is convinced that specific ideas of what is right and wrong are not innate, but the general capacity for conscience exists in everyone. Conscience is Allport's good word, then, for describing the heart of ethical behavior. For Freud, remember, it was something negative, a wrong track. Allport admits that conscience may originate as a lingering vestige of parental discipline and childhood fears, but he points out important differences. While training is important, there are basic structures within the mind that are gradually developed. Allport explains these differences by use of the terms "must" and "ought." One "must" get gas for the car, but one "ought" to write a letter to a relative or friend who deserves or needs it. The unpleasantness resulting from the violation of an "ought" is quite different from the fears of physical sanctions that would result from the violations of laws of mechanics, nature, or society (1950, pp. 99–100).

Conscience should not be conceived of as "man within the breast" or as a disjointed collection of fragments of the personality. It is not a little person, a voice inside, but rather, "it is the knife edge which all our values press upon us whenever we are acting or have acted contrary to these values." Nor is it a collection of fragments, because miscellaneous fears and discomforts would not motivate overall behavior. "Conduct out of line with minor sentiments troubles us little," Allport says, "while deviations from the principal highway of our lives are marked by a sense of guilt" (1950, pp. 101–2).

Although we can point to psychological research that examines the role of religion as an integrating factor in people's lives, the greater amount of research has been on a basic insight of Allport's: that "religion" cannot really be measured unless it is divided into intrinsic and extrinsic religion (King and Hunt, 1972). In general, intrinsic religion is dedicated, prayerful, and interior, while extrinsic religion is more a matter of official, patriotic, and exterior practice. Chapter 7 will show how Allport and other researchers made use of and refined these distinctions.

Maslow's Interpretation of the Religious Experience

Abraham Maslow said of his youth:

> With my childhood, it's a wonder I'm not psychotic. I was a little Jewish boy in the non-Jewish neighborhood. It was a little like being the first Negro enrolled in the all-white school. I was isolated and unhappy. I grew up in libraries and among books, without friends. [Maslow, 1968b, p. 38]

The son of immigrants who had no formal education, Maslow received every encouragement from the parents. He went to the University of Wisconsin to study psychology, Watson's behaviorism in particular, coming immediately under the influences of Thorndike and Hull, among others. His dissertation was on monkey behavior, a subject to which he never returned. The experience of reading Bergson and Whitehead and the birth of his first child turned his interests completely away from behaviorism to a type of "humanism." After several teaching jobs, a two-year fellowship, and even a stint in a managerial position, Maslow went on to Brandeis, where he was a professor of psychology from 1951 until just before his death.

A few days after Pearl Harbor, Maslow was profoundly moved by a simple daydream of people seated at peace table watching a raggedy military parade move on before them. He felt that his calling was to develop a "psychology for the peace table," that is, a "theory of human nature that could be tested by experiment and research." Thus he began to develop his notion of humanism:

> I wanted to prove that human beings are capable of something grander than war and prejudice and hatred. I wanted to make science consider all the problems that nonscientists have been handling—religion, poetry, values, philosophy, art.
>
> I went about it by trying to understand great people, the best specimens of mankind I could find. I found that many of them reported having something like mystical experiences. [Maslow, 1968b, pp. 54–55]

These were the interests that guided the rest of Maslow's career as a psychologist. He wished to theorize about personality in order to improve it, and so turned to the study of the best persons rather than the worst. His own personal experience of meaning and goal after Pearl Harbor was so important that he was motivated to conceptualize it as a "peak experience," an intense dreamy or mystical experience that profoundly changes a person in a moment.

Maslow was more or less the leader in humanistic psychology, even though Allport's theorizing was more clear and complex. He coined the word "Third Force" to distinguish this psychology from psychoanalysis and behaviorism.

Maslow himself had high hopes for understanding better the

most intense specifically religious experiences by way of theorizing on the peak experience:

> The peak experience may be the model of the religious revelation or the religious illumination or conversion which has played so great a role in the history of religions. But, because peak experiences are in the natural world and because we can research with them and investigate them, and because our knowledge of such experiences is growing and can be confidently expected to grow in the future, we may now fairly hope to understand more about the big revelations, conversions, and illuminations upon which the high religions were founded. [Maslow, 1970, pp. 26–27]

Peak experience is a general term for the range of experiences that go from mostly intellectual/slightly emotional to mostly emotional/slightly intellectual. They can be introvertive or extrovertive, pure examples of one attitude or a mixture of many. Almost anything can be a peak experience. It is a "self-validating, self-justifying moment which perceives the greatest values of a being's existence." Maslow lists these values as wholeness, perfection, completion, justice, aliveness, richness, simplicity, beauty, goodness, uniqueness, effortlessness, playfulness, truth, self-sufficiency (1968a, p. 83).

But we must try to limit the types of experience that can be given the name peak experience. Maslow has a very restricted type of intellectual—emotional gestalt in mind. There are no limits with respect to the cause or content of the experience—it can be caused by a sunset or a vision of Christ's love—but there are real restrictions of ethics or character. To have a true peak experience in the Maslow sense, an individual must have begun to develop toward maturity. For such individuals, motivation must be growth motivation and not deficiency motivation; in the case of love, "being" love and not deficiency love. Also, of course, "being" cognition is preferred to deficiency cognition. Maslow's views serve as moral reminders more than anything else. If you love the being of other persons, you love them for what they are and what they can be (growth or being love motivation) rather than because of your own needs and problems (deficiency motivation or love). Intellectual activity is superior when you seek to know something for what it is (being cognition) rather than for what it can do for you (deficiency cognition).

In his discussion of the understanding of life and sense of reality found in peak experiences, Maslow says: "The emotional reaction in the peak experience has a special flavor of wonder, of awe, of reverence, of humility and surrender before the experience as before something great." With specific reference to religion, he says:

> In some reports, particularly of the mystic experience... the whole of the world is seen as unity, as a single rich live entity. In other of the peak experiences, most particularly the love experience and the aesthetic experience, one small part of the world is perceived as if it were for the moment all of the world. [1968a, p. 88]

Maslow even posits a moral goodness that is associated in religious tradition with imitation of, or identification with, the divine: "The person at the peak is godlike not only in the sense that I have touched upon already but in certain other ways as well, particularly in the complete, loving, uncondemning, compassionate, and perhaps amused acceptance of the world and of the person" (1968a, pp. 87–88).

The ultimate goal is self-actualization. The term is similar to Jung's, but there is nothing of Jung's mythology of the unconscious. Self-actualized persons live in accordance with a system of values that Maslow believes is basic to human nature: "The study of the human being by science or by self-search can discover where he is heading, what is his purpose in life, what is good for him and what is bad for him, what will make him feel virtuous and what will make him feel guilty, why choosing the good is often difficult for him, what the attractions of evil are" (1968a, p. 205). Self-actualized individuals balance off "the conative, the cognitive, the affective, and the motor" (p. 208). They transcend conflict, anxiety, frustration, sadness, hurt, and guilt. They can live introvertively and extrovertively.

Maslow gives similar lists of values at different points in his book: When he is talking about growth-motivation, being love, being cognition, peak experience, or self-actualized persons, the same list comes up again. For Maslow self-actualized religious people possess and develop a variety of good qualities. They accept themselves, others, and the natural world at the same time as they strive for something better. They are spontaneous and task-oriented rather than self-preoccupied. Although they have a sense of privacy and independence, they have also a sense of identity with others and can be vividly appreciative of their values. Their democratic openness does not rule out the cultivation of intimacy with a few loved ones. They recognize the difference between means and ends and possess a humor that is philosophical rather than hostile. Nonconformity is only the other side of creativity, which they arrive at only in their moments of highest poetic, self-transcending experience. Of course, not only technical creativity is involved, but natural, aesthetic, parental, orgasmic, "oceanic feeling" types; also, they have high moments in the arts and athletics. These experiences include and can culminate in what should be called religious experiences, because they are identical to the sublime moments described in religious literature (1968a, pp. 97–98).

Maslow, like Allport, concerns himself with two levels of human functioning. He uses the terms "survival tendency" and "actualization tendency" to describe these levels. The survival tendency is the push toward satisfaction of needs ensuring physical and psychological survival. Maslow also calls this deprivation motivation: The person has need of certain things that he or she should not be deprived of. There are physiological needs such as food and water; safety needs such as the avoidance of pain; needs for belongingness and love such as intimacy, gregariousness, and identification; and esteem needs, such as the approval of self and others. This list of needs is one of increasing human refinement in that a set of needs becomes important only when those preceeding it on the list are satisfied.

An actualization tendency grows out of the survival tendency. This is the push toward realization of special capabilities for cognitive understanding (with emphasis on the hunger for stimulation and information). Maslow calls this growth motivation, because the person does much more than "get by." It is the self-actualizing person who is the candidate for what some call the religious experiences of life. Maslow's description of self-actualized people who develop themselves according to a genetic blueprint includes elements of openness to contemplation of beauty and realistic good behavior that are also part of religious belief and behavior.

Maslow's is a simple, positive description of human nature, an attention to a particular brand of happy human experiences, and a statement of ideals for members of the affluent, somewhat introspective, artistic, intellectual, and somewhat leisured Western society.

Some research has been done on the relationship between religious experience and self-actualization (Stones, 1980), and the motivational maturation scale based upon Maslow's ideas has been developed and used in religious research (Alker and Gawin, 1978). But humanistic and existentialist psychology emphasizes such all-pervading features of the personality that it is difficult to isolate basic notions for research. Some progress has been made, for example, in sorting out what Maslow and others mean by maturity (Browde, 1976) and in distinguishing purpose in life from personal values (Jacobson, Ritter, and Mueller, 1977). In the last analysis, self-actualization might simply be another word for self-coherence—when you have it "together" you are self-actualized (Stark and Washburn, 1977).

The Existentialist Interpretation of the Religious Experience: Rollo May

Rollo May and other psychologists today who would call themselves "existentialist" are concerned about many of the same problems and issues as Allport and Maslow, but their intellectual origins and outlooks are distinctly different. While modern schools of European existentialism derive from the Danish philosopher and theologian Soren Kierkegaard, the central influence has been Martin Heidegger. Issues such as the relation of the individual to systems, intentionality, communication, being and absurdity, freedom and choice, and, of course, anxiety concerned all the existentialists. Heidegger attempted to answer the basic question, "What is it to be?" with an elaborately developed philosophy of "Being-in-the-World." Heidegger's philosophy forms the basis of European existentialist psychology, the foremost exponent of which is Ludwig Binswanger. There is no alternative to a profound philosophy of existence, Binswanger says, because "knowledge of the structure or basic constitution of existence provides us with a systematic clue for the practical existential—analytical investigation at hand" (Binswanger, 1958a, pp. 200–201). If the mentally ill live in their own worlds, they can be judged as aberrant only if we understand the structures of the normative world; and they can be helped only if we understand the structures of the normative world. Second, speech can be studied as the means by which the content of existence is best expressed: Binswanger says that everything depends upon the precise criteria by which the language phenomena are studied as expressions and manifestations of world design or world content.

Traditionally, existentialist analysis has distinguished three modes of world. Three German words expressive of these three modes have become famous. *Umwelt* means the natural world, the world of objects around us. It includes needs, drives, and instincts, and is the world, as Rollo May puts it, "that one would still exist in if, let us hypothesize, one had no self-awareness" (May, 1958, p. 61). The *mitwelt* is the world of interrelationships with human beings. There is an exchange that goes on: People influence and at the same time are influenced by those around them. The *eigenwelt* is the personal basis on which we react to the world around us. It presupposes self-awareness but is not merely a subjective inner experience. The human being should live in these worlds simultaneously; if he or she lives only in one, then there are bound to be deep problems for living (1958, p. 63).

Binswanger's case of "Ilse" is a good illustration of how analysis and therapy must deal with these three modes of being.

Ilse was an intelligent thirty-nine-year-old woman, more or less happily married, Protestant, religious, mother of three children; her father was proud and tyrannical, her mother self-effacing and kind. One day, in a planned attempt to achieve the long-term goal of persuading her father to treat her mother more considerately, she put her right hand into a fire-filled stove right up to her forearm. Then she held out her hands to him saying, "Look, this is to show you how much I love you" (Binswanger, 1958b, p. 215). After that she began to interpret herself as the absolute center of attention, even thinking during the reading of a work of fiction that it referred directly to her.

The two themes Binswanger develops in his analysis are *father* and *sacrifice*. Although he makes use of some psychoanalytic connections, he sees the woman's problem in relation to her overall life and the lives of those around her: "The entire dialectics of her relation to her father continue in the dialectics of her relations to her fellow men in general" (1958b, p. 222). The adored father is the life problem that dominates the life history. When the pressure of his tyranny became intolerable she believed that only a violent solution could change things: The sacrificial burning was the solution. After that she was sidetracked by a number of ancillary concerns, until finally she could achieve control.

This woman's problems, crisis, and later stabilization are interpreted relative to her relationship to the people around her (*mitwelt*) and her overall context (*umwelt*) and not simply limited to her interior problems. The strength of her father problem caused her to meet her father in the people around her. And then, "just as the father's harshness and coldness, inaccessibility to love and sacrifice, turned into a tortuous riddle for Ilse, so the entire environment now becomes an enigmatic power" (1958b, p. 224).

The basic solution was Ilse's reconciliation with the *mitwelt* and *umwelt* when she grew into and was helped into a readiness to assist and work for fellow human beings. For Binswanger, Ilse's cure depended on her ability to deal with her present situation rather than remember the past.

The present and the future are what counts if people are to do any significant reflection on the worlds they have inhabited in the past. Problems occur when people do not think of, hope in, and set goals for the future—"their past does not come alive because nothing matters enough to them in the future" (May, 1958, p. 70). More broadly speaking, people have to transcend their own situations. This looking to a future is at the center of what existentialists take to be the most important human power, the ability to self-transcend. Beginning with an awareness of this world and of others around them, and of themselves, people can move beyond themselves by discerning possibilities and choosing from among them. And the motivation to choose comes from the ability to care (May 1958, p. 76).

Living in one's worlds, knowledge of one's worlds, imagining of one's worlds, and care-motivated structuring of one's worlds make the human being unique. These ideas of existentialist philosophers, as they are funneled into psychology by Binswanger, May, and others, are considerations about the nature of life and human uniqueness that are the grounding of Allport's and Maslow's view of optimal personal, human functioning: seeking future goals in personal freedom. These are issues with which theologians and philosophers of religion have often concerned themselves. None of our psychologists, however, had more specifically religious concerns than Rollo May.

Born in Ohio and educated at Oberlin College, Rollo May traveled and taught for several years in Europe before returning to the United States. He enrolled at Union Theological Seminary and helped out very briefly at a parish in Montclair, New Jersey. At Union and later while a Ph.D. candidate in clinical psychology at Columbia he was a student of Paul Tillich, whose terminology influenced May's own notions of centeredness, courage, intentionality, and anxiety of meaninglessness (Reeves, 1977). Another important influence was the Gestalt psychologist Kurt Goldstein. May started in private practice but soon became connected with the William Alanson White Institute, and in subsequent years he taught at the New School for Social Research and New York University while continuing his association with the institute.

Anxiety was May's first full scholarly preoccupation (May, 1950). *The Meaning of Anxiety* was derived from his Columbia dissertation, a combination of his own concerns and his dialogue with Paul Tillich (see May, 1973). The book was written in the style May was to use in all of his later works: filled with historical, literary, and philosophical references, and shaped by his growing experience in psychotherapy and maturing experience of social problems.

Its argument boils down to this: The first step in psychotherapy is to understand the nature and cause of the problem, and the fundamental cause of human problems is anxiety. Anxiety, if we are to follow Kierkegaard and Freud, is "ontological," inalienable, and inevitable in human existence. While May has reservations about Freud's theories, he admits that they clarify what happens in anxiety. But the ultimate cause of anxiety is much better explained in Kierkegaard, because for Kierkegaard anxiety is ontological, that is, it belongs to the very being of existence (the Greek *ontos* means "being"). Accordingly, May defines anxiety as "the apprehension cued off by a threat to some value which the individual holds essential to his existence as a personality" (May 1950, p. 191).

Religion is at the center of the problem of modern anxiety, because it is at the center of people's lives in any given culture. When the religious beliefs and symbols that enabled people to ward off anxiety no longer work, everyone is threatened by the apparent meaninglessness and chaos of the universe. By becoming aware of the disintegration of their symbols, human beings can establish the basis for a new morality. May's writings are themselves often a search for a new morality. In this search, no work is more important than *Love and Will* (1969). Here May sketches the basic challenges of loving and willing today. He attempts to aid people to arrive at goals the same as or similar to Freud's teaching and therapy goals, *lieben* and *arbeiten*—love and work.

People are split off from their personality centers of thinking and feeling, he says, referring to the collective problem as a "schizoid world." But May wants to discover the constructive elements of the schizoid attitudes, because it can make for good living in a hectic and troubled modern world. Speaking of those who can "make it" in this world, May says this: "They preserve the inner world which the very hyperstimuli of our age would take away. These introverts can continue to exist despite the overpowering stimuli or lack of it, for they have learned to develop a 'constructive' schizoid attitude toward life" (1969, p. 33).

The primarily ethical concerns of May become as prominent as ever when he examines the paradoxes of sex and love. The new sexual freedom (sex without love) makes people more anxious and introduces a new sexual puritanism. For some reason he associates the mechanistic with the puritanical, and he defines puritanism by naming three elements: "a state of alienation from the body," "separation of emotion from person," and "the use of the body as a machine." He places the blame for this type of puritanism upon psychoanalysis, because it presumably views the body and self as a mechanism for gratification by way of sexual objects. He quotes a later-1930s statement of a past president of the American Psychological Association to this effect: "Psychoanalysis is Calvinism in Bermuda shorts" (1969, p. 49).

Very readable complaints about the modern sexual wilderness have become so standard by now that they sound like everyday ideas. May decries, for example, the danger of "making one's self feel less in order to perform better," warning that in the end "the lover who is more efficient will also be the one who is impotent" (1969, p. 55). Here May's readers will find the standard complaints about *Playboy,* quotes from the *Times Literary Supplement,* and the likes of T. S. Eliot, David Riesman, Sophocles, and Marshall McLuhan.

The words that May analyzes in his discussion of love are *eros* and the *daimonic.*

"We fly to the sensation of sex in order to avoid the passion of eros," says May (p. 65). By choosing the Greek word eros as the peg on which to hang his discussion of love, May is able to discuss elements of passion, self-giving, mystery, and death. Eros is a combination of mental, emotional, and physiological intensities that give life to the sexual interaction and is not to be symbolized by the chubby little Cherubs with bow and arrow, who in fact represent the tritest aspects of love.

> We have arrived on the wings of eros, if I may put it so, at a new concept of causality. No longer are we forced to understand the human being in terms of billiard-ball cause-and-effect, based solely on the explanations of "reason why" and susceptible to rigid prediction.... I am proposing a description of human beings as given motivation by the new possibilities, the goals and ideas, which attract and pull them toward the future. [1969, p. 93]

Instead of being driven from behind, people are inspired and attracted by the "future," a species of vision or intentionality. May, like Allport, bases his discussion of intentionality on the writings of Franz Brentano.

There is a somber element, however: Love is possible only in connection with death. May even thinks that love is possible only if a sense of mortality is combined with it. Sex emptied of eros is obviously used to ward off death anxiety or a sense of mortality. Love has an element of the tragic, because there is the constant potential to destroy and the inevitability of separation. But the energy generated by the presence of the tragic is not necessarily evil. May believes that the Greek notion of *"daimonic"* (as against the notion of *"demonic,"* or profoundly evil) entwined with the tragic is the basis of eros.

The daimonic may be defined as "any natural function which has the power to take over the whole person" (1969, p. 123). It is sometimes creative, sometimes destructive, and normally both. The classical example is Socrates' description of his own "daimon" in The *Apologia,* the mysterious drive that made him the searcher for truth. So demon possession or violence is the daimonic gone bad. And the daimonic can go bad if it is not recognized for what it is. The passions have to be identified, controlled, and taken into oneself. You take in the daimons which would possess you if you didn't. The one way to get over daimonic possession is to possess it, by frankly confronting it, coming to terms with it, integrating it into the self-system. People must take a stand, assert themselves, and give themselves. And this, of course is what May considers essential in the love relationship.

To profit from the presence of the daimonic in the personality, May requires entry into "dialogue." We must enter into dialogue with other people and with ourselves, or else we project our own passions in their worst form upon an enemy. And this can be the neighbor in the next house or the next country. The daimonic has to be known, to be named in dialogue, so that its energies can be harnessed. May quotes William James on the curative effect of naming one's problem: "The effort by which [the patient] succeeds in keeping the right *name* unwaveringly present to his mind proves to be a saving moral act" (1969, p. 167). Thus can a variety of drives, passions, insights, and inspirations be named and organized. They then become a pull toward the future that causes people to communicate themselves creatively, that is, to enter into a love relationship.

The will has not been helped by the new freedom. People are unable to decide anything, one way or another, in the context of liberation, physical and intellectual. May is concerned to show that psychoanalysis and psychology assume a determinism that contradicts the notion of freedom, even though aimed at a certain liberation of the human personality from unhealthy inner constraints. But Freud did not take will power to be a positive force, believing it to be more or less the instrument of repression. *Wish* is for Freud a good word—to May's joy, because he wants to valorize the term. "Wish is the imaginative playing with the possibility of some act or state occurring" (1969, p. 218). Wishing is valuable because it sets the stage for the movement of the *will*, "the capacity to organize one's self so that movement in a certain direction or toward a certain goal may take place" (1969, p. 218).

At the heart of wishing and willing is intentionality, which is, as in Brentano and Allport, a movement toward something:

> You cannot understand the overt behavior except as you see it in relation to, and as an expression of, its intention. Meaning has no meaning apart from intention. Each act of consciousness *tends toward* something, is a turning of the person toward something, and has within it, no matter how latent, some push toward a direction of action. [May, 1969, p. 230]

A good example is found in Freudian therapy when patients are unable to remember something. When they can remember, it is because something has changed in their intentionality—"the patient cannot remember something until he is ready to take a stand toward it" (1969, p. 232). Memory in this sense depends upon intentionality.

Taking a stand toward something is the dynamo that causes all forms of personal interaction, intellectual and emotional. We perceive things, we conceive things by acting, and by acting with genuine bodily involvement. May helpfully illustrates this richer meaning of intention with a quotation from a Shakespeare sonnet on thinking about his love when going to sleep:

> *For then my thoughts—from far where I abide—*
> *Intend a zealous pilgrimage to thee,*
> *And keep my drooping eyelids open wide.*

May says that today we would write "intend to make a zealous pilgrimage," while Shakespeare gave the word "intend" its full active meaning. To intend a pilgrimage is to make one in some way (1969, pp. 241–42). Clearest illustrations of intentionality, of course, come from therapy sessions where patients do not admit that thoughts and emotions are really theirs. They refer to "the" hatred, "the" despair, or they label one of their problems with some catchword from psychological literature. "What such a patient is doing is taking the intentionality out of the experience," May says (1969, p. 260).

When people can act, they are free. May believes this in spite of the great amount of evidence that in so many various ways we are all determined: He appreciates the idea of Spinoza that "freedom is the recognition of necessity" (1969, p. 269). We exercise our freedom by taking up a certain relationship to what determines us: death, growing old, limitations of intelligence and upbringing.

It can often happen that love and will can get in each other's way, that people can be so developed in one area that the other is damaged. Take the example of the business executive with limit-less drive who walks all over his sensitive son. Or take the exam-ple of the young man who becomes impotent when he does not genuinely care for the person he is making love to: The "patient is trying to will his body to love when he does not love" (1969, p. 280). In fact, it is in care that love and will unite.

Care is the opposite of apathy, and is the notion that things do matter. May vividly describes a scene in Vietnam that he wit-nessed on television. A black American soldier is looking down on a Vietnamese child whose family had just been flushed out of a hiding place by some kind of gas. The bewilderment and sorrow on the man's face May takes to be care. The Roman poet Lucre-tius—in spite of his Epicurean theories of detachment—can be taken as someone who cares because of his engagement with the profoundest human issues in living and dying. Heidegger made care the source of will and probably the basic phenomenon that constitutes human existence.

The ultimate goal of May's presentation of love and will is the communion of one person with another. Love and will are both forms of communion of consciousness. "Both are also *af-fects*—ways of *affecting* others and our world. . . . An affect or af-fection is also the way of making, doing, forming something" (1969, p. 309). Whether making love to a beloved, dealing with friends, or relating to the social environment, we both love and will at the same time: "For in every act of love and will—and in the long run they are present in each genuine act—we mold our-selves and our world simultaneously. This is what it means to embrace the future" (1969, p. 325).

In *Power and Innocence* May examines the distortion of the structures of existence that underlie contemporary violence and hostility. He refers to Vietnam, American protest movements, ghetto living, and the structure of minority groups in America. He warns that a false innocence is no protection against violence; what is needed is a recognition of everyone's right to power: "Power is the birthright of every human being. It is the source of his self-esteem and the root of his conviction that he is interpersonally significant" (May, 1972, p. 243). Power is con-nected to love and is not antithetical to the Christian ethic, be-cause, for May, power is the assumption of one's rightful respon-sibility for another person. Again we encounter the issue of one person's communing with another. May, like Freud, is a demanding moralist, but like Allport he is more optimistic about the results.

Allport, Maslow, and May speak of the personality in ways quite different from Freud and Jung. On paper they do not differ much from one another. To read Maslow as simply a theoretician of personality somewhat like Allport is to miss his distinctiveness. And to see May as philosophically murky is to be fooled by the "existentialist" label. Allport was a very clear, almost hardheaded writer, who wanted to understand individuality and rationality. For him the role of religion was different in each human being, because it helped people to achieve mature rationality in a mysterious world. Maslow was also interested in the individual, but he wanted to get at the indescribable self-experiences by which people seemed to unify and perfect their lives relative to the situation around them. May explored the nonrational as an energizing drive in people, enabling them to both be and share themselves.

The psychologies of Allport, Maslow, and May are really the philosophies of strong and generous individuals. But the more we become removed from their individual personalities, the more the impression fades. They will probably not remain as distinctly influential as Freud or Jung.

PART III

Religious Development Through Social Interaction

W<small>E</small> have already begun the study of the development and growth of the religious personality. The relationship of young boys to their fathers, the development of individuals out of opportunistic functioning into propriate functioning, and so on, are related to the development of belief and morality. However, more specialized and wider-ranging explanations of religious development have been worked out over the years: Emphasis has been on the step-by-step development of children in accordance with some kind of inner "blueprint" or "program." Erik Erikson and Jean Piaget—at times isolating a religious component—explain the emotional and cognitive steps that people pass through on their way to fuller development and maturity. And others, like James Fowler and Lawrence Kohlberg, have discussed these steps relative to faith development and moral development. All these studies are related to the personality theories of the preceding section of the book: The work of Erikson coordinates with the conflict version

(Freud and Jung) with some important differences that we need not emphasize here; and the work of Piaget coordinates with the fulfillment version (Allport, Maslow, and May) with some important differences. Whereas in the last section we were more concerned with the results or goals of development, in this section we are concerned with the process of development.

We have to be at least partially convinced that religious development occurs in visible stages if we are to benefit from the studies of Erikson and Piaget. And if we are only partially convinced, it will still be drudgery to go through a discussion of the stages. A student or educator who is only partially convinced would do better to read the first and last sections of Chapter 5 and then zero in on the issues that might seem to be personally interesting. For example, if you are interested in the ways children think about their individuality in the world, the breath of life in things, or the way the elements of nature and people are created, or if you are interested in how children begin to follow rules, their sense of fair play, communication of the truth, and the dispensing of justice, turn to the appropriate sections of the discussion of Piaget. If you are interested in the sources of truth, will power, and sensitivity in the lives of young people, turn to the appropriate sections of the discussion of Erikson. If you find that neither Erikson's nor Piaget's presentations seem explicitly "religious" enough, then you might concentrate on Fowler's and Kohlberg's discussions of Judeo-Christian faith and morality.

The social psychology presented in Chapter 6 is not totally removed from developmental psychology. A developmental psychology that emphasizes interaction with social environment is assumed by a number of social psychologies. Psychologists who emphasize social environment make development dependent on interaction with adults and accordingly take an inner plan or staged development far less seriously than Erikson or Piaget, for whom the adult environment is the trigger for the performance of development tasks and the formation of schemata. To integrate developmental and social psychology we shall have to assume that development is caused by interchange—"interaction" is the more commonly used word—between children and those who take care of them (and with their peers, especially those one developmental level higher). Children's control over their personalities and behavior is, in effect, shared with adults. In a given situation the adult has an understanding of the basic goal to be achieved, but the child does not. The child has the necessary subskills and can carry out the behavior necessary for attaining the subgoals but does not know how to organize them; the child does not know what the situation *is*. As children struggle to make sense of the situation, the adults steer their behavior so that the children accomplish the tasks as if they knew what they were doing. During this process an adult overinterprets a child's behavior as appropriate (even though the child may not realize the behavior is appropriate) and thereby imparts to the child the sense that this is what one should be doing in that situation. The end product on the part of the child is a sequence of behaviors that constitute appropriate activity in the given situation. But—note—the responsibility for these behaviors rests with the adult. Only when children have been told that the task is complete can they reflect on what they "did" and treat the sequence of subgoals as part of a single routine or a new goal-directed activity.

Social psychology assumes that human beings continue to determine the behavior of one another far beyond the years of earliest and most intense formation. No one is ever completely formed, because everyone continues to behave in relationship to other people. When I act I do so on the basis of my interpretation of what people are thinking of me at the moment I act, what people seem to have thought of me in the past, and what I expect them to think of me in the future. We deal with this kind of social interaction in social psychology. We study how people are what they are religiously, and every way, because of their exchanges with others. Then we can turn to an analysis of the attitudes that people form as a result of the exchange with or simple reflection about other people and situations; the study of attitudes has been at the center of social psychology research since social psychology had its own separate identity. But first we examine here the basis for both interactions and related attitude formation, namely the fundamental drive for consistency, either cognitive or emotional. Such a drive causes people to reject viewpoints that are inconsistent with their views of themselves. In religion a famous example of this is the failed prophecy—when a prophet's followers completely change their interpretation of a prophecy, such as the date of the end of the world, so as to make it consistent with what really happened.

Thus three areas of the social psychology of religion are presented. First, consistency theory: We examine the theories of Leon Festinger, George Kelly, and the combined efforts of Salvatore Maddi and Donald Fiske. Second, social interaction and small-group theory: We examine the views of George Herbert Mead, Erving Goffman, and the appropriate small-group-research. Third, attitudes: We discuss the nature of attitude study and the general categories of religious attitude research.

Religious Development: The Traditions of Erikson and Piaget

EMOTIONAL AND MOTIVATIONAL development is the subject of Erik Erikson's work, and he links religious development to general development, sometimes explicitly and sometimes implicitly.

Describing eight stages of development (see table), Erikson cites a principle that he thinks is operative in all of life: Anything that grows has a ground plan; each part has its time for special ascendency, until all parts have arisen to form a functioning whole. This means that the qualities that emerge at various points in life—trust, autonomy, and so on—are all operative from the beginning and throughout life. But there is a proper point, a proper age in life, for each one to take over center stage, as it were. These qualities have a religious aspect also, insofar as they determine the way individuals relate to God and regulate their behavior. For example, Erikson connects Martin Luther's personal to his religious development in this way:

> The characteristics of Luther's theological advance can be
> compared to certain steps in psychological maturation which

Eras and Ages	Erikson	Piaget	Fowler	Kohlberg
Infancy (0–1½)	Basic trust vs. basic mistrust (hope)	Sensorimotor	Undifferentiated faith	
Early childhood (2–6)	Autonomy vs. shame and doubt (will) Initiative vs. guilt (purpose)	Preoperational or intuitive	Introjective–projective faith	Preconventional level 1. Heteronomous morality 2. Instrumental exchange
Childhood (7–12)	Industry vs. inferiority (competence)	Concrete operational	Mythic–literal faith	
Adolescence (13–21)	Identity vs. role confusion (fidelity)	Formal operational	Synthetic–conventional faith	Conventional level 3. Mutual interpersonal relations
Young adulthood (21–35)	Intimacy vs. isolation (love)	—	Individuative–reflective faith	4. Social system and conscience
Adulthood (35–60)	Generativity vs. stagnation (care)	—	Conjunctive faith	Postconventional principal level 5. Social contract, individual rights
Maturity (60+)	Integrity vs. despair (wisdom)	—	Universalizing faith	6. Universal ethical principles

every man must take: the internalization of the father–son relationship; the concomitant crystallization of conscience; the safe establishment of an identity as a worker and a man; and the concomitant reaffirmation of basic trust.

God, instead of lurking of the periphery of space and time, became for Luther "what works in us." The way *to* Him is not the effortful striking toward a goal by "doing what you can"; rather, His way is what moves from inside: God, now less of a person, becomes more personal for the individual; and instead of constituting a threat to be faced at the end of all things, He becomes that which always begins—in us. His son is therefore always reborn: . . . It therefore behooves us to be reborn, renovated, regenerated. To "do enough" means always to begin: . . . The intersection of all the paradoxes of the vertical and the horizontal is thus to be found in man's own divided nature. The two [kingdoms], the realist sphere of divine grace and the naturalist sphere of animality, exist in man's inner conflicts and in his existential paradoxes: . . . the two personalities and the two callings which a Christian must maintain at the same time on this earth. [Erikson, 1962, pp. 213–14]

Note the explicit linking of developmental stages in the first paragraph: theological advance accompanies psychological maturation. Erikson becomes something of a theologian himself in the second paragraph: Luther's internalization of the father–son relationship is accompanied by an internalization of God, whose image, then, is no longer external and threatening. Initiative and industry must be carried out in spite of inner conflicts.

As an example of Piaget's explanation of cognitive development, take the following discussion of the child's ideas on how things are made.

To regard this artificialist interest as entirely due to religious education is a hypothesis that cannot be borne out by analysis. A very pronounced artificialism may, in fact, be found among deaf-mutes or with children who are too young to have understood or generalised the religious teaching they may have received. . . . But even supposing—what is far from proved—that all the children between the ages of 4 and 12 examined had been directly influenced by the theology of the Book of Genesis, there remain three reasons for maintaining the artificialist tendency we have noted is in part at least spontaneous.

In the first place, we have been struck by the fact that the majority of children only bring in God against their will as it were, and not until they can find nothing else to bring forward. . . .

Secondly, even if we admit that the child's artificialism is an extension of the theological artificialism imposed by education, it remains to be explained why the child, as has been shown, thus extends to everything conceptions wherein the religious significance remains so vague, and still more why this extension obeys laws instead of differing from child to child. . . .

Thirdly, and this is the most important objection to be opposed to the theory under discussion, the child's real religion, at any rate during the first years, is quite definitely anything but the over-elaborated religion with which he is plied. [Piaget, 1972, pp. 353–54]

Piaget is convinced that the religious instruction of youngsters is something foreign to their thought, because their God references are not nearly as subtle or intricate as their other artificialist ideas about the origin of the stars, weather factors, and so on. Nor can the simple religious description of creation, since it is so "vague," cause children to be so like one another in their description of details. Piaget notes, too, that the child attributes powers to the parent that are only later transferred to God. "God is either a man like other men, or else the child is always romancing when he speaks of him, in the same way that he speaks of Father Christmas and the fairies" (1972, p. 354).

We can see that the concerns of our two developmental psychologists are different: Erikson explains how children develop personally and emotionally as a background to their cognitive development. Infants develop a sense of trust or mistrust depending upon the care they receive; very young children develop a sense of autonomy or shame depending upon the encouragement they receive; slightly older children develop initiative or feeling of guilt, depending upon the initial success of their endeavors; children who are able or who fail to keep their initiative on an ongoing basis develop a sense of industry or inferiority. In adolescence, the primary activity is the development of identity; failure to do so, of course, results in identity confusion. Moving into adulthood, young people make use of all the previous stages to achieve intimacy with others; otherwise, they fall into isolation. Adults must develop faculties of generativity in the sense of personal and especially family productivity, or they fall into stagnation. And finally, when well into mature life, the highest development and a full integrity are reached, because life is complete and satisfying; total failure means despair (Erikson, 1968, ch. 3).

Jean Piaget calls the basic principles of human functioning organization and adaptation. All species organize their physical processes into coherent systems, and all species are born with a tendency to adapt to the environment, either by accommodating themselves to it or assimilating it into their own habitual patterns of behavior. These tendencies to organize and adapt result in psychological structures or operations called "schemata" that take different forms at different stages of child and adolescent development.

Piaget explains how children develop their conception of the world and a sense of moral selfhood in conjunction with basic developmental tasks. Children from approximately two to six years old are at a *preoperational* stage of cognition: Egocentric in their thought, they cannot take the viewpoint of other persons, differentiate the psychical from the physical, or understand different types of animation. Play rules are just a matter of fantasy. They do develop representational thought during this period, becoming adept at images and symbols to represent their knowledge and communicate it to others. From approximately seven to twelve years the children are at the *concrete operational* stage of cognition. They begin to appreciate a large group of actions that can be performed on objects *mentally,* such as conservation (a tall water glass is no longer considered to contain more when water is poured into it from a short, broad container), classification, and combination. Children are capable of more cooperative play here, but rules are considered sacred and untouchable, coming from adults. Loyalty to peers will always give way to adult rules. For the next few years, until puberty, children advance in skills learning and social cooperation. Intellectual skills involving hypotheses and evidence, as well as artistic skills, can be developed, and almost every adult sport becomes possible. Responsibility and punishment are evaluated more in terms of motivation and the complexities of justice (Ginsberg and Opper, 1979).

As children move into adolescence, their thinking becomes

more abstract. The stage Piaget speaks of is called *formal operational*. Adolescents can generate hypotheses about events that have never been perceived. Thoughts are governed by logical principles. The ability to hypothesize regarding logical consequences of action, conceptualize regarding change, and anticipate consequences of actions, all serve to make the future an important part of life.

The table at the beginning of this chapter offers a coordination of the Eriksonian and Piagetian stages. It helps to refer to the table before and after the reading of each section.

Emotional and Motivational Development: Erikson

Erik Erikson, born of Danish parents, grew up in Germany. At first he tried his hand at art, but he said of that early career that "artist" was at that time a "European euphemism for a young man with some talent but nowhere to go" (Maier, 1969). When he began teaching at a small American school he began psychoanalytic training with Anna Freud at the Vienna Psychoanalytic Institute. During the 1930s he taught at both Harvard and Yale. Later he taught at the University of California and at several psychoanalytic institutes. In 1951 he returned to the East Coast to join the staff of the Austin Riggs Center at Stockbridge, Massachusetts, and joined the staff at Harvard ten years later. His major collections of essays, *Childhood and Society* and *Identity, Youth, and Crisis*, gained widespread recognition, even fame, in the United States.

Erikson analyzes social–emotional more than cognitive development. His emphasis has to do with all aspects of the personality rather than mental faculties alone. His eight-stage description is thought by many to be a true-to-life presentation, or at least an artful idealization of life. The reception of this view of human development has been so favorable that we must base our acceptance of the truth of the description more on the popular acclaim it has received than on any confirming systematic testing. Throughout the years of human growth different attitudes or virtues are developed that can be properly called religious; as we move through Erikson's eight ages of "man," we can note the elements of trust, autonomy, initiative, industry, identity, intimacy, generativity, and wisdom that determine religious belief and behavior.

Personal and Religious Development

Babies first of all, according to Erikson, have a sense of relationship to their mothers and, probably in a secondary way, to their fathers. The way they are suckled, treated generally and have parental atittudes conveyed to them determines whether they will basically trust or mistrust life around them. Naturally, their earliest concerns are oral, so the way their food needs are responded to determines that initial sense of wellbeing that we call trust. If infants are neglected or ill-treated, deliberately or by force of circumstances, there will always be an element of mistrust in their personalities, even though an initial bad situation is basically compensated for later on (whatever happens to a quality at its moment of ascendency is more important than what happens to it at other times; the lower the age level at which a problem arises, the greater problem it is). Trust is developed as the religious quality of hope—in various imaginable worlds, including a perfected world here and the future joyful world of heaven (1968, pp. 96–107).

As time moves on, children establish a wide, for them unlimited, radius of goals, perfecting their language so they can ask innumerable questions. They expand their imagination to include all types of roles for themselves. They can thus emerge with a sense of initiative as a basis for a realistic sense of ambition and purpose. By the end of the third year children are walking with ease and becoming aware not only of what they can do, but of what they may do. And a genuine, though infantile, sexual initiative is developed as the essence of an overall style. In the boy the emphasis is on intrusion and head-on attack; in the girl, on aggressive snatching, attractiveness, or self-endearment. Erikson describes the Freudian phallic state in his own way: "The child thus develops the prerequisites for masculine and feminine initiative and, above all, some sexual self-images which will become essential ingredients in the positive and negative aspects of his future identity" (1968, p. 118). Here an initial sense of purpose is developed. Goals, without which conscience does not exist, are set up, along with appropriate response patterns. Purpose is a genuine strength of conscience. Here, play and fantasy end and irreversible purpose begins. We have the earliest integration of conscience activity, because fantasy is no longer permissible, and to-be-learned reality all-demanding (1964, p. 122).

When they are not able to make things and make them well, children can come up with the well-known sense of inferiority. If things go well, they develop, rather, a sense of industry. Since a child has to be integrated into the technology of a culture, teachers are highly important. Awareness of opportunities for making and doing in a society and the ability to teach the needed skills, as well as the ability to bring out the child's potential, are the necessary talents of a teacher. This does not deny that children wish to be mildly but firmly pushed into the adventure of finding out that they can learn to accomplish things they would never have thought of by themselves. This is the decisive age for establishing capacities for technical and occupational success. Morally, children develop a sense of competence in personal achievement that can really be helpful in developing ego strength, the ability to achieve the goals set for them by their conscience. A genuine moral dexterity and a sense of morality are present (1964, pp. 122–24).

All the foregoing stages bequeath some problems to adolescents, and they need time to deal with the various identity elements that emerged while they were going through the earlier stages. In fact, the earliest moments of falling in love are not necessarily sexual first of all; falling in love, puppy-love, is really an attempt to unify and confirm the sensibilities already acquired. Erikson says, "Adolescent love is an attempt to arrive at a definition of one's identity by projecting one's diffused self-image on another and by seeing it thus reflected and gradually clarified" (1968, p. 132). Often they have to work with negative views of themselves, images that result from things that did not work out right in previous stages. Sometimes young people can be so bewildered by the roles pressed upon them that they are unable to cope. They leave school or jobs, behave in bizarre ways, and withdraw into themselves. If, however, we look at the lives of creative individuals, we can see that their resolution of identity problems can provide a model for others who can then follow their lead. When distinct and creative persons forge new identities, they do so because something has changed in the culture or in the society, and the old identities do not work. Ordinary people—young people, we are speaking of—cannot find themselves, because their old-fashioned upbringing does not prepare them for a new style of life.

According to Erikson, the basic virtue bound up with this experience is fidelity. Young people need to give it and receive it: A sense of duty, accuracy, truthfulness in explaining reality is helped by confirming ideologies and affirming companions. Such loyalty enables young people to preserve their orientations to the image of divinity that have come to have power for them and the orientations toward the members of society that have need of support. There is an integration: Religious belief is in the service of religious behavior, and vice versa (1964, pp. 125–26).

In more recent essays Erikson has expanded his descriptions of individual stages; he emphasizes less the "versus" and more the complementarity of each stage. For example, hope emerges from the struggle of trust versus mistrust in the child's personality, and a total victory of trust over mistrust is not expected (Erikson, 1982).

Sexual Identity and Religious Behavior

There is more to human development than what happens in the years generally studied in developmental psychology. Erikson speaks of intimacy and generativity in adult love and of the mature integrity of the older person. He says that intimacy means mature genitality and all that goes with it. It is obvious that sexual intimacies often precede the capacity to develop a true and mutual psychosocial intimacy. Before genital maturity, much of sexual life is of the self-seeking, identity-hungry type, each partner trying to reach himself/herself, or it remains a type of combat in which each tries to defeat the other. Intimacy becomes possible when, in the words of Erikson, differences between the sexes become a "full polarization within a joint life style" (1968, p. 137).

Love, care, and wisdom are virtues developed through the adult's life, with love being the beginning of all things here. It is the goal of previous virtue development and the guarantee of subsequent virtue. "Love, then, is mutuality of devotion forever subduing the antagonisms inherent in divided function" (1964, p. 129).

A theme that runs through all of Erikson's theory is the personal importance of the sexual development of male and female in relation to each other, the mutuality and complementarity of male and female in their life together. Erikson has further interpreted the meaning of this complementarity in all areas of life, including the most specialized religious search for ultimates (as we have continually noted, general virtues are the results of good development at each stage). The influence of love–sexuality on very specific religious attitudes can be traced through a number of essays and in two books on religious figures.

"Anatomy is Destiny" is Erikson's key phrase, much criticized since its publication and still defended by Erikson himself (1975, pp. 225–47). Observing the way children manipulate certain kinds of toys, we see that they push them around and position them in ways resembling, in fact, the shape of their bodies: The little girls arrange blocks in circles or build little enclosures, while little boys arrange or build pointed, tall, "erectile" structures. Boys draw scenes of houses with walls and façades protruding, high towers, and exclusively exterior views. In the boys' constructions more people and animals are outside, and more vehicles and animals are on the streets. High structures predominate. The typical girl's scene is a house interior or a simple enclosure built with blocks. People and animals are mostly within the enclosure, mainly in a static sitting or standing position. Walls are low, interiors peaceful. In some cases the interior is invaded by animals or dangerous men, but this does not necessarily lead to a counteracting or defensive construction of walls or doors. There is an element of excitement and pleasure in the intrusions (Erikson, 1950, p. 106).

Similar results were observed in other settings. Take the example of the young Sioux, the plains people whom Erikson observed so closely. The boys have a game that is a configuration of phallic aggressiveness, which in the culture is equated with the ferocity of the hunter. The game involves small, phallic-shaped bones called "bone horses." According to shape they are called horses, cows, or bulls and are used in games simulating horse racing and buffalo hunting. This allows little boys in the phallic and locomotor stage to cultivate competitive and aggressive daydreams that are common to all the tribal males. The games of the girls are not described at any length by Erikson, because they had been so affected by the experiences of their older sisters at school, despite a home education that pointed toward being a hunter's helper and, later, a hunter's mother. Erikson draws the following conclusions:

> It is clear by now that the spatial tendencies governing these constructions are reminiscent of the *genital modes*. . .and that they, in fact, closely parallel the morphology of the sex organs: in the male, *external* organs, *erectable* and *intrusive* in character, *conducting* highly *mobile* sperm cells; *internal* organs in the female, with a vestibular access leading to *statically expectant* ova. [1950, p. 106. Emphasis in original]

Erikson argues that this "reflects a profound difference in the sense of space in the two sexes, even as sexual differentiation obviously provides the most decisive difference in the ground plan of the human body, which, in turn, codetermines biological experience and social roles" (1950, p. 106).

In more recent years Erikson has refined his interpretations of children's play and the toys they use (Erikson, 1977). He now gives more attention to the individual expression of the child than to the expressions of basic sexual identity. Describing the building-block structure of a black male child, he ignores the phallic imagery and reports the child's own explanation of the structure. The youngster imagined a tall structure with children in it; he himself was on the top, but in supine position. Erikson offers these remarks:

> To compare any unique construction with others equally unique would be a time-consuming thing, and so I must ask readers to accept this one performance as an example of a five-year-old's eagerness and capacity to use a toy inventory on a given table for a relevant and yet probably only vaguely conscious "statement" which dramatizes the solution of a deep uncertainty—an uncertainty which, we may now add, is not restricted to this one boy and his individual fantasy life: for many black youngsters share the dilemma of a relative imbalance of their physical vigor, their power of expression, and a certain inhibition in school learning. [1977, p. 36]

Erikson has found that the interpretation of play with toys must include analyses of the child's individual social and personal setting. This he takes to be more important now than the relationship to sexual morphology; such play can provide useful information in conjunction with other forms of observation of children.

In his essays Erikson concentrates principally on the development of the female, no doubt because the ideas of Freud on the subject are especially inadequate. Instead of the girl experiencing penis envy and a sense of loss of an external organ, she moves simply from a sense of difference to an awareness of inner potential. Because of her anatomy and the psychological qualities that go with it, the little girl comes to a solidarity with her mother and other women and to a purposeful and competent pursuit of activities and qualities consonant with the possession of ovaries, uterus, and vagina, including the ability to stand pain specific to her feminine human experience.

A proper awareness and promotion of the destiny of women, heretofore so often stereotyped, should lead to a new balance of male and female, Erikson says. "A new balance of Male and Female, of Paternal and Maternal is obviously presaged not only in contemporary change in the relation of the sexes to each other, but also in the wider awareness which spreads whenever science, technology, and genuine self-scrutiny advance" (1968, p. 264). In these wider areas of life women should play a part of ever increasing importance. In the realm of body awareness, women can create in children a specific sensual and sensory basis for their physical and cultural identity. Beyond this is a specific psychic influence of the woman upon others derives from her active female, personal strength—in effect, her ego strength. Intellectual and emotional emphasis proper to individual women can assist in the formation of a balanced society.

The more widely extended social life is the sphere of citizenship of city and country. The opportunities, tasks, and roles within the city, and the actual organization of the city are all at present shaped by the masculine personality. Reorganization of societies resulting from the greater influence of women's being themselves will change society and culture into something that is more fully human. Erikson concludes: "A truly emancipated woman, I should think, would refuse to accept comparisons with more 'active' male proclivities as a measure of her equivalence, even when, or precisely when, it has become quite clear that she can match man's performance and competence in more spheres of achievement. True quality can mean only the right to be uniquely creative" (1968, pp. 290–91).

Because his "inner space" aroused more discussion (and antagonism) than any other of his views on sexuality, Erikson has taken some pains to clarify and extend his meaning. In response to several feminist writers, he says that anatomy is destiny for men also, and more importantly that the destinies of men and women are combined and may be interchanged. This takes place in the everyday lives of children and adults. Both live in high-rise apartments and both live in enclosed rooms, for example. Activity characteristic of the sexual morphology of the opposite sex belongs to males and to females. There are constant teaching and learning, exchange and combat, activated often by the natural presence of defenses. "A specifically psychoanalytic re-evaluation of sexual differences must ask not only what defensive deals individuals make with their own manifold identifications but also what deals men and women have made or are making with each other, in order to complement each other's defenses, and to come to some workable division of roles" (Erikson, 1975, p. 240). Erikson still clings to his original notion that the self-expression, the goals, and, in that sense, the destiny—of children and adults is related to their bodily structure and sexual morphology, but he puts more emphasis on the cultural conditioning of the self-expression and the goals. And, as with his later essays on toys, he makes the dynamics of sexual difference and complementarity more general as regards the species (there is "something" that is female, though we may not wish to stereotype it as "interiority") and more specific as regards individuals (a career woman contributes to the firm because of her own individual qualities, "female" or otherwise).

All stages of personal development have a religious quality, according to Erikson. The type of trust developed is the basis for religious belief, and a proper balance of independence and competence leads to sexual identity and intimacy, both of which very much determine the way many individuals see themselves in relation to God. And, too, identity and intimacy determine how people form the religious belief and behavior of the next generation. Erikson illustrates how the process might work in his books on Martin Luther and Mohandas Gandhi, *Young Man Luther* (1962) and *Gandhi's Truth* (1969).

Martin Luther's view of God, scripture, and Church was definitely the result of his experience of his father's mindless discipline and his mother's genuine but somewhat diffident love. Luther's handling of his own sexual drives was related to his upbringing. And all ultimately came together in his formulations on sexuality and marriage. In the case of Gandhi the dynamics are the same, but the specific connections are different: The end results were Gandhi's attempts to reduce completely the violence of his own phallicism in order to achieve a holiness that he felt was a proper combination within himself of paternal power and maternal care.

Cognitive Development: Piaget

Jean Piaget began observing and recording behavior at a very early age. When he was ten years old, he published his first article, which dealt with a rare albino sparrow. In the years following, he turned his attention to the study of mollusks. While engaged in higher studies, both in the *gymnasium* and in the university, he became more and more concerned with psychology and development. At twenty-five, when he began his professional career, his primary goal was to find a logical link between psychology and biology. In effect a zoologist, a logician, and a psychologist, Piaget—with his associates—developed more than fifty techniques for measuring and interpreting the cognitive achievement of children. He has taught at the Sorbonne and has received honorary degrees all over the world, but most of his research (from sparrows and mollusks on) and writing have been done in his native Switzerland (Maier, 1969).

According to Piaget, the religious cognitive activity of adults is built on the way they come as children to experience the world as separate from themselves, and how they see the animation of nature and the creation of things. For example, babies first see everything around them as real extensions of themselves ("realism"), only gradually coming to see that they are separate units and that not everything moves in phase with their sense of reality. Little children at first think everything is animated from within (animism) and only later develop the understanding that only animals and people have an inner animation. Connected with this is the early idea that everything is created or concocted directly (artificialism), an idea that then develops to the understanding that only manufactured items are deliberately fashioned; otherwise, people and things in nature grow directly from or otherwise evolve out of what directly precedes them.

The elements of adult religious behavior depend upon the way children come to cooperate with their fellows and to follow rules. For example, at the beginning they consider rules an "absolute" that they themselves decide upon and change according to whim. When they come to the end of this arbitrary and whimsical style of changing things, they really absolutize rules. But this absolutizing means that they see rules as the results of others' work and contributions, so they gradually come to understand rules as the results of mutual consent. Their ideas on honesty and justice go from objective to contextual.

Conception of the World and Structures of Belief

Children consider all things around them, all reality, part of themselves. Children believe that their own perspective is immediate; they are not individual, existent selves looking on objectively but *are* all of reality (this is a kind of "realism," but hardly what we adults call objectivity). When children evolve out of this, *going from preoperational to concrete operational thinking*, they change their views on thoughts, names, and dreams. Very "realistically," children think that thoughts are brought into existence by the mouth; then they think that the head produces the thought; finally thought is no longer materialized. Piaget has recorded this changing viewpoint on thoughts. Presented here, and in the material following, are quotations from his interviews with a variety of Swiss children through the years, retaining the original abbreviated Swiss names (ages in years and months are in parentheses). The mouth is the cause of thought:

> Mont (7;0): You know what it means to think?—Yes.—Then think of your house. What do you think with?—The mouth.—Can you think with the mouth shut?—No.—With the eyes shut?—Yes.—With the ears stopped up?—Yes.—Now shut your mouth and think of your house. Are you

> thinking?—Yes.—What did you think with?—The mouth.
> [Piaget, 1972, p. 39]

The head is the cause of thought:

> Kenn (7½): What do you think with?—Inside my head.—Is the
> head empty or full?—Full.—If someone opened your head,
> would they see when you were thinking?—No, because they
> couldn't see.—If they look inside your head without your dy-
> ing, would they see your thought?—You can't hear it when
> you speak gently.—What do you think with?—The head. [p.
> 41]

Thought is immaterial:

> Visc (11; 1): Where is thought?—In the head.—If someone
> opened your head, would he see your thought?—No.—Could
> he touch it?—No.—Feel it if it was air?—No. [p. 54]

In regard to names, the child absolutizes at first but gradually comes to realize how things are named by contract with
others and the process of discussion. Here, too, children come to
understand their objective nature and become aware of the process of thought itself:

> May (10): Could you have been called Henry?—Yes.—Could
> the Jura have been called "Saleve" and the Saleve
> "Jura"?—Yes, because men could have changed names or
> made them the opposite.—Could the sun have been called
> "moon"?—Why not?—Could it have? Could that (a table) have
> been called a chair, and that (a chair) a table?—Yes.—If the
> sun had been called "moon," would we have known it was
> wrong?—No.—Why not?—We couldn't have known it was
> wrong.—Why not?—Because they would have given the name
> "moon" to the sun." They wouldn't have seen any difference.
> [pp. 82–83]

When reflecting on dreams, the children begin with crude notions on the origin, place, and organ of dreams. They think that
dreams come from material around them or fly in materially
from the outside.

Children's animism is their sense of the consciousness and
spirit in things (the latin "anima" means soul). In attributing
consciousness to all things, they pass through the following
states: (1) All things are conscious; (2) things that move are conscious; (3) things that move of their own accord are conscious;

and (4) consciousness is restricted to animals. *Most of this development takes place at the concrete operational stage.*

> Vel (8½) says that only animals could feel a prick, thus showing he is able to differentiate in his answers. What he means, as a matter of fact, is that only animals can feel pain. Clouds, for example, would not feel a prick.—Why not?—Because they are only air.—Can they feel the wind or not?—Yes, it drives them.—Can they feel heat?—Yes.

> Mont (7; 0): Does the sun know it gives light?—Yes.—Why?— Because it is made of fire.—Does it know that we are here?—No.—Does it know it is fine weather?—Yes. (So, too, the wind, the clouds, the rivers, the rain are regarded as conscious.) Does the wind feel anything when it blows against a house?—Yes, it feels it can't go any further.

> Ross (9;9) started by ascribing consciousness to animals but refusing it to the table: Would a table feel if I were to prick it?—No.—Why not?—Because it is not a person.—Can the fire feel anything?—No.—If someone threw water on it, would it feel that?—No.—Why not?—Because it is not a person.—Does the wind feel anything when the sun is shining?— Yes.—Doesn't it know it is blowing?—Yes.

> Cel (10;7) denies consciousness even to the sun and the moon—because it is not alive.—What things can know and feel?—Plants, animals, people, insects.—Is that all?— Yes.—Can the wind feel?—No.

> Visc (11;1) justifies the same standpoint by saying each time: No (it doesn't feel anything) because it is a thing, it isn't alive.

> Falq (7;3) gives as proof each time the matter of which the object is made; thus fire can't feel—because it's burnt wood—clouds—because they're made of rain—the sun— because it's made of fire—the moon—because it is a little cloud—the wind—because it hasn't got a head. [pp. 174, 179, 182-83, 187]

Their concept of life evolves through the same stages as their views of consciousness: Life is attributed to activity in general, then is attributed to movement, then to spontaneous movement.

In the child animsim is more a general trend of mind, a framework into which explanations are fitted rather than a continuously systematic belief, and sometimes older children show more animism when they momentarily find a need for it.

Children's artificialism is their tendency to think of things as resulting from a specific act of creation outside those things. Children think of sun and moon as made artificially. And so on: The night, the clouds, thunder, lightning, snow, ice, cold, rivers, lakes, sea—all are derived from something else, from some artificial cause. Piaget insists that the child's artificialism is literal, fundamental, and not due to romantic daydreaming or education or religion. Perhaps children's awareness of their own ability to make and cause things—and, for that matter, their curiosity about birth—is the source of their notion that everything is made or manufactured by something else. They also have a sense that all nature centers on themselves and seems to have been organized by their parents or by human beings in general. Even after children develop away from crude notions of artificialism, they retain a sense of their own ability to cause things by means of their bodies and by means of manual activity.

While theories about the origins of artificialism are open to speculation, we can note more concretely that there are several stages of artificialism in children. These can be illustrated by the ways they understand the sun and the moon. First, diffuse artificialism at the *preoperational stage:*

> It is only necessary to glance through a list of questions put by children of from 3 to 5, to find examples like this: Fran (2;5) asks—Who made the sun?—The very form of this question is artificialist. Stanley Hall quotes the following examples: At 5 years of age—Why is there a moon?—At 3½ years—What makes the sun shine?—and—Who is it puts the stars in the sky at night?—At 5 years—Who is it makes the stars twinkle? [1972, p. 256]

Passing into the *concrete operational stage,* children attribute to the different parts of nature origins that are half-natural and half-artificial. And finally they believe that all elements of the cosmos are fashioned by nature.

Piaget himself has not applied all the different evidence about realism, animism, and artificialism to faith development.

But it should be clear that children's developing concepts about their faith world is related to the increased sophistication of their concepts of the material world.

These schemata of realism, animism, and artificialism are the mental building blocks of faith. The mental schemata that children develop at each level of their growth is assumed into the schema immediately developing next. In a sense, each one of the schemata leaves its "mark," so that these early, cruder senses of thought, names, dreams, life and animation, growth, evolution, and manufacturing contribute to the basic understanding that lies beneath their scientific knowledge.

As children move out of realism, understanding that thoughts, names, and dreams are not a part of them and are not material, they gradually develop a sense of "other." Growing out of crude animism, they gradually come to a knowledge of life and animation that is objective and enables them to have a sense of the material and immaterial. Growing out of crude artificialism, they gradually come to a knowledge of growth and evolution through a knowledge of end results, thus distinguishing manufactured items from the living and feeling things around them. And so children build up schema upon schema, developing the knowledge that there is a distinct world, that there is life in it, that some things are made, some born or evolved or manufactured, and that the ultimate source cannot be seen. Since each schema does not annihilate the previous one, there is a backlog of more primitive ways of understanding the world that can contribute to a conceptualizing of the mysteries of meaning that are beyond the powers of the more sophisticated, "higher" schemata. If they encounter mysteries or problems they cannot master, the earlier schemata will be used again. The schemata for understanding the mysteries of childhood are used to conceptualize the mysteries of adulthood. These notions are yet more refined by psychologists who have studied religious development in particular. We examine the research of Lawrence Kohlberg and James Fowler later in the chapter.

Moral Judgment

Piaget carefully observed the details of children's games of marbles from the simple repetition of the tiny child who drops the marbles according to a pattern or transfers them from the floor to crannies in an easy chair and back again, through the preadolescents who understand the whole business of rule codification.

In the practice of game laws the child passes through phases. First comes the *preoperational stage,* where the laws are not yet coercive in character. Tiny children, in effect, just play around with marbles. While there is lack of continuity and direction in the sequence of behavior, there are certain regularities of detail in which particular acts become schematized and even ritualized. They develop their own little rituals by playing by themselves and setting up their own little goals.

> Jacqueline has the marbles in her hands and looks at them with curiosity (it is the first time she has seen any); then she lets them drop on the carpet. After this she puts them in the hollow of an arm-chair.—Aren't they animals?—Oh, no.—Are they balls?—Yes.—She puts them back on the carpet and lets them drop from a certain height. She sits on the carpet with her legs apart and throws the marbles a few inches in front of her. She then picks them up and puts them on the arm-chair and in the same hole as before. (The arm-chair is studded with buttons which create depressions in the material.) Then she collects the lot and lets them drop, first all together, then one by one. After this she replaces them in the arm-chair, first in the same place and then in the other holes. Then she piles them up in a pyramid:—What are marbles?—What do you think? She puts them on the floor, then back on the arm-chair, in the same holes. We both go out to the balcony: she lets the marbles drop from a height to make them bounce.
> The following days, Jacqueline again places the marbles on the chairs and arm-chairs, or puts them into her little saucepan to cook dinner. Or else she simply repeats the behaviour described above. [Piaget, 1965, pp. 29–30]

Second is the egocentric stage (*concrete–operational*), where laws are regarded as sacred and untouchable. Children state laws that seem to come from outside sacred authority but adopt the laws to their own ends, and they insist that those who are playing with them follow suit. They seem to be dominated by a whole set of rules and examples imposed from outside, but since they cannot place themselves on a level of equality with their elders they use for their own defense all they have succeeded in grasping of the organized life around them, unaware of their own isolation and concentration upon themselves—in other words, unaware of their egocentrism. Working with their own separateness and trying to imitate their elders' ways with rules, in practice they simply enter into competition with their own individual selves.

Mae (6) and Wid (7) declare that they are always playing together. Mae tells us that they both—played again, yesterday.—I first examine Mae by himself. He piles his marbles in a corner without counting them and throws his shooter into the pile. He then places 4 marbles close together and puts a fifth on top (in a pyramid). Mae denies that a square is ever drawn. Then he corrects himself and affirms that he always does so.—How do you and Wid know which is to begin?—One of the two throws his shooter and the other tries to hit it. If he hits it, he begins.—Mae then shows us what the game consists in: he throws his shooter without taking into account the distances or the manner of playing ("piquette"), and when he succeeds in driving a marble out of the square he immediately puts it back. Thus the game has no end.—Does it go on like that all the time?—You take one away to make a change (he takes a marble out of the square, but not the one that he has touched).—It'll only be finished when there's only one left (he "fires" again twice). One more shot, and then you take one away.—Then he affirms—Every third shot you take one away.—He does so. Mae removes a marble every third shot independently of whether he has hit or missed, which is completely irregular and corresponds to nothing in the game as habitually played, or as we have seen it played in Neuchatel or Geneva. It is therefore a rule which he has invented then and there but which he has the impression of remembering, because it presents a vague analogy with what really happens when the player removes the marble he has just "hit" (touched). This game of Mae's is therefore a characteristic game of the second stage, an egocentric game in which "to win" does not mean getting the better of others, but simply playing on one's own. [pp. 38–39]

When they get a little older, children reach a cooperation stage where law is looked upon as due to mutual consent. The child's interest is distinctly social. In other words, to dislodge a marble from a square by manual dexterity is not longer an aim in itself. Instead of fighting the other boys, they wish to regulate the game with a whole set of systematic rules to ensure that everyone "gets along." At this point, however, cooperation exists mainly in intention. As Piaget says, "Being an honest man is not enough to make one know the law." Children at best succeed in setting up a "provisional morality" and do not really take up the task of developing a code of laws until the next stage. They attempt to discover rules that are fixed and common in order to get along with one another; but in practice it is a case of the individual's relating to society.

Finally, children arrive at the codification stage (*formal-operational*), where they seem to take a peculiar pleasure in anticipating all possible cases and in codifying them. Piaget reports the complications figured out and reported upon by three older boys.

> In addition, there is a whole set of rules, unknown to the younger boys, which bear upon the position of the marbles in the square. According to Gros—the first boy who says "place-pour-moi" (English, "place-for-me") does not have to place himself at one of the corners of the square—and—the one who has said "place-des-marbres" (English, "place-for-the-marbles) can put them down as he likes, in a "troyat" (all in a heap) or at the four corners.—Vua is of the same opinion and adds—If you say "place-pour-toi-pour-tout-le-jeu" (English, "You place for the whole game"), the other chap (the opponent) must stay at the same place. [p. 48]

Piaget feels that the boys' enjoyment in complicating things clearly indicates that the quest is for rules for their own sake. The rules, with their overlapping and their exceptions, can be almost as complicated as the rules of spelling. Game practice is just about completely wrapped up in the codification of rational rules.

In their *consciousness* of what is going on, it is obvious that children in the first two stages have only a sense of coercion. The youngest children keep up rituals for their own sake and for personal pleasure, but these motor rules never give rise to a feeling of motivation proper. Then they want to play in conformity with certain rules received from outside: As soon as they are in possession of a new rule, they are sure that it has been in existence since the beginning and are hostile to any innovation. But in the second and third stages some kind of mutual respect predominates. A rule is considered a by-product of actual, individual

minds, so this and other new types of consciousness lead to genuine observation of the rules; insistence upon democracy takes
the place of willing acceptance of constraint from older children.

Moving on to other things from literal game playing, Piaget
seeks to examine the effect of adult behavior on the child's own
notion of *responsibility,* first of all, and then on the child's own
idea of *justice and punishment.* All this takes place as children
develop from the preoperational through concrete operational
stages.

A growing sense of responsibility is shown in the way
children interpret clumsiness and stealing. First of all they proportion sense of guilt to amount stolen or damaged: the larger
the amount, the greater the guilt, regardless of motivation. It is
strictly objective responsibility that counts. Later children see a
person's motivation as the primary determinant of guilt and
punishment. There is a reasonably long period, however, when
both attitudes exist side by side, the child giving evidence of the
one on certain occasions, and the other on other occasions (pp.
124–26).

Perhaps the children's approach to lying is the best indication of their growth in responsibility. Piaget finds that the
average age for objective responsibility is seven; otherwise,
children alter truth spontaneously. They have a great deal of difficulty in distinguishing error from lying; in general lies are
evaluated from the point of view of their content—the more its
contents mark a departure from reality the worse it is. They pass
through these stages: The lie is wrong because it is punished,
because it is wrong in itself, because it is in conflict with mutual
trust and affection (pp. 168–74).

The idea of justice and punishment has its own development. In relation to retribution for individuals, children think at
first that punishment should be proportioned to merit and second that it should be equal for all. They move from expiation
punishment ("you must suffer for what you've done") to
reciprocity punishment ("you get the punishment that goes with
your crime"), at first thinking—with a strong element of
vengence—that well-punished children will not repeat the
misdeed. In letting the punishment fit the crime they go from
the more to the less severe: exclusion from the social group,
punishment related to the immediate material consequences of
the act, depriving the guilty ones of the thing misused, doing to

the transgressors exactly what they have done themselves, and simple restitution by paying for or replacing what it broken. Then they move to the idea that punishment is educationally useful to prevent relapses, and finally to the idea that there are other ways of educating to avoid relapse (pp. 212–18).

Stages of Faith and Morality:
Fowler and Kohlberg

Having highlighted the very general religious aspects of Erikson's work and suggested how religious development is implied in the cognitive development schemata of Piaget, we now explore religious development explicitly. We have at our disposal two systematic attempts to show the development of religious faith and morality: James Fowler's and Lawrence Kohlberg's. To remind ourselves how all these ideas integrate we should continually refer back to the table at the beginning of this chapter.

James Fowler's career has included Christian ministry, theology teaching, and counseling. His deep interest in the relationship between psychological development and faith has led him to formulate a stage theory that artfully combines the insights of both Erikson and Piaget with his own observations of the faith experience. *Stages of Faith* (1981) is his principal book.

Lawrence Kohlberg is Professor of Education and Social Psychology at Harvard. When completing his Ph.D. in 1958 at the University of Chicago, he began his still continuing longitudinal study of the moral reasoning of then preadolescent and adolescent boys. In 1974 he found at Harvard a Center for Moral Development and Moral Education, which sponsors moral development research and other projects in schools and prisons in New England. His research and writing have been prolific, and a three-volume collection of his principle articles over the years, *Essays in Moral Development* (1981), has recently appeared.

Faith Stages: Their Strengths and Deficiencies

It is Fowler's way to describe a faith stage and then point out the possible strengths and deficiencies of the stage and the patterns of transition to the next stage.

For infants in the first months "faith" is something of a misnomer, Fowler says, because theirs is an undifferentiated sense of what adults call trust, courage, hope, and love—as well as, at times, abandonment, inconsistencies, and deprivations:

> Those observers are correct, I believe, who tell us that our first *pre*-images of God have their origins here. Particularly they are composed from our first experiences of mutuality, in which we form the rudimentary awareness of self as separate from and dependent upon the immensely powerful others, who were present at our first consciousness and who "knew us"—with recognizing eyes and reconfirming smiles—at our first self-knowing. [Fowler, 1981, p. 121]

The strength possible at this stage would come from the basic trust experience of the caring relationship of the family. The danger is narcissism or isolation, depending upon the infant's demands for attention or feelings of neglect. The transition to stage one involves those first convergences of thought and language that open the way to the use of symbols in speech and play.

Intuitive–projective faith constitutes the first stage. Thought patterns are fluid, so that the stage is fantasy-filled. Because the child is uninhibited by logic, images and feelings can be very effective. Self-awareness is still quite centered upon the self, but the surrounding family with its cultural patterns of sex and dying deeply affect the sense of self. To illustrate this, a quote from Bruno Bettelheim shows how fairy tales—Bible narratives should work the same way—can help children to express their anxieties and use images and stories to make sense of their lives:

> Encouraged by discussion about the importance fairy tales have for children, a mother overcame her hesitation about telling such "gory and threatening" stories to her son. From her conversations with him, she knew that her son already had fantasies about eating people, or people getting eaten. So she told him the tale of "Jack the Giant Killer." His response at the end of the story was: "There aren't any such things as giants, are there?" Before the mother could give her son the reassuring reply which was on her tongue—and which would have destroyed the value of the story for him—he continued, "But there are grownups, and they're like giants." At the ripe old age of five, he understood the encouraging message of the story: although adults can be experienced as frightening

giants, a little boy with cunning can get the better of them. [quoted in Fowler, 1981, p. 130]

The strength possible at this stage would come from the birth of the imagination nourished by the powerful images and stories about the ultimate questions in life. The danger is that the child's imagination will be haunted by images of terror and destructiveness, and fearsome taboos will have a negative effect on later doctrinal and moral development. The transition to stage two is caused by the emergence of concrete operational thinking: The child wants to understand the bases for distinguishing what is real from what only seems to be.

Mythic–literal faith constitutes the second stage. The stories, beliefs, and observances of the child's family and community are appropriated as personal. Symbols, stories, and moral rules are taken literally. The children search for coherence and meaning. Reporting on his interview with a youngster named Millie, Fowler sums up the child's notion of God at this stage.

> With Millie's mentioning that God's doing what he thinks best is like parents doing what they think best for their children we are in position to grasp a useful insight. Millie's God-image takes forms offered by her culture, both the larger Western culture and the most particular Protestant culture of her family. But the forms are filled with the contents of Millie's perspective . . . . [1981, p. 141]

The strength possible at this stage would be an ability to find and give coherence to experience. The danger is that literalness will result in a stilted perfectionism or a deep sense of badness that is impossible to get away from. The transition to stage three comes from the discovery of contradictions in authoritative stories and disillusionment with authority figures.

Synthetic–conventional faith constitutes the third stage. Faith provides a unified orientation in the midst of a diversified range of interests and values. However, being very much attuned to the expectations and judgments of others, it is conformist. Such faith does not allow the young person to step outside the faith-world and examine its content. Fowler supports this interpretation of adolescent faith referring to those other principal features of adult life already discussed.

By the time of the teen years a young person has begun to relate to a widened set of environments. In addition to the sphere of the family now there are spheres of influence represented by peers, by school or work, by media and popular culture, and perhaps by a religious community. In each of these spheres of influence there are peers and adults who are potentially significant others. With this term I refer to those persons whose "mirroring" of the young person has the power to contribute positively or negatively to the set of images of self and of accompanying meanings that must be drawn together in a forming identity and faith. [1981, p. 154]

The strength possible at this stage would enable the young person to form a personal myth of identity and faith, incorporating past and future in a mental image of the perfect environment. The double danger is that the young person will internalize too much the evaluations of others or reject others so much that religion becomes an otherworldly intimacy with God that is totally divorced from life. Transition comes when the young persons' nicely ordered world is broken up by changes in the religious format that the young person depends upon.

Individuative–reflective faith constitutes the fourth stage. In young adulthood the individual can establish an identity and world that are distinct from the compositive view of others. In other words, an individual sense of ultimate goals and what hangs together is developed. Symbols are translated into conceptual meanings, and so this is a demythologizing stage. For Fowler's "Jack," who came from a lower-class neighborhood, life in the armed services provided a new context for individuative–reflective faith:

But when Jack identified himself with that group of black soldiers, held together by their commitment to soul music and the Panther ideology, he burned his bridges. Without full assurance of where it would lead, he began to shape a new identity and faith. His identity had previously derived from and been a function of the groups he grew up with in fated membership. Now, as is the case in any genuine Stage 4, his choice of groups, with the ideological perspectives they bear, became a function of the identity he was forming. He shaped his new identity in relation to the groups and outlooks whose invitation to life-redefining memberships he accepted. [1981, pp. 178–79]

The strength possible at this stage would be a superior ability to reflect critically on the life around one. But dangers are inherent in this superior ability, because confidence in one's reasoning powers can leave one relatively defenseless in the face of the anarchy in the environment and inner meaninglessness.

Some adults reach the stage of conjunctive faith. They have solved some of life's challenges and have been hurt by others. They have listened to the inner voices and have resolved some conflicts while learning to live with others. Ultimately a universalizing faith may be reached. This is a norm of love and acceptance in working for a better world that is seldom found but can yet be considered a model. It is the faith of Gandhi, Martin Luther King, Jr., Mother Theresa, Dag Hammarskjold, Dietrich Bonhoeffer, Abraham Heschel, Thomas Merton. Fowler says about such people:

> I believe that these persons kindle our imaginations in these ways because, in their generosity and authority, in their freedom and their costly love, they embody the promise and lure of our shared futurity. Those persons embody costly openness to the power of the future. They actualize its promise, creating zones of liberation and sending shock waves to rattle the cages that we allow to constrict human futurity. Their trust in the power of that future and their trans-narcissistic love of human futurity account for their readiness to spend and be spent in making the kingdom actual. [1981, p. 211]

To describe faith in such stages is establish a hierarchy, to state a series of steps to a goal. The conjunctive and even universalizing faith of the mature and even heroic adult can be set up as an ideal only if a preexisting ideology or creed establishes these stages as ideal. Fowler admits this. So we must judge his stages accordingly. If you set up a series of stages progressing toward an ideal, people can be grouped accordingly, and not just infants, children, adolescents, and young adults. Fowler describes the faith of a number of adults on the lower developmental stages. For a Mrs. W., on the mythic–literal level (stage two), and sometimes even on the fantasy level (stage one), the meaning of faith is contained in stories—the Christ Child, St. Anthony, Pope John Paul. For a Mr. D., on the synthetic–conventional level (stage three), faith is seen as being everybody's faith system or the faith system of the entire community; his loosely gathered collection of opinions or convictions are just the views of one common man. For many, individuative–reflective faith (stage four) ideally arrived at in early adulthood, can be arrived at much later. Only a select group arrives at conjunctive faith, and only prodigies of dedication arrive at universalizing faith. Obviously, we have here a hierarchy of values that is not based on simple social-scientific observation.

Moral Development

In an influential early article Lawrence Kohlberg (1964) summed up previous work on the moral behavior of children as a preface to his own theories and studies of the stages of moral development. There he said that most researchers, without getting into complicated problems of definition, have been content to consider morality quite simply as "conscience" and moral development as an increase in the internalization of basic cultural rules. Theories about this development tend to divide up into three categories: (1) the behavioral type, concerned with the conditioning required to resist temptation to go against values of the culture; (2) the guilt-emotion type, concerned with the experiential causes of this emotion; and (3) the judgment–standard type, concerned with the capacity to make judgment in terms of a standard along with the justification to oneself and others of keeping up to the standard. In behaviorist theory, moral character is generally seen as good habits; in guilt-emotion theory, character is generally seen as ego strength.

For Kohlberg, as should become obvious, the most successful researchers are the judgment–standard type. He believes he begins where Piaget, the most important of the judgment–standard theorists, leaves off. Piaget says, remember, that the cognitive limitations of children of three to eight lead them to confuse moral rules with physical laws and to view rules as eternal things rather than as instruments of human purposes and values. These cognitive limitations may be described as "realism," or the inability to distinguish between the subjective and objective aspects of experience, and as "egocentrism," or the inability to distinguish personal perspective on events from that of others. In addition to seeing rules as external absolutes, young children feel that their parents and other adults are all-knowing, perfect, and sacred. This attitude of unilateral respect toward adults joined with children's realism is believed to lead them to view rules as sacred and unchangeable.

Of the eleven different aspects of moral judgment implied by Piaget's stage concepts, Kohlberg calls five into question because he takes them to be social–emotional rather than cognitive elements of development. For example, as regards Piaget's concept of a shift from unilateral respect for adults to a mutual respect for peers, findings do not support his idea that there is a general trend of moral development from an authoritarian to a democratic ethic, although they do support the notion that the child's earliest morality is oriented to obedience, punishment, and impersonal forces and progresses toward more internal and subjective values. A problem with Piaget's research is that the stages of development are so general and unified that they do not allow for separate development of the separate aspects of moral judgment (Kohlberg, 1964, p. 399).

Kohlberg says he feels that clearer distinctions are possible between moral and intellectual maturity. Further distinctions can be made regarding types of guilt—fear of punishment is different from guilt, which in turn is different from making a confession—and further work is needed on the relation of parental influence to conscience.

Kohlberg's writing has been prolific, but it always involves the presentation of his six-stage theory of moral development in order to test it in different ways or clarify it for different audiences. His 1976 overview of the cognitive–developmental theory of moralization suffices for our purposes. His basic contention is that the correctness of the stages as description of moral development is a matter of empirical observation, not social science theory.

The six moral stages are grouped into three major levels: preconventional level (stages one and two), conventional level (stages three and four), and postconventional level (stages five and six). The word "conventional" means "conforming to and upholding the rules and expectations and conventions of society for authority just because they are society's rules, expectations, or conventions (Kohlberg, 1976, p. 33). One way of understanding the three levels is to think of them as three different types of relationship between the self and society's rules and expectations. For this point of view, level one is a preconventional person for whom rules and social expectations are something external to the self; level two is a conventional person in whom the self is identified with or has internalized the rules and expectations of others, especially those of authorities; and level three is a postconventional person who has differentiated himself from the rules and expectations of others and defines his value in terms of self-chosen principles. Within each of the three moral levels there are two stages. The second stage is a more advanced and organized form of the general perspective of each major level.

Kohlberg has a methodology for assessing moral judgment. First, he developed a definition of religion in terms of twenty-five aspects grouped under the headings rules, conscience, welfare of others, self welfare, sense of duty, role taking, punitive justice, and motives. Subjects were presented with sentences and stories. Sentence scoring used a manual listing prototypical sentences on each aspect of each moral dilemma presented. Using a second method, a subject's total response to a story was assigned a stage.

Here is seventeen-year-old Joe's response to the question, "Why shouldn't you steal from a store?" "It's a matter of law. It's one of our rules that we're trying to protect everyone, protect property, not just protect a store. It's something that's needed in our society. If we didn't have these laws people would steal, they wouldn't have to work for a living and our whole society would get out of kilter." Joe is concerned about keeping the law, and his reason for being concerned is the good of society as a whole. When Joe was ten, at the preconventional level, he answered the same question this way: "It's not good to steal from a store. It's against the law. Someone could see you and call the police." Being "against the law," then, means something different at the two levels.

Kohlberg notes that the postconventional level is like the preconventional perspective in that it returns to the standpoint of the individual rather than taking the point of view of "us members of society." The individual point of view taken at the postconventional level, however, can be universal; it is that of any rational moral individual. It is with this mind set that Joe responds to the question at age twenty-four. "Why shouldn't someone steal from a store?" "It's violating another person's rights, in this case to property." "Does the law enter in?" "Well, the law in most cases is based on what is morally right, so it's not a separate subject, it's a consideration." "What does 'morality' or 'morally right' mean to you?'' "Recognizing the rights of other individuals, first to life and then to do as they please as long as it doesn't interfere with the rights of others.'' The interpretation Kohlberg offers is this: "The postconventional perspective, then, is *prior to society:* it is the perspective of an individual who has made the moral commitments or holds the standards on which a good or just society must be based" (1974, p. 36).

Kohlberg then describes how he sees two stages to each level. At the preconventional level, in stage one only the concrete individual's point of view is involved, whereas in stage two there is an awareness of a number of other individuals, each having other points of view. At the conventional level an individual is at first less aware of society's point of view than of shared relationships between two or more individuals (stage three), whereas in stage four the member-of-society perspective is a system perspective. At the postconventional level, a typical stage five orientation distinguishes between a moral point of view and a legal point of view but finds it difficult to define a moral perspective independent of the perspective behind contractual-legal rights. In stage six, the person recognizes that individuals are ends in themselves and must be treated as such.

Although a summary and brief report on research in religious development will be given in Chapter 7, some examples of representative research should be cited here. We can suggest how the initial theories and research of Erikson, Piaget, and Kohlberg have motivated further theorizing and research along the same lines.

Erikson's theories on overall development relative to parents and significant peers has given rise to a variety of research. Regarding the child's overall religiosity, for example, there is some evidence that alienation from religion correlates with the young people's relationships with parents and other religious authority figures. The amount of alienation depends on the inconsistency between the adults' profession of faith and their style of life (Dickinson, 1976). Among older students the number of college students rejecting the home religious tradition increased in the 1970s (Hastings and Hoge, 1974). Students from very conservative religious backgrounds, such as the Mennonites, are substantially more in agreement with parents than liberal Protestant students (Hunsberger, 1976). Other research indicates that adolescents view themselves as somewhat like their fathers in theoretical, social, political, and religious values but closer to the peer group than to either parent (Munns, 1972).

Differences between middle-class or upper-middle-class life and ghetto life have been examined to see if the Piaget–Kohlberg stages are truly built in, as the theses insist, or are due to environment. Behavior that may be delinquent from a middle-class perspective may represent survival in the ghetto environment (Sams, 1975). An even more basic challenge to the Piaget–Kohlberg theses is the evidence that moral judgment can be based on empathy and imaginal thinking as much as, if not more than, cognitive thinking (Dykstra, 1980). It has also been said that cultural differences in moral teaching and in the structure of intelligence cast doubt on Piaget's and Kohlberg's theories about the universality of developmental stages. Perhaps the dilemma-posing stories of Piaget and Kohlberg require problem-solving abilities rather than moral judgments relevant to life (Stanton, 1976). But in more familiar (that is, Western, Judeo-Christian, middle-class) situations it is possible to list the experiences that might cause development from one level to the next (Gorman, 1977).

The formation of a concept of self can be examined in ways complementary to cognitive developmental theories as an active process of interpretation of behavior. This would mean, for example, that the acquisition of a self-category of gender might facilitate the process of sex-role behavior (Lewis, 1979).

Important questions about these theories of stage development have been posed by those who see interaction with adults and the effect of environment as the vital determining factors in religious and moral thinking. They do *not* insist that these interactions cause development in stepwise fashion. A study of the individual person in a unique context is emphasized in social psychology, whether the issue is the child or adult personality. The effect of the social environment on the shaping of the religious elements of a personality is examined next.

The Influence
of Society

SOCIAL ENVIRONMENT shapes every kind of behavior. When people go to a church or synagogue to pray, they not only engage in unique conversations with their God but pray in the midst of, and as the result of, an influential social environment.

A study of synagogue life some years ago showed how religious behavior is "a collective, intersubjective definition of the situation which has moral authority over any individual participants' view of the setting and of any activity in it" (Heilman, 1976, p. 131). Liturgy is at the center of synagogue life, but all sorts of involvements are associated with the public assembly: sociability, machinations of collective control and maintenance, gossip, joking, and information exchange. There are connected involvements such as the putting on or taking off of prayer garb, arrangement of ritual articles, moving of chairs, occasional pacing back and forth in the aisles, and boys punching out an "I-got-you-last" game. Some people are quite sociable and warm up by indicating awareness of others' presence, perhaps opening with a remark that can be developed in conversation, such as a joke or a bit of gossip. When there are fewer than the required number present for prayer, members are summoned according to certain social estimates. On the Sabbath, since riding to synagogue is forbidden on principle, the walk to the synagogue from nearby neighborhoods where one has parked the car has its own measure of sociability. Further shifting involvements are shown by the ways of inviting friends to the Sabbath dinner, an important social adjunct to the synagogue service. Here a set of unspoken yet unbreachable conventions and procedures is in operation. Each invitation is subject to repayment, and another is tendered, always in alternating order. Repayment for invitations from members who are not within the same clique may take other forms, so when a guest brings along a bottle of wine, flowers, chocolates or some other gift, he is both repaying his host and signaling him not to expect a reciprocating dinner invitation. The exchanges found in this type of synagogue life can be observed in almost all religious group life. Significant small-group research has been done on contemporary cults. Even more basic than the type of interchange found in this synagogue example is the tension between the individual human being's need to master and comprehend the social surroundings and the facts that present themselves for belief. This drive for consistency often causes religious believers to reject the evidence of their senses. The famous example here is a cultlike group that believed in the coming of a terrible flood, which never came. The attempts to make do with this obvious disconfirmation of personal beliefs can be studied as efforts to achieve an equilibrium with the social environment. Attempts to achieve consistency can also lead to rejection of personal beliefs and acceptance of evidence presented. In any case, we see here the roots of social action and interaction.

Social psychologists are most interested in the attitudes that result from the drive for equilibrium with the social environment and social interaction. The attitude that most affects social and political behavior is prejudice against people who are different. It affects presidential elections and stimulates wars; it determines everything from immigration patterns to real estate sales. If we want to understand why a Muslim religious leader would order the execution of countless political dissidents or how churchgoing is related to increased prejudice, we must study attitudes. Though we discuss the study of attitudes last here, it is the central issue in present-day social psychology.

We examine now the fundamental consistency drive, interaction and small-group research, and attitude development insofar as these social–psychological factors affect religious experiences.

Consistency Theory

We can sum up the consistency theories simply: What people think, feel, and do is determined more by what they experience in interaction with the world around them than because of built-in psychological qualities (though the conflict, fulfillment, and developmental theories we examined give important place to relationships to other people, they hold that the basic drives and attributes one is born with count the most). Consistency viewpoints can emphasize thoughts, expectations, opinions, and perceptions—activities that are more cognitive than anything else. The consistency considered also might be much more general—the level of tension or activation: Emphasis is on the compatibility of different thoughts or different feelings.

As the first example of the effect of the consistency drive on religious experience, we offer the case of believers for whom a prophecy has failed. Leon Festinger, who originated the term cognitive dissonance, studied the group several decades ago. Another relevant discussion of the importance of cognitive consistency with the social environment arises in the work of George Kelly. A discussion of the tendency to general bodily—cognitive and emotional—equilibrium with the social environment will be based on the studies by Salvatore Maddi and Donald Fiske.

Cognitive Dissonance and Religious Group Expectations

The movement studied by Leon Festinger was able to adapt when a specific prophecy failed to come true: a catastrophic flood was expected to cover the world on a given date, and the flood never took place. The way members of the movement tried to reduce the genuine dissonance between their belief in something and its obvious failure to come true clearly shows how a theory on the reduction of cognitive dissonance can help us understand at least some forms of religious experience (Festinger, Riecken, and Schachter 1956).

Festinger's basic hypotheses about cognitive dissonance are these:

1. The existence of dissonance, being psychologically uncomfortable, will motivate the person to try to reduce the dissonance and achieve consonance.

2. When dissonance is present, in addition to trying to reduce it the person will actively avoid situations and information likely to increase the dissonance. [Festinger, 1957, p. 3]

People can try to reduce the dissonance in different ways: They can change their actions and so reduce the dissonance, or they can change their "knowledge" about the effects of the actions. For example, learning that smoking is harmful to the health, a person might give up smoking or redo his or her knowledge about the harmfulness by deciding that the outlet it provides for pent-up nerves more than compensates for the harm it does to lung tissue. It frequently happens that a person or source of information for which one has a high regard supports something for which one has a very low regard. One can reduce the dissonance by changing either the evaluation of the person/ source or the evaluation of the opinion involved. Festinger works with some related hypotheses about the reduction of dissonance and the magnitude of dissonance. He maintains that the pressure to reduce the dissonance is a function of the magnitude of the dissonance and that the maximum dissonance possible between the things depends upon the total resistance to change of the less resistant element.

A great deal of research underpins the theory of cognitive dissonance. Festinger sums up pre-1957 research on the consequences of decision, effects of forced compliance, voluntary and involuntary exposure to information, and the role of social support. Regarding the consequences of decisions, the data show that following a decision there is active seeking out of information that produces cognition consonant with the action taken and an increase in confidence in the decision, along with a de-

crease of the attractiveness of the alternatives. Increased difficulty in reversing a decision follows situations in which people's
viewpoints or actions are forced (1957, p. 122). Regarding voluntary and involuntary exposure to information, the data show
that when dissonance exists, people will be able to avoid the impact of dissonance-increasing information by such means as
misperception and denial of the validity of the information
(1957, p. 176). If people do not expect a source of information to
produce dissonance, the information will have more impact.
Regarding social support, the data show that some social influences lead to the reduction of dissonance. The most striking
social influences involve mass phenomena where dissonance is
reduced through rumors, the maintenance of invalid beliefs, or
mass proselytizing.

All of Festinger's principles have many religious applications, but we shall concentrate on the failed-prophecy situation
Festinger himself examined in detail.

Referring to a number of instances of failed prophecy in
history, Festinger notes that when an expectation is frustrated
(the better terminology is "when a belief is disconfirmed"), there
is often increased promotion of the belief, increased proselytizing. People do not cease to believe, but on the contrary they
become even stronger in their faith. He lists the conditions required for this to happen:

1. There must be conviction.

2. There must be commitment to this conviction.

3. The conviction must be amenable to unequivocal disconfirmation.

4. Such unequivocal disconfirmation must occur.

5. Social support must be available subsequent to the disconfirmation [Festinger, Riecken, and Schachter, 1956, p. 216]

These conditions are fulfilled in the story of the flood expectation group that followed a female leader whom Festinger calls
Mrs. Keech. Most members of the group believed in Mrs.
Keech's prediction and were heavily committed to their belief.
Disconfirmation was unequivocal, because the disaster simply
did not take place, and the attempted rationalization was never
completely successful in dispelling dissonance. With some exceptions, members of the group faced disconfirmation and its af-

termath together. Following are examples of their publicity-seeking, personal proselytizing, secrecy, and persistence of prediction.

There was a quick change in attitudes toward the press. Whereas previously the press received an almost hostile reception and resistance to their story-seeking attempts, after the definitive disconfirmation the press was invited for interviews by Mrs. Keech and the principals in the story. Previously all proselytizing had been discrete: The principals preached and practiced caution. In general people were treated well, but they were never given exhortations and were not invited back. After December 21, the date of definitive disconfirmation, almost every visitor was admitted, and one of them was even nominated to membership in the inner circle. In the months prior to disconfirmation the group became quite secretive about its ideas and activities. Passwords and secret signs were developed, and members were careful to admit only true followers to their meetings. After disconfirmation Mrs. Keech revealed the existence of a secret book and released tape recordings to the press; the public was invited to a Christmas vigil in the street in front of the Keech home. Intense proselytizing characterized almost every member of the group following disconfirmation.

New predictions were made after the disconfirmation, and there was a growing tendency to identify visitors as spacemen! Festinger summarizes this total deterioration where even random visitors were labeled spacemen:

> It seems fairly clear that their intent on such occasions was to win guidance and direction. Floundering, increasingly disoriented as prediction after prediction failed, they cast about for clues, watching television for orders, recording phone calls the better to search for coded messages, pleading with spacemen to do their duty—all in a desperate attempt to discover a clearly defined next step on the path of salvation by saucer. [Festinger et al., 1956, p. 215]

So when the expectation of the flood was disconfirmed, a number of people went on with their proselytizing; others did not. Kurt and Arthur (to use the fictitious names of the book), who were slightly committed to begin with, completely gave up their belief in Mrs. Keech's writings. Five members of the group, including Mrs. Keech, all of whom entered the precataclysm period strongly convinced and heavily committed, passed through this period of disconfirmation and its aftermath with their faith firm, unshaken, and lasting. Cleo and Bob, who had their conviction strongly shaken at one point, actually emerged from the major disconfirmation more strongly convinced than before. Bertha and Clyde started out with doubts; they reacted to the disconfirmation with doubts, disillusionment, and confusion but did not completely disavow Mrs. Keech's beliefs. Bertha and Clyde were forced to face disconfirmation in isolation, so this may account for the difference between their reactions and those of Cleo and Bob. Ultimately the followers reacted in the two possible ways of reducing dissonance. Those who were from the same city as Mrs. Keech and maintained close contact with one another held fast to their beliefs and tried to create a broader circle of supportive believers; a second group, from another city, reduced the dissonance by giving up the belief.

Two Versions of Consistency Theory: Cognitive Dissonance and Activation

George A. Kelly, onetime director of the Psychological Clinic at Ohio State University and a professor at Brandeis at the time of his death, developed the purest form of the position we call (after Festinger) the cognitive dissonance version. He said that discrepancies, whether large or small, produce discomfort, anxiety, and tension. These emotions, in turn, produce behavior aimed at reducing the discrepancy and ensuring that it will not occur in the future. Donald Fiske and Salvatore Maddi, professors at the University of Chicago, saw the need to introduce a major modification of this view. They found sufficient evidence to state that people will try to maintain the level of excitement to which they are accustomed; and so, they said, some cognitive dissonance is acceptable and may even be necessary. Note—to distinguish clearly between the two versions—that Kelly emphasizes the attempt to predict and control the events one experiences, whereas Fiske and Maddi emphasize the attempt to maintain the level of activation to which one is accustomed. Neither Kelly nor Fiske and Maddi have much to say explicitly about religious ideas and behavior, but the principles would apply to the way a person practices religion as much as to anything else. It is better to review the elements and dynamics of the theories and then, very briefly, to find some religious applications.

Since an individual's basic need is to predict and control his experience, Kelly says that the basic activity is the construing of events in order to give them proper shape and meaning. The process of construing is one in which certain events are classed together with others that are considered similar, and contrasted with others that are considered different. *Constructs,* then, are categories of thought that grow out of the interpretations we place on events. Kelly sees constructs as paired opposites such as good-bad, satisfying-dissatisfying, creative-banal, or productive-nonproductive, which the individual uses to judge other people and events. That listing is just one set of constructs that an individual might use, let us say, in judging personal friendships; he will have many other sets of constructs and eventually tend to organize them into a construct system.

In developing a construct system to predict and control events, there are two strategies open to the individual. The first is to develop a construct system that works well for a given set of events and then to construct the world of your experience to just those events or very similar ones. The second is to develop a construct system that is so comprehensive and valid that no restriction of experiential possibilities is necessary because virtually any event can be accurately anticipated. In either case, the emphasis is on prediction and control, so that in building up a system only those constructs that permit accurate prediction of events are useful. A person's construct system represents the results up to that time of a process of rational trial and error in the development of what amounts to a theory of the world of experience. To sum up, the person tries to develop a predictive system that is *consistent* with the real world of events.

Religious ideas and behavior are part of the surrounding world, in relation to which people define themselves. Kelly puts it this way:

> Certain common features of one's social surroundings are often described as his *culture.* It is important that the clinician be aware of cultural variations. Yet, from our theoretical view, we look upon the "influence" of culture in the same way as we look upon other events. The client is not merely the product of his culture, but it has undoubtedly provided him with much

evidence of what is "true" and much of the data which his personal construct system has had to keep in systematic order. [1955, II: 688]

Individuals—clients if it is a clinical situation—develop their construct systems in relation to size of population, economics and social change in the community, school and recreation resources, and certainly religious organizations and norms of behavior. "Religious sects and denominations frequently represent the characteristic cultural controls which operate in the construct systems of a group of people" (II:702). For Kelly, religion exercises an influence primarily in the area of negative control, taboo, and not only on members but on all in a community where a given religion has influence. He cites, among others, the examples of limitation of recreation and use of medicine and says, "These taboos are important in understanding the personal construct systems of persons who live in communities where they are extensively observed, not only because of the restrictions they tend to place on specific forms of behavior, but also because of the difficulties they may interpose in the establishment of role relationships." (II: 702). Any influence upon the establishment of role relationships is significant in the buildup of a construct system, so the more power religion has in a given society, the more power it has in the life of an individual. Even when people are not formal adherents of a given powerful religious tradition, they cannot help but be affected by it through the surrounding culture. Notice the implicit evaluation of religion in Kelly's description of it, however: negative control upon constructs, signaling to the individual what he had better not think of doing. While Kelly does not have anything condemnatory to say about religion, he does not develop any notions about the possible guiding or healing influences of religion on a person's development of a construct system. But if normative religious thought and behavior in a culture enable people to predict and control events, to achieve a consistency between their lives and the world around them, to handle the dissonances and difficulties— those negative elements which are a part of life—then, presumably, religion, like other basic, neutral factors in life, can be a good and healthy thing. A serious problem can arise if people have need of a more flexible construct system than the religious laws of a culture allow.

Both Donald W. Fiske and Salvatore R. Maddi, professors at the University of Chicago for a number of years, came under the influence of Gordon Allport and Henry Murray at different points in their psychological training. Fiske has specialized in the measurement of personality variables and the conditions under which variability takes place, whereas Maddi's principle interests have been in personality change and existential psychology. In their work on consistency Fiske and Maddi report that an individual will hold and maintain an accustomed level of activation. Hence they are concerned with the things that determine this level of activation. They speak of the three dimensions of stimulation as intensity, meaningfulness, and variation. Intensity, such as the difference between a loud noise and a soft noise, is an obvious attribute of stimulation; meaningfulness is the underlying attribute of importance—"love" and "fire" have more significance than "glove" for example; and the variations provided by change, novelty, and unexpectedness are all related to changes where a current stimulus is different from that which preceded it. For Fiske and Maddi, it is highly important that a definite level of interesting dissonance or excitement be kept up, and kept up in various ways. On this issue they differ from Festinger and Kelly, who say that the person strives to reduce the dissonance.

The intensity, meaningfulness, and variation that come from sources outside and inside the person produce an impact. And human behavior—the behavior that maintains the proper amount of intensity, meaningfulness, and variation—is called impact-increasing and impact-decreasing. A person, of course, acts to increase or decrease the effect of the stimuli that have an impact upon his life.

Such a discussion about the activation of the personality by environment does not contain any judgments about religion. Maddi alone, reflecting upon his work with Fiske, says that the two of them "are eclectic with regard to content, in that their conceptualization of man and society includes little that is necessary and immutable (Maddi, 1972, p. 178). While Maddi has elsewhere expressed himself on the issue of religion, there is nothing in his personality theory to constitute a value judgment of religious thought and behavior. But, according to the Fiske–Maddi theory, religion is significant whenever it enables people to hold and maintain an accustomed level of activation. Since they have concerned themselves, generally speaking, with those three dimensions of stimulation, they would take an interest in those occasions when stimulation—intensity, meaningfulness, and variation—is provided by religion.

People's relationship to the dissonance-producing or activation-producing environment can be examined on the personal interaction level. Instead of analyzing basic cognitive and emotional energies, as we have just done, we may look at specific, very describable human interactions. The interactionist viewpoint is an interpretation of the social production of the adult religious experience. Here we analyze the personality as a part of group cooperation, insofar as this cooperation takes place by means of signals and gestures.

The Analysis of Interaction

George Herbert Mead and Erving Goffman say that the self is the result of interaction between an individual and the surrounding group. For Mead (1962), consciousness emerges from social behavior and not the other way around. Thinking is really the internalization of gestures shared socially. The meaning of any event is not necessarily in the direct experience of it but rather in the response we make to it. This is why the same stimuli can mean very different things to different people: They respond to stimuli from different social perspectives. Recall the almost totally different responses of military officers and radical college students to the American flag during the Vietnam years. Human social life consists in a series of symbolic interactions with the surroundings in which people experience themselves. These interactions are not individual but collective, plural, and social processes. Mind, Mead says, emerges in communicative interactions with others and continues to have a life only with regard to others.

Erving Goffman, a student of one of Mead's students, in a major work entitled *The Presentation of Self in Everyday Life* (1959), used the metaphor of the theater to express the process by which the self comes into existence. In this perspective the self is seen as a staged production, a series of masks that people present to those who, in the role of audience, observe the production. Or better, the interaction between actor and audience produces the self. Rather than being tied to a given personality, the self is a continuously shared interactive phenomenon.

Interaction in a Religious Setting

Goffman's basic notion is that in any kind of interaction those taking part contribute a single overall definition of the situation that is not an agreement about reality but rather an agreement "as to whose claims concerning what issues will be temporarily honored" (1959, p. 10). Individuals who come into a group project a definition of the situation while the others present, however passive their role, will project a definition of the situation in response to the new individuals and because of the communications they themselves wish to project. The result is a kind of working consensus as to how everyone is to operate vis-à-vis one another. Goffman labels as *front* that part of the individual's performance that regularly functions in a general and fixed fashion to define the situation for those who observe the performance. Part of the front, then, is the *setting* involving furniture, decor, physical layout, and other background items that supply the scenery and the stage props for the human action. *Appearance* refers to those stimuli that function to tell us of the performer's social stature; *manner* refers to those stimuli that function at the time to warn us of the interaction role the performer will expect to play in the oncoming situation (pp. 22–24).

Using in a very general way the theater metaphor, a Goffman student, Samuel Heilman (1976), describes a particular orthodox Jewish synagogue in the United States. In this synagogue individual performances range from president of the synagogue, through a rule-following gossiper, to a youngster trying to get away with as much as possible. People take turns performing and being audiences, of course, and the performances change from day to day.

Roles are basically the same in all synagogues, in all orthodox synagogues at any rate. The role of the rabbi as scholar, teacher, and in more recent years guide is well known. Less familiar, perhaps, are the roles of treasurer and president of the congregation. The treasurer appoints various members of the congregation to honorable liturgical duties, such as the reading of the Torah. These honors are given out on the basis of the individual's past record at the synagogue and bring about a strengthening of obligation and commitment to the synagogue. The president, being more directly responsible for the good order of synagogue life, has important mediating (procedural issues) and conciliating (in the personal realm) functions. The cantor really can be regarded as a more important liturgical functionary than the rabbi: He prays on behalf of the congregation and is at the center of all sung prayer. There are, in addition, temporary cantorial roles, which can be very indicative of specific religious standing in relation to the synagogue. Among regular members, those categorized as mendicants (needing or raising money) have a distinct effect on common life—those who are needy plain and simple, those who have special and temporary problems, and those who solicit funds for various purposes (Heilman, 1976, pp. 69–127).

People will highlight certain facts of their performance that they are afraid will remain unapparent or obscure. If the individuals want to become significant to others, they must mobilize their activity so that it will express during the interaction what they want to convey. For example, umpires, prizefighters, policemen, and surgeons must act with a sureness of movement designed to convey competence, which might be better served, in fact, by less sureness of movement (more time to reflect, or a deliberate pace that allows for last-minute change). If an individual is to give expression to ideal standards during a performance, then he or she will have to forgo or conceal action that is inconsistent with these standards. Profitable activity that is opposed to goals of visible performance must be whitewashed; errors and mistakes must be corrected before the performance takes place; end products will be highlighted rather than problems in development; "dirty work" will be covered over; and ideal motives will be publicized so as to hide selfish and mechanical ones. Performers will try for a unified and smooth performance, making sure that as many as possible of the minor events, however inconsequential, will occur in ways compatible with the overall definition of the situation being fostered. Misrepresentation is difficult to analyze, of course, because a performance has a basic simulative quality, and activities that are thought to be legitimate by some audiences in our society are thought to be rackets by others. But terms such as "outright impersonations" or "barefaced lies" by common agreement are a form of straight dishonesty or misrepresentation (Goffman, 1959, pp. 61–62).

In Heilman's synagogue various officials of the congregation had to give expression to ideal standards during the performance, and minor discrepancies had to be made inconsequential in relation to the overall definition of the situation. Appropriate whitewashing and the harmless expression of antagonisms were accomplished by joking remarks. On one occasion the president of the synagogue had just finished explaining how he tried, illegally, to evade responsibility for causing a car accident. When the story was finished, he looked around for some sort of ratifying response from his audience. One member responded, "I don't know if we should allow you to be president." There was laughter, but the point was clear that, although the action might be overlooked this time it should not be repeated often, because it reflected unfavorably on the president's right to moral leadership of the group. Heilman concludes with a psychological explanation of the constant joking and gossip that make up synagogue conversation:

> Finally, a psychotheological explanation may be offered for the incessant joking and gossip that constitute shul conversation. This "light" chatter of sociability, almost compulsive in character, blocks out—literally as well as symbolically—the possibility of the speakers' having to come to terms with deeper antinomies inherent in their modernity and orthodoxy. To talk about such matters of the spirit would be to open a Pandora's box of anxieties and theological conflicts with which the everyday shul Jew refuses to deal. The "small talk" of joking and gossip is infinitely safer and more manageable. [Heilman, 1976, p. 209]

Often a unit performance is given by what Goffman suggests we call a "team." Whether the members of a team stage similar individual performances or stage dissimilar performances that fit together into a whole, an emergent team impression arises that can be conveniently treated as a fact in its own right, as a third level of fact located between the individual performance on one hand and the total interaction of participants on the other. Goffman defines a team as "a set of individuals whose intimate co-operation is required if a *given* projected definition of the situation is to be maintained." A team is a grouping, but it is a grouping not in relation to a social structure or social organization but rather in relation to an interaction or series of interactions in which the relevant definition of the situation is maintained (Goffman, 1959, p. 104).

Members of a team find themselves related to one another in various ways. Negatively, any member of the team has the power to give the show away or to disrupt it by inappropriate conduct. Positively, teammates, in proportion to the frequency with which they act as a team, tend to be bound together by rights of what might be called "familiarity," a kind of intimacy without warmth. A teammate, then, may be defined as someone on whose dramaturgical cooperation one is dependent in fostering a given definition of the situation. To withhold anything from certain teammates means you are in jeopardy of ruining their performances, of withholding their characters from them. And if a member of the team makes a mistake or somehow offends in the presence of an audience, the other team members often must suppress their immediate desire to punish and instruct him until the audience is no longer present. Naturally, someone cannot be a member of both performing team and audience, because a variety of impressions will be given away or lost (of course, the audience in many circumstances can be considered a team also) (Goffman, 1959, p. 283).

The synagogue membership can be conceived of as one team in relationship to outsiders, even though there are a number of shifting involvements within the total group. Heilman says:

> Beyond the various perspectives which emerge from shul roles and their expectations, and "preliminary to any self-determined act of behaviour," is a collective, intersubjective definition of the situation that has moral authority over any individual participant's view of the setting and of any activity in it. Any behavior or assertion of a situational definition [of prayer] results in the perpetrator's being defined as an outsider, one not familiar with the claims of the setting. [Heilman, 1976, p. 131]

For example, there is a complex relationship among sociability, conversation, and prayer–reverence that occurs in the midst of the service. Certain portions of the service are considered more sacred than others. Participants are aware of these distinctions, so the more sacred the moment, the more sociability and conversation are inhibited and impaired. If a person has entered the sanctuary during a solemn period, little conversation will take place, but if a service has few prohibitions, the set of involvements and associated situational definitions will be broad-ranging. Long periods of prayer are too demanding socially, so synagogue members have in practice redefined prohibitions.

For performances to be brought off properly, the various performers must possess certain attributes and express these attributes in practices employed for saving the show. Goffman speaks of loyalty, discipline, and circumspection. Perhaps the key problem in maintaining loyalty in team members is to prevent the performers from becoming so sympathetically attached to the audience that the performers disclose to them the consequences for them of the impression they are being given, or in other ways make the team as a whole pay for this attachment. Performers who are disciplined remember their parts and do not commit unmeant gestures or faux pas in performing them. They have discretion; they do not give the show away by involuntarily disclosing its secrets. They have the presence of mind to cover up on the spur of the moment for inappropriate behavior on the part of teammates while at all times maintaining the impression that they are merely playing their parts. To show circumspection, members of a team need to exercise foresight and design in determining in advance how best to stage a show. Prudence must be exercised. When there is little chance of being seen, opportunities for relaxation can be taken; when there is little chance of being put to a test, the cold facts can be presented in a glowing light, and the performers can play their part for all that it is worth, investing it with full dignity. If no care and honesty are exercised, then disruptions are likely to occur; if rigid care and honesty are exercised, then the performers can be greatly limited in what they can build out of the dramatic opportunities open to them. Simple etiquette and tact will, of course, assist in all this (Goffman, 1959, Chapter 6).

If we think about the way people relate to other people as performances, teams, roles, and impression management, then we will think of religious practice and behavior as the performance of a cast of characters in a house of prayer with its shifting involvements, its relationship of background and personality to liturgical behavior, and the various interpersonal meanings expressed by everything from gossip and joking through formal study and assembly. We shall see that the psychology of religious experience emerges as people deal with one another, both in formal worship and in the communal life that surrounds the formal worship.

In the synagogue life described here a variety of people take turns performing and being audiences. Individual performances, as noted, range from president of the congregation, down through a rule-following gossiper, to a youngster trying to get away with as much as possible. Their performances change from day to day. Various officials of the congregation had to give expression to ideal standards during the performance, and a minor event such as a brush with the law had to be made inconsequential in relationship to the overall definition of the situation being fostered.

The appropriateness of being the performer and being the audience varied with the occasion. Teams form on the basis of common sentiments about belief and behavior, though there is the constant regulation of the Torah. One would gather that those who have come to the head of the congregation join forces with one another to convey the idea that loyalty to Torah in serious orthodox fashion renders one just and good in daily living. Adults will join forces in conveying this to children, and children end up on teams that sometimes compete in pious conformity and other times in mischievousness. As outlets, the gossiping and joking performances enable people to express the tensions they feel between obligations to adhere strictly to the Torah and the other roles they are called to play in modern society.

To understand the performances fully we would have to know what areas of Jewish teaching, thought, and life provide the occasion of performances on the part of people who have other roles to play in life. But we can be sure that the Jewishness of Samuel Heilman's synagogue is the result of a multitude of interactions that make the variety-filled theater of the synagogue a unique collection of unique performances.

The Application of Small-Group Research to Religious Research

We have featured interaction descriptions composed of theater metaphors, but there is a collection of theory and research that might simply be called "small group" study. Across the decades there have been studies of the significance of group size or of the "geometry" of the relations among group members (e.g. where people spontaneously sit in relationship to one another). Encounter groups have been the subject of intense study in recent years. Since religion is so often a social function, some of the psychologists involved in small-group research have had occasion to study a variety of religious experiences. They ask how religious groups form around a founder, how divisions form when a group becomes larger or more diverse, how mutual support causes or influences the individual's religious experience, the extent to which an "individual" experience is, in fact, "social," and how small groups can be part of larger groups. Often these studies are related to sociological discussions of "churches," "sects," and "cults"—definition of the different types of religious groups being the main problem. If it is obvious that religion can be a family or a tribal affair to begin with, then a given group can spread throughout a city or a country; members can break off and start their own version of the group, or alien groups can come from outside a geographical area. Think of the beginnings of Christianity or Islam, the relationship of tribal gods to ancestors, missionary efforts, revolts, and reformations. The data are quite varied, but we can note one basic fact, namely, that the beginnings of all religious activity and the wide varieties of religious change are all related to the small group.

The varieties of religious groups can be classified. Conversionist groups believe that salvation can be achieved only by profound inner change; introversionist groups believe in withdrawing from the world; revolutionist groups believe that the world must be overturned totally and supernaturally. Utopians believe, obviously, that only in a completely rebuilt world can salvation and happiness be attained; manipulationist groups believe in the use of supernatural powers and secrets to attain their ends (Wilson, 1978). Within these groups common patterns or dynamics are assumed. The goal of small-group research is to discover the nature of these patterns and dynamics, examining the form and content of social interaction in a group, the norms and social control established, the decision-making process, the way the group develops, and styles of social perception. These processes and structures depend for their uniqueness on a group of interaction variables: personalities involved; age, sex, and other social characteristics; group size; tasks to be performed; the type of communications network that is in place; and the nature of the leadership (Hare, 1976).

More recently, attempts have been made to systematize contemporary methods of group observation (Bales and Cohen, 1979). Basically small natural groups were studied, such as families, teams, or classroom groups. But such systematization has not yet been extended to religious groups. While popular reports abound, there are very few properly psychological studies. Studies of sects in general (Ellwood, 1973; Wilson, 1978), American communes (Zablocki, 1980), the Jesus movement, and the Unification Church (Bromley and Shupe, 1979; Robbins et al., 1976) were primarily sociological studies. Psychological studies deal with the psychological traits of both those who stayed in and those who left religious groups. The more recent the study, the more precise the discussion of the psychological details in this decision-making.

Perhaps no group has received more attention than the Unification Church (generally, and disparagingly, called the "Moonies"). One researcher studied the psychological qualities of the conversion process that took place during twenty-one-day workshops (and their subdivisions) set up to introduce people to the Unification Church. Subjects were given a variety of tests at different times during this time period. After the initial two-day sequence 71 percent dropped out; the 29 percent who remained had greater affiliative feelings toward the group and greater acceptance of the church's creed than the early dropouts. The 9 percent who ultimately joined the church had weaker outside personal ties than the later dropouts, although their beliefs in and sense of cohesiveness with the church were the same as the late dropouts (Galanter, 1980, p. 1574). For the researcher, this latter fact was the interesting one: Those who dropped out at the end had, still and all, the same commitment to the group and its beliefs as those who stayed—"apparently, at least at this stage in the affiliation process, considerable enthusiasm for the group may be countered by the strength of outside ties" (p. 1578).

Comparing this study with earlier research on long-standing members of the Unification Church, the author found that new members of the church had significantly lower general wellbeing scores than long-standing members. Regarding specifically psychological wellbeing, the author found that both members and workshop guests scored considerably lower than a control group. The favorable interpretation of this is that there is a considerable amount of social disruption experienced by those who elected to come to workshops. A more negative interpretation is possible, because considerable pathology unrelated to situational issues is found among the membership. The author concludes:

> For the potential members perhaps only a certain degree of absent meaning in life is necessary to elicit interest in the Unification Church. The church must present its belief system in such a way that the potential innate resistance is relieved and the creed can be accepted. To this end, the social context plays an important role to rapidly generate a strong sense of cohesiveness during the workshops, as observed here. This was promoted when the workshop guests continued through the initial workshop segment in close relationships with the hosts who originally invited them [Galanter, 1980, p. 1579]

In fact, sometimes studies of the dynamics of group membership are called "large-group" psychology (!) because of the connection of the local group with a larger group (Galanter, 1980). For example, members of a religious sect who meet in some local situation interact on the basis of the local group's participation in a larger group. But the borderline between "small" and "large" tends to get blurred in these discussions. In the last ten years the literature on sects, cults, and the use of group dynamics research to anlayze larger churches has increased enormously. Some strategies have been developed for the application of small-group study to macro-systems: first, one must study the relationship of the variables in small groups without regard to their existence in natural group situations; then, one should make a naturalistic study of small groups to see how they interact with larger systems, relying upon life-stage theories in developmental psychology. It would be going beyond the evidence, however, to say that small-group study gives anything more than guidelines for study of larger areas of society (Back, 1973). Studies have been made of small-group dynamics suggesting the importance of Freudian and Jungian theory for understanding the development patterns of small groups, small religious groups, and religion in general: themes of group murder, autonomism, and feared king were examined (Slater, 1966).

There are also a number of studies of ingroup and outgroup feelings to see how religion stands up relative to other issues in causing "ingroup" feeling and determining relationships to outgroups. Obviously, there is greater interaction of groups with greater physical proximity. And there is greater outgroup interaction when people know the language of those belonging to the other groups. India, Lebanon, and other such places where religious differences are coupled with ethnic differences are especially good fields for such study. In one cross-cultural study, it was reported that members of an Israeli kibbutz were more willing to experience interaction with others than were Israeli city dwellers; both Israeli groups were less willing to experience interaction than Jewish and non-Jewish subjects in the United States (Pirojnikoff, Hadar, and Hadar, 1971).

The Study of Attitudes

Attitudes are part of, or are connected to, interactions. An attitude is a consistent manner of thinking (based upon a variety of experiences) about such things as people, groups, social issues, or events in the environment. The term includes a wide variety of thoughts and beliefs, feelings, emotions, and tendencies to react. Attitudes develop in the course of coping with and adjusting to the environment. Sometimes they are formed in an interaction—one can form a positive attitude toward serious churchgoers or political liberals. Or they can be formed because of a lack of interaction—prejudices toward other races and ethnic groups are often established in this way. Of course, people are not always aware of their attitudes, of the range of thoughts and emotions involved, or of the contradictions found within a given expressed attitude. Often people regulate their own attitudes by inferring the attitudes of present or absent others: They decide that someone is liberal, understanding, or unprejudiced and then try to react appropriately. Attitudes influence the speed and efficiency of learning, groups associated with, professions chosen, and philosophies lived by. Attitudes are influenced by interaction and in turn, influence further interaction.

Much of the research in social psychology is centered on the learning and changing of attitudes. In fact, expressed ideas about anything and everything can be called "attitudes." The next chapter considers many types of research that social psychologists would call social psychology under other headings (for example, research on the formation of God-image might be considered "attitudes toward" God, but I prefer to consider this research relative to an earlier chapter in the book, namely, the study of Freud and Jung). This chapter discusses religious attitude research in general.

There are two major problems in determining or understanding the attitudes of others. It is difficult, first, to know whether an attitude someone expresses is really what he or she thinks and feels or is simply a response to the questioning situation—perhaps those who do the questioning are really hinting at the proper attitude to have (Salancik and Conway, 1975). But even when we know the authentic attitude, we cannot be sure that this will have any effect on their behavior (Bagozzi and Burnkrant, 1979). We all know the cases of the pious person who is a horror to deal with, and those vicious-sounding individuals who are, in the last analysis, always ready to help.

We can give a profile of attitudes toward or based upon religion without delving into problems of the formation of those attitudes or their expression, because so much research has been done on correlations. The religious attitudes themselves can be divided into attitudes toward God (theism), the church and its members (church orientation), the Bible (Fundamentalism), other people (altruism), visionary moral principles (idealism), formal worship and one set of ways of relating to the deity (ritualism), informal worship and prayer experience (mysticism), and luck, omens, magic, and forces in the universe (superstition) (Maranell, 1974).

Note that a number of things elsewhere called dimensions or experiences or whatever are here called attitudes. The psychologist who formulated this particular list calls them "attitudes" toward and responses to the crucial aspects, symbols, and practices of religion. The author studied the religious attitudes of clergy, college professors, students, citizens of a small Southern city, and citizens of a Midwestern community. Other attitudes and experiences correlated with religious attitudes in the research. As a sample of how this works we quote the summary of research results on Fundamentalism—the literal interpretation of scriptures (Maranell, 1974, pp. 247-248):

1. Seventh-Day Adventist, Lutheran, Catholic, Church of Christ, and Baptist clergymen are highest in Fundamentalism, whereas Unitarian–Universalist clergyman are lowest.

2. Southern clergymen are most Fundamentalist, followed in order by those of the Pacific Coast, New England, and lastly those in the Midwest.

3. Older clergymen are significantly more Fundamentalist than younger clergymen.

4. Professors in denominational colleges and universities are significantly more Fundamentalist than those in public universities.

5. Professors in larger colleges and universities are less Fundamentalist than those in small colleges.

6. Full professors are significantly more Fundamentalist than assistant professors.

7. Behavioral science professors are significantly less Fundamentalist than professors of physical sciences and fine arts professors, who are the most Fundamentalist.

8. Fundamentalism is not often positively correlated with political conservatism.

9. Fundamentalism scores of the various socioeconomic classes of a Southern city are not significantly different.

10. Fundamentalism is inversely related to socioeconomic status in the Midwestern community studied; that is, Fundamentalism is highest in the lowest class and lowest in the highest class.

11. Active church members score higher on Fundamentalism than inactive members.

12. Fundamentalism is not affected by either arrogation or derogation.

13. Fundamentalism is not related to suggestibility.

14. Fundamentalism is not related to perceptual rigidity.

15. Fundamentalism is generally inversely correlated with scholastic aptitude in the Southern student sample only.

16. Fundamentalism is significantly and positively correlated with dependency and inversely correlated with ego strength as both are measured by the MMPI.

17. Fundamentalism is highly related to orthodoxy and less, but significantly, correlated with fanaticism and the importance of religion.

18. Fundamentalism is not generally correlated with alienation.

19. Fundamentalism is significantly higher among Southern female students than among Southern male students.

20. Fundamentalism is clustered with theism and superstition in a common factor among clergymen.

21. Fundamentalism is clustered with superstition, ritualism, theism, mysticism, and church orientation and not with altruism or idealism in the attitude system of professors.

22. Fundamentalism is clustered with theism, altruism, mysticism, and idealism and not with church orientation, ritualism, or superstition in the attitude system of Methodist church members.

In the foregoing a variety of religious attitudes were correlated with the one specific religious attitude, Fundamentalism. But religious attitudes can be correlated with a number of other attitudes and factors in life. Religious attitudes are believed to be correlated with sex differences, childrearing differences, achievement motivation, education, intelligence, creativity, authoritarianism, dogmatism, suggestibility, political attitudes, ethnocentrism, prejudice, physical health, neuroticism, mental disorder, adjustment to life crises, suicidal behavior, alcoholism, crime and delinquency, sexual activity, birth control, sexual attitudes, marital adjustment, fertility, social class, minority group membership, urban–rural differences, social organization, and economic conditions (Argyle and Beit-Halahmi, 1975).

For example, the data indicate that women are more religious than men in every way, including church membership and attendance, beliefs, and mystical experiences. The experiences of religiously reared children are different as regards authoritarian relationships, the use of physical punishment, and training for independence. Jews have more achievement motivation than Protestants and Catholics, and earlier in history Protestants were more notable in this regard than Catholics. In the case of academic and scientific achievement, some religious groups are overrepresented. Early studies found negative correlations between intelligence and measures of religious conservatism. There are denominational differences in authoritarianism; the only fully significant item is that those with no religion score lowest on authoritarianism. Social suggestibility (everything from dependence on group opinion through hypnosis) is greater in religious people. Political and social attitudes reflect people's beliefs regarding the social order, the divisions of power and positions around them, those more fortunate than themselves, and those they consider distinctively different from themselves because of race, nationality, or tradition. The data indicate that religious people, apart from the most devout, are more prejudiced both because religion can in some way cause prejudice and because religion and prejudice together can be caused by a third factor. Pro-religious attitudes and self-expression can be related to individual wellbeing, happiness, and peace of mind in some cases and psychopathology in others (though it may be simply that emotionally disturbed people turn to religion to help them with their problems). And people who are pro-religion generally speaking are less sexually active, though more happily married. Ideas about different forms of religious expression—restrained through ecstatic—are affected by social class.

Of course, these research results can be so general as to be misleading. The next chapter will discuss the problems inherent in the research that leads to such conclusions. Some social psychologists believe that we can explore correlations and arrive at some type of unified psychology of religion (Hunsberger, 1980), but others question the possibility of a general social psychological profile of "the religious person" (Gorsuch and Malony, 1976). There is also a problem of refining the notion of what attitudes are supposed to be toward—what do people mean when they say they have a particular attitude toward the *church*, for example? This and many other problems are addressed in the chapter on research that follows.

PART IV

Religion
in Psychological
Research
and Therapy

A DISCUSSION of psychological research and a presentation of types of therapy and guidance are not arbitrary additions to our study. For so many of us today psychology *is* research. When we "coordinate" a variety of research reports with the preceding chapters, we are not adding a series of little research games as proofs of the good old theories. The theories are the source of hypotheses for the research psychologists do, and that research gives rise to new theoretical insights. We shall see this when going over summaries of research on God-image, conversion, or prejudice. Also for many of us today, therapy and guidance are the most significant practical applications of the science of psychology. In fact, therapy itself is a subject for research. Do not take these chapters, then, as token offerings to research psychologists and therapists or those planning careers in these areas. There is an intimate connection: You will have noted that we integrated a number of research results in earlier chapters, and you will now note that the research chapter is built on theories already discussed. The connection between therapy and psychological theory is already obvious, but the connections will be spelled out in Chapter 8, with a focus on religious issues. Research designed to explore Freudian hypotheses has been centered on the range of people's defensive behavior or the special qualities of oral, anal, and phallic personality types. Piaget's research, originally put together in interview and clinical situations, is tested in a number of cross-cultural studies. In social psychology, various attitudes are correlated or the interrelationships involved in group behavior are studied. Remember too that specific religious issues are associated with those psychological approaches: Freud and conflict theory—projection of divinity figures and conversion on various levels of the personality; Allport and fulfillment theory—integration of personality and prejudice; developmental studies—measures of the development of belief schemata and morality schemata; social psychology —correlation of religious attitudes with other areas of social life.

The basic problem in research would appear to be the labeling of variables within hypotheses, e.g. God-image in the context of the oedipal hypothesis. Although I have identified themes with theories, in reality little of the research is strictly bound to one theorist. Research on divinity figures, for example, may derive from hypotheses that are not Freudian or Jungian. Ideas about the dynamics of projection might be retained without any attempts to explore the oedipal theory. In general, then, we must allow that researchers just may be using an idea or portion of theory outside of its original context. In that case we cannot say that a given piece of research is "Freudian," "Allportian," or anything of the sort. To associate Freud, Allport, Piaget, and others with given themes, as I have done, is a matter of impression and happenstance: impression, for example, because Freud's discussion of God as a projection of the father-figure is so famous that it immediately comes to mind when any research on God-image is suggested, and happenstance, for example, because Allport himself happened to have done a great deal of research on the problem of prejudice. What we have, then, are useful generalizations.

Even when an idea or hypothesis obviously drawn from a given theory is supported by the research, it may be only a partial answer. Processes can be accounted for by hypotheses drawn from different theories: Relation of God-image to experience of the father may be accounted for in different ways. Several processes may be involved in the same phenomenon: Both father experience and self-image may regulate belief in God. In these cases, if the processes are separate, both theories can be retained. If the processes are joined, they can be accounted for by one theory that contains the other (the cognitive dissonance theory about self-image could be understood to contain the Freudian Oedipus complex theory).

Therapies, secular and religious, are also derived from personality theories and from developmental and social psychology. Just as we speak of research topics and methods in relationship to conflict and fulfillment theory and to developmental and social psychology, so we can speak of therapies and their relationships to theories and psychologies. Material in Chapter 8 is related to Chapters 2 through 6. Choosing the therapies and/or counseling approaches that are clear and developed, we proceed now to representative examples of religious problems. Since a "conditioning" approach can be applied to religious problems, it is included, even though conditioning has received only passing mention in the earlier chapters. We see that the varied approaches are ready-made for handling different types of religious problems. In fact, many therapists today are quite eclectic in their work, using conflict, fulfillment, and conditioning approaches as the need arises.

Whether therapies are based solely on one or another of the old orthodox theories (Freudian, Allportian, and so on) or on an eclectic combination of several, they have regular features and qualities that enable us to classify and understand them.

For example, among the regular features of the therapies themselves we can see the different roles that therapists and subjects play: the role of the present-day nondirective counselor is different from the Christian monastic spiritual director who is thought to be experienced in a divinely revealed system. We can see the way they come together also: Is it just therapist and patient, or is it a specially composed group, such as a family or alcoholics? We can see the way they schedule their meetings. There are, obviously, a physical locale (therapist's office or secluded sanitarium), props (writing pad, furniture, splendid view), and appropriate costumes (clinical or everyday, attractive or sloppy), and everything functions symbolically or as nonverbal background communication. We can learn of the views about the human personality held by both therapist and patient (on human nature, ideals for human fulfillment, how people get sick, techniques that should be used to make them whole). And we can learn of the type of exchange that goes on in the various settings. Involved here are the conduct and experience of the participants at the individual level (tasks and techniques can be assigned to different participants, while internal experiences—emotions, intentions, and evaluations—are going on at the same time).

A knowledge of the setting of all these activities is equally useful for understanding therapy. Where do the directors and subjects come from? What kinds of institutions are involved? The values and beliefs about guidance and healing found in the surrounding culture, as well as those who in general enter more fully into the spiritual guidance system itself, need to be examined. Psychological characteristics of the individuals who come to the guidance session should be known also: their motivations, their expectations, the particular qualities of their personal situation. If we can inform ourselves about these regular features, we can grasp the ways therapy and guidance are mediated to people.

And ultimately psychology is for people. The personality of the human being is the center of most religious practices and studies (with that personality most often seen in relationship to a God and another world). It is difficult to see what use this information about human beings will be unless it somehow enlightens and changes us for the better, and unless it makes us capable of enlightening and changing.

Psychological Research on the Religious Experience

CONSIDER WHAT INFORMATION is actually conveyed by the following abbreviated and paraphrased research report titled "Sex Differences in Symbolic Conception of the Deity" (Larsen and Knapp, 1964):

Introduction and hypotheses. When Freud's theory of the Oedipus complex is used to interpret belief in God, then we have the following hypothesis: "God is psychologically nothing more than a magnified father." Following the oedipal theory in its entirety, we must presume that the Father-God image of the Judeo–Christian tradition would be seen by the male with latent fear and hostility, while the female would react in a less complicated and more receptive way. The research is designed to explore attributes ascribed to God by male and female subjects.

Research design and methods. The subjects were twenty men and twenty women chosen from a mainline Protestant denomination. Seven ink blots, identified by letter, were presented to the subjects. Subjects were required to order them on a scale from one to seven to the degree that they might symbolize the subjects' concept of God. The scales used involved going from benevolence to malevolence and from potency to weakness.

Data analysis and discussion. There was a reliable difference between men and women in the manner in which blots were ranked as symbols of God. Because of the nature of the difference it could be said that "fear of God" characterizes the male much more than the female. These results suggest that acceptance of the Judeo-Christian God and submission to religious discipline involve different and probably more problematic psychodynamic adjustments for the male than for the female. Whether this information might be generalized to include other religious groups remains a question.

The results do not conclusively show that men will have more difficulties with the mental image of a Father-God, but the quick reader is left with the impression that this is probably so. There are other issues involved, as we shall see when examining more detailed research.

For a better understanding of psychological research on the religious experience, this chapter will offer representative psychological research that is coordinated with all of the preceding chapters. The variety of research reports chosen sustain the hypotheses expressed in the James–mysticism, Freud–Jung, Allport–Maslow–May, Piaget–Erikson, and social psychology chapters.

Surveying and Evaluating Religious Research

Psychological research has ranged across many different types of religious data under the headings of God-image, conversion, integration of personality, prejudice, the relationship of religious cognition and moral judgment, and the development of personal religious identity, among others. A variety of mental and emotional activities have been scaled (less or more religious) and correlated (the less-or-more-religious activity with other aspects of mental and emotional life).

When the varieties of religious research are surveyed, four primary topics emerge (and perhaps the case can be made that the topics are the basic elements of the religious experience). *God-image* is the type of divinity figure or figures that predominate in people's imagination or the type of mental concept of divinity that they have. While it is not a static image, it is what predominates in people's minds and emerges in varieties of projective testing and questioning. *Conversion* refers to the special activation of intellectual and emotional forces by divinity images or ideas of divinity. *Integration* of faculties refers to the drawing together, sustaining, and inspiring effects of religion on the personality. Sometimes this integration can be effected by, or is at least concomitant to, conversion. But at other times it simply develops early in the life of the believer, who in the course of a life of faith may have periods of agnosticism or atheism. *Prejudice* is the opposition placed between one's own religious personality and that of other people. Those for whom religion has provided a means of straightening out their lives may deal confidently with the religious or irreligious ways of others or may fearfully reject others, depending on the quality of this integration of faculties. The themes coordinate nicely with the approaches presented in this book.

Today researchers start with a *hypothesis* they want to test. Next they decide what factual *evidence* they need (reliance on views of authorities, the opinions of other people, or one's own impressions is not sufficient), and their plan for gathering data is called the *research design.* To obtain these data they systematically observe and record the phenomenon they wish to study, trying to do so in an unbiased way; this procedure requires measurement, and so then they choose specific scales, questionnaires, and procedures called research *methods.* Fourth, results and scores of the various tests and measurements are checked and interpreted by statistical techniques; this is called *data analysis.* Tables and graphs are often used to present the data clearly. Finally, the researchers return to their hypotheses to discuss how it was supported or contradicted by the research; alternative explanations and broader general implications are discussed in the presentation of results and conclusions (Lewin, 1979).

The wholesale publication of tests for use in research resulted from the great interest in clinical and educational testing following successful mass testing of soldiers in World War I. Tests of intelligence or other general abilities that had widespread or national use were valued the most, because testing was previously decentralized, with every college, business, and clinic planning and administering its own program. Today intelligence is measured by various tests, abilities are sorted out by factor analysis, interests are inventoried. Personality measurements are really attempts to assess typical behavior and the typical reactions and perceptions that occur within individuals (e.g. self-concept, feelings of hostility, attitudes toward authority).

Personality tests of the projective, self-report, and performance varieties, which will be presented below, have made possible inquiries into social relationships, character, learning, and so on. Psychologists and sociologists interested in religion have constructed tests for their purposes. Psychologists have been concerned with the religious experiences of individuals, such as their feelings, attitudes, and beliefs about the supernatural, and sociologists have been concerned with empirical studies of church attendance and related facets of organizational membership, but both have tended to use the same measures of religious adherence (Robinson and Shaver, 1973).

The fundamental problem in psychological research has been to agree on the nature of the data (it is difficult, after all, for psychologists of very different orientations to agree on the nature of religion). Some of the data that researchers have discussed is observable: It is hard to imagine any type of psychologist who would be unwilling to discuss the relationship of brain functions to contractions within the eye, vibrations within the ear, and so on. Other types of data, such as an attitude toward a group of people, are more complex, involving a variety of sentiments and motivations, the existence of which would be argued over by psychologists of the varying approaches—conflict, fulfillment, and conditioning. But all of the adult, developmental, and social elements of the personality, if properly delimited and described, can be made the objects of measurements and experiments. So the problem is to delimit and describe the data properly or—in psychological terminology—to label the variables properly.

Variables can be best labeled if certain factors are attended to. Obviously the measurement of the *same* property in all subjects is necessary for basic research. One can deal with the frequency, intensity, and rootedness of a religious thought or emotion in a variety of people, but it has to be the same property, the same unit. The measurement operations must be public and communicable; neither the observations of highly individualistic therapists on a neurosis nor the observations of a visionary believer on the origins of a religious phenomenon can be shared by others, very simply because they cannot *observe* the same things. Science is built on the consensus of informed scientists. And since the human personality is complex, and several factors can produce the same feeling or action, the important thing is to measure each variable separately, standardizing or controlling all possible influential variables except the one being measured. Such control of variables is so important that it has become the central task in personality measurement. Researchers must make sure that the setting in which the measurements are made has basically the same meaning for all subjects and minimize the extent to which the setting itself contributes variance to the responses. The subjects must have a task to perform that is unambiguous, which is within their powers, and which is acceptable and interesting to them. Stimuli must be selected that will be perceived and interpreted in the same qualitative way by all subjects. A response format must be devised that will enable subjects to indicate their responses readily and feel confident that these responses represent what they wish to express (Fiske, 1971).

Furthermore, the usefulness and complementarity of different types of tests must be agreed on. Salvatore Maddi (1972) suggests that different types of tests and measurements be used in order to serve as controls of one another, and that tests be constructed to handle different aspects of the personality. Thus projective tests, such as Rorschach and TAT, by eliciting motivation can give the general orientations of the personality and the role of religion within the personality. Questionnaires concerning the directions and goals in people's behavior tend to elicit their values and sense of social roles. A third type of test, in which familiar circumstances are created so people will perform actions that reveal the regularities of their functioning, is especially useful for measuring traits.

Research Reports

In the research reported below a number of test combinations were used in order to examine a wide variety of hypotheses. Hood's research shows that environment and susceptibility can induce religious experiences. Dealing with the projection of divinity figures according to the conflict version of personality, Antoine Vergote and his associates sought to discover personal images and emotions toward parents and their effect upon belief images. Relating conversion to anxiety, Spellman, Baskett and Byrne submitted a variety of simply categorized religious people to a test that scaled levels of anxiety without attempting to discern the causes of their anxiety. Examining integration of personality according to the fulfillment version, Pargament, Steele, and Tyler used a battery of question-and-answer scales to assess attitudes towards self and the world, and to measure coping skill, dealing with a number of items so as to eliminate as many hidden factors as possible. Allport and Ross brought together the results of years of prejudice studies and by analysis of previous results and indirect measures sought to relate prejudice to indiscriminate thinking. In developmental psychology, the direct questioning methods described in Chapter 5 were used by Hoge and Petrillo and by Saltzstein and Osgood to understand cognitive development in religious belief and morality. And in social psychology King and Hunt studied the dimensions or attitudes that constitute religiosity.

The Mystical Experience

Much of the research in the 1970s on the nature of the mystical experiences was dominated by the work of Ralph Hood. The following is an example of the kinds of issues researchers deal with.

HOOD, RALPH W., AND RONALD J. MORRIS. "Sensory Isolation and the Differential Elicitation of Religious Imagery in Intrinsic and Extrinsic Persons," *Journal for the Scientific Study of Religion* 20 (1981): 261–73.

Within the emerging body of altered-states-of-consciousness literature it is well noted that meditation is likely to be characterized by imagery. Persons well practiced in prayer come to anticipate such imagery and define it as a category of religious experience. In sensory isolation research, isolation tanks have proved to be most effective in eliciting imagery under appropriate set conditions. While early isolation research reported imagery only infrequently, continued research found that imagery could be elicited if subjects were relaxed and unfearful in the isolation tank and were given specific instructions to attend to internal mental states, contents, and processes. Under such conditions imagery is more frequent, especially unstructured phenomena such as diffuse white light or various geometric forms.

Hood and Morris designed this study as a pilot effort to fulfill two major goals. First, they wanted to produce set conditions to maximize the elicitation of meaningful imagery. Second, they wanted to identify persons whose religious orientation facilitated the production of meaningful religious imagery. In a first study, three hypotheses were tested: (1) Persons given set instructions to perceive meaningful imagery in the isolation tank situation would report more set imagery than persons not given set instructions. (2) Intrinsic religious persons would report more meaningful religious imagery under appropriate religious set than would extrinsic religious persons. (3) Extrinsic and intrinsic persons would not differ in the amount of imagery where no set instruction was given or where the set given was irrelevant to religious orientation. The intrinsic–extrinsic distinction belongs to Allport, whose work with these categories is described on p. 194. In a second, supporting study (which will not be reported on here) Hood and Morris asked participants to interpret ten Rorschach cards. Here intrinsic persons did not give a significantly greater number of responses than extrinsic persons. This indicated that simply being part of a test did not automatically elicit religious responses from intrinsic types.

Research design and methods. Persons participating in this study were selected from a pool of 394 introductory psychology students who took the Intrinsic/Extrinsic scales as part of the course proceedings. From these scores, the upper 25 percent and the lower 25 percent on the intrinsic scale were offered a chance to participate in the isolation tank experience. For ethical and health reasons certain careful selection procedures were followed. These procedures probably had the effect of assuring an increased frequency of imagery, since only persons comfortable and inquisitive enough to participate in an unusual psychology experiment volunteered. Participants were read the appropriate set instructions and were led to the isolation tank room and left alone to undress and enter the tank. Then the experimenter closed the tank and simply monitored the tank in case the participant chose to exit before the hour. After completing one hour in the tank, participants were allowed to shower and dress. Immediately afterward all participants filled out a questionnaire. Included in the questionnaire were five items directly relevant to the hypotheses tested. These were items referring to experiences of white light, geometric shapes, meaningful figures (nonreligious/non-cartoon), cartoon figures, and religious figures. Each specific item was rated from "frequently experienced" to "never experienced." In addition participants were debriefed by talking in open-ended terms about their isolation experiences and probing the experimenter regarding any problems they might have had regarding their experience.

Data analysis and discussion. Overall it is clear that the data offer support for the hypotheses tested. Intrinsic persons at least *report* more religious imagery under an appropriate set than do extrinsic persons. If we ignore the issue of demand characteristics for a moment, these data indicate that when instructed to experience religious imagery in a situation likely to elicit imagery, intrinsic persons in fact report the experience of such imagery more than extrinsic persons. These data are especially crucial in light of the cartoon set condition, in which it was demonstrated that no differences between religious types occur when appropriate instructions are given merely to experience cartoon imagery. Hence the differential intrinsic/extrinsic report of religious imagery under appropriate set conditions is a specific function of religious orientation and not one of *general* tendencies to imagery.

Although persons may be willing to *report* religious imagery on the posttank questionnaire, since they were expected to experience it in terms of anticipatory sets, this is not equivalent to *experiencing* imagery in the tank situation. The problem of imagery assessment in isolation research is well noted in the literature. But the fact that intrinsic persons may acquiesce to demand characteristics to report religious imagery while extrinsic persons do not itself indicates intrinsic persons are more likely to respond religiously in appropriate circumstances. Likewise, it remains intriguing that even when instructed to experience cartoon imagery, intrinsic persons still report an incidence of religious imagery in excess of that of extrinsic persons under religious set conditions. Whether or not one wishes to make demand characteristics carry so much weight remains problematic, especially in light of the card study. That genuine imagery is elicited in the isolation tank experience, especially when participants are appropriately "set," remains an intriguing possibility.

In combination these studies certainly suggest the importance of imagery among intrinsically religious persons. The isolation tank setting appears to elicit religious experience in a way that avoids the dilemma of controversial or simply ineffective drugs. Furthermore, the card study indicates the minimization of indiscriminate religious responses from intrinsic participants in appropriate settings. Hence it would appear that under relevant conditions, probably including but not restricted to appropriate physiological arousals, religious set persons of intrinsic orientation can readily experience religious imagery.

BASIC CONCLUSION: *Intrinsically Religious People Are More Apt to Experience Specifically Religious Imagery in Appropriate Circumstances.*

There is no need for physiological change in the brain for a mystical sense to come over people, because normal cognitive processes can account in large part for experiences of surprise, conflict, tension, timelessness, and ambiguity. For example, a cognition can involve the active conceiving of two or more opposite or antithetical ideas, images, or concepts simultaneously (Rothenberg, 1978–79). These contradictory images or concepts can then be brought together in a composite religious symbol such as the notion of an all-good God "allowing" evil for the sake of a greater good.

Often altered states of consciousness are produced socially. There is something to be said for the sharing of altered states in small groups or even by whole societies (Ben-Yehuda, 1978–79; Rosegrant, 1976). It is not necessary to be a member of a crisis cult or to experience significant social unrest to be involved in a group consciousness change. One study of speaking in tongues indicates that altered-states-of-consciousness "readiness" exists in any given population: The alteration can be triggered by minimal stimulation unrelated to deprivation, acculturation, or other social stress (Goodman, 1980). In a study of the social evolution of altered states of consciousness in the context of religious ritual, it appeared that the combination of such psychological factors as repetitive stimuli and sensory inhibition, and such social influences as expectation and motivation resulted in the achievement of intense mystical experiences. These experiences have both social and therapeutic advantages in that they increase prestige in a clearly defined subculture with tension release and anxiety reduction on a short-term basis (Ward and Beaubrun, 1980). And some people require ecstatic experience as an alternative to the struggles of everyday life (Ennis, 1967). Social support within the religious group influences the generation and maintenance of religious experience.

At times religious experience influences a society's values.

In one survey it appeared that the general values and beliefs of contrasting groups of Asians and Americans (with the principal religions of their respective regions predominating) directly influenced the nature of their life satisfactions. The Asian group considered religious faith, service to others, family ties, and luck to be important factors contributing to life satisfaction. U.S. subjects reported that hard work, personal abilities, travel, recreation, and social status had significantly affected their life satisfactions (Fry and Ghosh, 1980).

Studies assimilating altered states of consciousness to creative activity underline the importance of an increase in environmental stimulation of motor activity and of increased or decreased alertness or mental activity. Such stimulation can cause alteration in time sense or cognition; changes in body, image, or emotional expression; perceptual distortion; a sense of the inexplicability of the experience; a feeling of rejuvenation; a change in meaning and significance; and hypersuggestibility (Khatami, 1978). Indeed, learning glossolalia and other intense experiences might best be studied in terms of learning variables (Spanos and Hewitt, 1979).

So for the religious interpretation of altered states of consciousness, some kind of belief environment is required. Religious attribution of any kind is sustained by strong beliefs. In ordinary states of consciousness, too, processes, functions, and relationships can have religious significance when so interpreted in a religious belief environment. Meaning systems are sustained best if based on supernatural beliefs and promulgated by formal church organizations (Bainbridge and Stark, 1981).

Issues Associated with the Conflict
Version of the Personality

PROJECTION OF GOD-IMAGE. A large number of studies have been made of the ways in which people have pictured God, which is to say the Judeo-Christian-Islamic God. At first researchers worked only with Freud's theory that an individual's sense of the human father was the primary element in that individual's God-image.

But more complex research done in Belgium by Antoine Vergote and his colleagues went beyond the simple Freudian hypothesis. A much wider range of parental images and stereotypes was correlated with the God-image.

ANTOINE VERGOTE ET AL., "Concept of God and Parental Images," *Journal for the Scientific Study of Religion* 8 (1969):79–87.

Introduction and hypotheses. The image of a parent is taken to be a combined cognitive and affective schema that results from individual experiences with particular parents, and from the structuring elements of family and society as these become integrated into the relationship between child and parent. Images may vary too because of the age, sex, and value orientations of the children.

Research Design and Methods. The researchers wanted to discover whether the image of God corresponds to the differential images of parents and, in addition, to attend to the differences between maternal and paternal characteristics: Although acceptance, warmth, and love are supposedly maternal, authority also is found in the mother. The research instrument consisted of a list of thirty-six characteristics—eighteen stereotypically maternal and eighteen stereotypically paternal—arranged randomly. Each characteristic was accompanied by a seven-point scale on which subjects rated the degree to which they associated that characteristic with a parent or with God. To develop this instrument, the researchers began with many more items, which were first validated by judges and then modified through group interviews. There was some final validity testing. The sample consisted of 180 American students and 178 Belgian students, all single, Roman Catholic, and from a middle socioeconomic level.

Data analysis and discussion. In general the image of the mother seems to be the most clearly perceived, receiving high ratings exclusively on maternal characteristics. The image of father is more complex, containing a relatively large component of maternal as well as paternal characteristics. The image of God, as expected, contains both characteristics, the paternal characteristics being more accentuated than the maternal ones. The image of God is especially strong in basic paternal qualities of knowledge, strength, power, justice, authority model, and law and order. Fathers tend not to be rated so high on these qualities as on those reflecting more concrete action: giving directions, taking initiative, making decisions. It also appears that the maternal qualities are most pervasive, applying to the image of father and of God as well as mother, and that the paternal characteristics assigned to father and to God tend to be different.

Researchers noticed some differences due to age and field of study. Divine image becomes more maternal as persons move from high school to college status. Liberal arts students have a more maternal mother than science students; this is especially true for females. The father of male science majors is more maternal than the fathers of male liberal arts students. For liberal arts students, the mother image is closer to the father image than the God-image. Other differences were found to depend on whether the researchers were reporting on the French- or Dutch-speaking sample of Belgian students or the American students.

Researchers concluded that while the paternal image is the most adequate symbol for the image of God, the paternal symbol attributed to God does not correspond to the image of a father to whom a person turns in situations of distress or frustration.

BASIC CONCLUSION: *"Maternal" Qualities Are Pervasive, Applying Also to the Concepts of Father and God; "Paternal" Characteristics Assigned to Father and to God Tend to Be Different.*

The reports given above and all experiments of this sort have more problems than other types of research on religiosity. It is especially difficult to control for different variables in projective tests, and there is a further problem of people's sense of what is basically masculine or basically feminine, what is basically paternal and what is basically maternal. After all, it has been the experience of many of us to learn our warmth and gentleness from our fathers and competitiveness and rigor from our mothers. But Vergote's research tells how different subjects ascribe stereotypical paternal and maternal qualities to their own mothers and fathers and to God. In the last analysis the God-image does not have the same paternal qualities as the concrete human father.

Other researchers, also working from conflict hypotheses, have discovered that images of mother and father naturally have less to do with the formation of the God-image in those who think abstractly. One should also examine concrete and abstract thinking (Tamayo and Desjardins, 1976).

Other research shows that God-image can be influenced by factors having to do with self-esteem and self-control (Benson and Spilka, 1973). This research is still based somewhat on conflict theory, because it is a question of image and not intention or orientation. But fulfillment theory (or some kind of consistency theory) provides the basis of the hypotheses here, because the researchers are examining fulfillment and integration of faculties. Self-esteem is related positively to loving God-images and negatively to rejecting, impersonal, controlling images of God. So self-esteem may be a more important determinant of God-image than the God-images resulting from early experiences of parents.

CONVERSION.   When we speak of conversion as taking place on various levels of the personality or as something that wells up from the unconscious, we are speaking of conflict theory approaches to this phenomenon. Conversion has been made the subject of a number of studies that result from other theoretical approaches, since it can be conceived of as search for a fulfilling unity and an attempt to achieve consistency. But whenever dramatic conversion has been explored in its suddenness and in its effects, it has generally been within the conflict theory approach.

In 1953 Leon Salzman made an excellent summary of the psychology of religion discussion on conversion since the beginning of the century. He presented a number of case histories.

For Salzman the conversion experience seems to be an attempt, especially by gifted, sensitive, basically decent people, to solve a problem of great magnitude in their lives. The religious solution is tried by those who have spiritual goals and whose philosophy encompasses magic and extreme dependency on strong, omnipotent figures. Occasionally in adults and often in adolescents, the inner struggle with the problem of hatred toward the father or toward father symbols—authority figures—results in overwhelming anxiety and can lead to the conversion experience, whether this experience is psychotic, neurotic, or normal.

Looking at the postconversion state, Salzman found that a person is more intense, hateful, self-righteous, and doctrinaire after conversion than before. Thus the overt behavior after conversion, whether religious or political, to some extent reveals the character of the conversion experience. Salzman saw these characteristics: (1) The convert has an exaggerated, irrational intensity of belief in the new doctrine, although this intensity quickly dies; (2) the convert is concerned more with form and doctrine than with the greater principle of the new belief; (3) the attitude toward previous belief is one of contempt, hatred, denial, and rejection of the possibility that there might be any truth in it. The convert also shows (4) intolerance toward deviates, with frequent denouncements of previous friends and associates; (5) crusading zeal and a need to involve other by seeking new conversions; and (6) engagement in masochistic–sadistic activities displaying a need for martyrdom and self-punishment.

At the beginning of the 1970s there was an important study of one implication of Salzman's hypothesis: that sudden conversion is related to manifest anxiety.

CHARLES M. SPELLMAN, GLEN D. BASKETT, AND DONN BYRNE, "Manifest Anxiety as a Contributing Factor in Religious Conversion," *Journal of Consulting and Clinical Psychology* 36 (1971): 245–47.

Introduction and hypotheses. The researchers based their work on Salzman's distinction between a gradual conversion and a sudden or abrupt conversion, and on his view that sudden conversion is a pseudo-solution to the convert's problems. The hypothesis, based upon these views, is that sudden converts should score higher on anxiety than should gradual converts.

Research design and methods. The researchers wished to study three categories of people in a town where the people's profiles are more visible to clergy: (1) those who are nonreligious, (2) regular attenders or those who belong to a church and attend frequently, and (3) those who experience a sudden religious conversion. Two ministers in a predominantly Protestant farming community in central Texas were asked to suggest the names of twenty persons whom they could both agree might fit each category. These sixty persons were then asked to take a Taylor Manifest Anxiety Scale.

Data analysis and discussion. Results indicated that, although age, sex, and interactions can produce a significant contribution to the variance of the Manifest Anxiety Scale scores, sudden converts were significantly higher than the other two groups —the ordinary regular attenders and the nonreligious—combined, and that these latter did not differ significantly from one another. The results provide tentative support for the hypothesis that those people having had a sudden religious conversion experience will score higher on anxiety than those who have not had such an experience.

Further considerations of the Manifest Anxiety Scale are necessary, according to the researchers. Since the Manifest Anxiety Scale and social desirability are highly related, the results of the present study may be interpreted as evidence that individuals who undergo sudden conversion are low in social desirability response set. However, since it has recently been well argued that the meaning of social desirability is unclear, this explanation seems less theoretically relevant than that which identified anxiety as the underlying variable. It might also be argued that the converts' higher Manifest Anxiety Scale scores reflect a lower defensiveness as a result of their being freed of their guilt. But if this were so, gradual conversions would react in the same way, which they do not.

Since Salzman described the sudden conversion as sometimes related to the psychotic process, one might wish to interpret the data as suggesting that sudden converts are less well adjusted. Their mean Manifest Anxiety Scale score is similar to that of psychiatric outpatients and neuropsychiatric patients, and higher than that of college students.

BASIC CONCLUSION: *Sudden Converts Have Significantly Higher Manifest Anxiety Scale Scores.*

Sudden and dramatic conversions certainly do correlate with anxiety. But another researcher wondered if some other element in the personalities of converts was also important. Accordingly, he tried to relate dogmatism to anxiety and conversion and found that anxiety and dogmatism combine in different ways to account for a change in religious affiliation: High anxiety and low dogmatism accounted for the majority of religious changes, because high-anxiety, highly dogmatic types tended to stay with their beliefs (Rappaport, 1978). In recent years researchers have focused on converts to cults. As expected, those who joined cults showed greater hostility toward parents than others, but those who were firmly grounded in their faith exhibited less neuroses (Galanter et al., 1979). Psychiatric reflections on certain troubled and dramatic conversions of religious history connected them with brain dysfunction (Dewhearst and Beard, 1970).

Issues Associated with the Fulfillment Version of Personality

INTEGRATION OF PERSONALITY. Gordon Allport's view of the integrating aspects of religious belief and practice has been studied in a variety of ways, but individuals' abilities to handle themselves in society form the central issue. The study of the psychosocial competence of the individuals is thus a primary test for those who follow Allport's (and Maslow's and May's) interests and theories. There is a distinction made between "intrinsic," and "extrinsic" religiosity in much of the research on integration of faculties and prejudice, and it was originally made by Allport. By intrinsic religiosity is meant dedicated, prayerful, self-giving, and by extrinsic religiosity is meant loyal, exterior membership, more of a patriotic, "stand-up-and-be-counted" kind of religion. One is loyally religious because of family background, level of society, political expedience, and so on. This is the most important single distinction in all of the research based on fulfillment theory.

KENNETH I. PARGAMENT, ROBERT E. STEELE, AND FORREST B. TYLER, "Religious Participation, Religious Motivation, and Individual Psychosocial Competence," *Journal for the Scientific Study of Religion* 18 (1979): 412–19.

Introduction and hypotheses. There is a current understanding of competent functioning based on three individual attributes: a favorable set of attitudes toward oneself (self-attitudes), a favorable set of attitudes toward others (world attitudes), and a set of problem-solving skills (coping skills). This study explores the relationships between that conception of individual effective functioning and two parameters of religion. Religious participation and religious motivation were selected for study by the researchers because of their centrality to a multidimensional definition of religion and their relevance to psychosocial wellbeing.

The very broad hypothesis was that parameters of religion would have significant implications for the effective psychosocial functioning of the individual, as they do for other dimensions of human behavior.

Research design and methods. The 123 participants represented four mainline Protestant churches, four conservative Jewish synagogues, and four Roman Catholic churches. They were mainly white, evenly divided into male and female, and equally represented three levels of society. Religious participation and motivation were measured by frequency of church attendance and Hoge's Intrinsic Religious Motivation Scale. Individual psychosocial competence was assessed by a variety of questions. Control, self-criticism and efficacy scales were used to measure the *self-attitudes* dimension. *World attitudes* were assessed by a trust scale; *coping skills* were measured by a behavioral attitudes of psychosocial competence scale. The researchers visited each congregation and administered questionnaires to those taking part in the study.

Data analysis and discussion. First, frequent attenders are distinguished from infrequent attenders by their greater sense of control by God, satisfaction with this control, and satisfaction with their congregation, but also by a lower sense of personal control, control by chance, self-criticism, and efficacy. Second, high-intrinsic members (those who score high on intrinsic religiosity according to Allport's classification) manifest a more favorable set of psychosocial competence characteristics than do low-intrinsic members, indicating a greater sense of personal control, greater satisfaction with the congregation, a more active set of coping skills, somewhat greater efficacy, and a lower sense of control by powerful others and chance. Third, only a marginally significant overall difference is found in individual psychosocial competence attributes as a function of the interaction between religious participation and religious motivation. Fourth, only nonsignificant overall differences in members' competence attributes are found as a function of the interaction between religious identification and religious participation, and between religious identification and religious motivation.

But an analysis of psychosocial competence as a function of the interaction between religious participation and religious motivation yields results that cause the authors to modify the general conclusion that less intrinsically motivated church/synagogue members reflect a less favorable set of psychosocial competence characteristics than more intrinsically motivated members. Of the less intrinsically motivated members, only those who participate in their congregations' activities frequently manifest less favorable competence attributes. This means that consistency of religious values and behaviors may be as important for the wellbeing of the individual as the nature of those values and behaviors.

Differences in effective functioning were not found to result from interactions between religious identification and religious participation, and between religious identification and religious motivation. This suggests that variations in participation and motivation have similar psychosocial meaning for Protestants, Jews, and Catholics.

BASIC CONCLUSION: *Less Psychosocial Competence Is Shown by Extrinsic Believers Who Are Very Active Church Members.*

Those who genuinely practice religion exhibit superior psychosocial competence, but we cannot be sure why. One researcher found that participation in secular organizations is more highly correlated with psychosocial integration than religious practice in itself, but the relationship between secular participation and integration is doubled in the case of strong belief and frequent practice (Schweiker, 1969). Recent research of social psychologists indicates that intrinsic religious orientation leads to freedom from existential concerns and to a feeling of strength based on a perceived good relationship with God; at the same time it involves bondage to the beliefs that sustain these feelings (Batson and Ventis, 1982).

Distinctions other than the intrinsic–extrinsic are made in the research. Authoritarianism correlates with dogmatism and concern for religiosity, while humanitarianism correlates with a religious value orientation (Fehr and Heintzelman, 1977). Types of religiosity are correlated with membership in different groups. In the study of fundamentalist religious participation it was found that consistency in participation and ritual was important for personality balance; people within a system can be greatly helped with psychological problems that take place within the system. Such groups pay less attention to secular life except in those areas of politics and social reforms that have bearing on specialized church doctrine (Ness and Wintrob, 1980).

Research has been done on the integrating influences of religion on youth, middle age, and old age. In youth identity achievers are religious because they have values, but not so much because they are orthodox. They look back on problems of autonomy and initiative relative to religious development (St. Clair and Day, 1979). For the middle-aged, religiosity correlated with life satisfaction in general but seemed to have neither a positive nor a negative effect on sexual and marital satisfaction (Wallin and Clark, 1964). Religious optimism does seem to decrease with age, however, which says nothing about other religious emotions such as resignation (Query and Steines, 1974). Relative to fear of death, some researchers found that neither the prospect of death nor serious illness induced belief in the afterlife. It did not intensify religious belief and practice, but it did cause those who already believed to believe yet more. Nor did belief in an afterlife relieve the pain and tension caused by fear of death, though it did seem to help alleviate painful memories (Osarchuk and Tatz, 1973).

Bringing these different research reports together, we see that religious beliefs and behaviors help to integrate and give purpose to disparate elements of life, generally facilitating people's relationships with surrounding society.

PREJUDICE. When religion does *not* help people to integrate their lives, it can serve as a means of communicating their worst qualities. Perhaps we could say that it serves as an offensive or defensive weapon. The connection between religiosity and prejudice has consistently attracted attention because of the past violence because of religious disagreements and the failure of religious groups to help people in pain. When individuals or groups react negatively to those around them, we say that prejudice—"prejudging"—is involved. Allport discovered that church attendance was positively related to prejudice. Following up on this phenomenon, he noted that the deeply committed were less prejudiced than those who used religion for personal ends or those for whom it was an element of their past family history or an element of their present socioeconomic life-style.

Allport's final say on the issue can be seen in this 1967 attempt to discern the basic religious attitude that related most closely to prejudice.

GORDON W. ALLPORT AND J. MICHAEL ROSS, "Personal Religious Orientation and Prejudice," *Journal of Personality and Social Psychology* 5 (1967): 432–43.

Introduction and hypotheses. Allport and Ross first summarize the results of a significant series of experiments, the first of which was made by Allport in 1946:

1. Church attenders are more prejudiced than non-attenders.

2. But a significant minority are less prejudiced.

3. It is the casual, irregular fringe members who are high in prejudice; their religious motivation is of the extrinsic order. It is the constant, devout, internalized members who are low in prejudice; their religious motivation is of the intrinsic order.

Now in this study the finding is that a certain cognitive style permeates the thinking of many people in such a way that they are indiscriminately pro-religious and, at the same time, highly prejudiced.

The intrinsic–extrinsic distinction is explained again, even though Allport had developed it in articles in '59 and '66. *Extrinsic orientation:* Persons with this orientation are disposed to use religion for their own ends. Such persons may find religion useful in a variety of ways—to provide security and solace, sociability and distraction, status and self-justification. The embraced creed is lightly held or else selectively shaped to fit more primary needs. *Intrinsic orientation:* Having embraced a creed, an individual endeavors to internalize it and follow it fully. It is in this sense that he or she lives religion. In the 1950s and 1960s a number of tests confirmed and discovered ramifications of all of this.

In 1964 J. R. Feagin developed a scale that measured both intrinsic and extrinsic religion. In his study of Southern Baptists, Feagin reached four conclusions:

1. Intrinsic and extrinsic did not fall on a unidimensional scale but represented two independent dimensions.

2. Only the extrinsic orientation was related to intolerance toward Negroes.

3. Orthodoxy as such was not related to extrinsic or intrinsic orientation.

4. Greater orthodoxy (Fundamentalism of belief) did, however, relate positively to prejudice.

Allport and Ross, relying on the results of earlier work, assume that inner experience of religion (what it means to the individual) is an important causal factor in developing a tolerant or a prejudiced outlook on life.

Research design and methods. Indirect measures of prejudice were developed, because direct measures were too sensitive, and a religious orientation scale was used. Sample consisted of 309 cases: 94 Roman Catholics, 55 Lutherans, 44 Nazarenes, 53 Presbyterians, 35 Methodists, and 28 Baptists.

Data analysis and discussion. Examination of the data reveals that some subjects are consistently intrinsic, having a strong tendency to endorse intrinsically worded items and to reject the extrinsically worded ones. Correspondingly, others are consistently extrinsic. They persist in endorsing any or all items that to them seem favorable to religion in any sense. No new criteria were developed to categorize religious types. Real consistency in answering was required before anyone could be considered intrinsic or extrinsic.

It was found that (1) the extrinsic type is more prejudiced than the intrinsic type for both direct and indirect measures, and (2) the indiscriminate type of religious orientation is more prejudiced than either of the two consistent types. The relationship between the indiscriminately pro-religious orientation and prejudice receives support when we compare subjects who are moderately discriminate with those who are extremely indiscriminate. It should be noted that the indiscriminate type had significantly less education than the intrinsic cases and somewhat less than the extrinsic. Low education does little to correct indiscriminate thinking, and the resulting mental confusion may have its own particular effects on religious and ethnic attitudes.

The argument about the tie between intrinsic orientation and tolerance, extrinsic orientation and prejudice holds that a person with an extrinsic religious orientation is using religion to provide security, comfort, status, or social support for herself or himself. Religion is not a value in its own right, because it serves other needs and is a purely utilitarian formation! Now prejudice, too, is a "useful" formation; it, too, provides security, comfort, status, and social support. A life that is dependent on the supports of extrinsic religion is likely to be dependent on the supports of prejudice, hence the positive correlations between the extrinsic orientation and intolerance. Contrariwise, the intrinsic religious orientation is not instrumental in character. It is not a mode of conformity, not a crutch, not a tranquilizer, not a bid for status. All needs are subordinated to an overarching religious commitment. In internalizing the total creed of his religion, the individual necessarily internalizes its values of humility, compassion, and love of neighbor. In such a life there is no place for rejection, contempt, or condescension toward one's fellow.

The researchers sought some functional tie between prejudice and the indiscriminately pro-religious orientation. The common factor seems to be certain cognitive style. Technically it might be called "undifferentiated thinking" or "excessive category width." In responding to religious items, the indiscriminate individual takes a superficial "hit and run" approach. The mental set seems to be, "All religion is good." And the question is, Why should such a disposition, whatever its source, be so strongly related to prejudice, in such a way that the more undifferentiated one is, the more prejudiced one is? Allport and Ross answer that prejudice is a matter of stereotyped overgeneralization, a failure to distinguish members of a minority group as individuals. It goes without saying that if categories are overwide, the accompanying feeling tone will be undifferentiated: Religion as a whole is good; a minority group as a whole is bad. It seems probable that people with undifferentiated styles of thinking (and feeling) are not entirely secure in a world that for the most part demands clear distinctions. The resulting diffuse anxiety may well dispose them to grab onto religion and to distrust strange ethnic groups.

The general conclusion is that prejudice, like tolerance, is often embedded in personality structure and is reflected in a consistent cognitive style. Both states of mind are enmeshed with the individual's religious orientation.

BASIC CONCLUSION: *Those Who Are Indiscriminately Pro-Religious Are the Most Prejudiced.*

Now that refined distrinctions have been made in the concept of religiosity, researchers are interested in refining the concept of prejudice so that elements of emotion, cognition, motivation, and general distaste may be examined. Results of prejudice are examined: People will assume that those who are less attractive to them are members of a disliked group (Himmelfarb and Fishbein, 1971), though some researchers found that students were more antagonistic to people of similar background who had different attitudes than to people of different backgrounds who had similar attitudes (Yabrudi and Diab, 1978).

Anti-Semitism and antiblack prejudice have been important research topics because of the horrendous results of these prejudices in Europe and America. One researcher found that Christian religious beliefs did not directly cause anti-Semitism, but socioeconomic status and social psychological variables were more important (Middleton, 1973). Since some researchers have found that anti-Semitism does not correlate with aggression (Rule, Haley, and McCormick, 1971), the task of tracking the causes of this and other prejudices remains vital. The research on racial prejudice in America has helped to clarify some further problems of the intrinsic–extrinsic distinction. Status concern and dogmatism have emerged as important correlates of prejudice (Bohra, 1979). The great importance of the dogmatism factor can be seen in a report comparing Unitarians with Southern Baptists: Members of the former group tend to be extrinsic and nondogmatic, and members of the latter, intrinsic and dogmatic. But the results indicated that the Unitarians are less prejudiced. Liberalism and permissiveness seem to count more than anything else (Strickland and Weddell, 1972).

Developmental Psychology

FAITH AND COGNITIVE DEVELOPMENT. In 1965 Ronald Goldman produced a study that purported to explore religious cognitive development relative to general cognitive development. He examined Piaget's three basic stages of cognitive development with a view to improving religious education. Goldman (1965) suggested that biblical stories be presented on such a graduated scale that the child would be properly prepared to understand them as symbols and avoid the pitfalls of Fundamentalism. But a few years ago another study was made of Goldman's application of Piaget to religious education. The results were against Goldman's earlier conclusions on the development of "higher," formal operational thought.

> DEAN R. HOGE AND GREGORY H. PETRILLO, "Development of Religious Thinking in Adolescence: A test of Goldman's Theories," *Journal for the Scientific Study of Religion* 17 (1978): 139–54.

Introduction and hypotheses. First, Hoge and Petrillo review Goldman's general achievements. In a number of his studies Goldman had adopted the Piagetian outline of three levels of thought (preoperational, concrete operational, and formal operational; see Chapter 5) and Piagetian interview methods. He found great variation in levels and types of religious thinking at any chronological age, and he carefully delineated factors accelerating or impeding the development of religious thinking. Goldman distinguished levels of cognitive capacity from levels of customary thinking in particular subject areas. He agreed with another researcher's conclusion that the entire religious development of the child has a much slower tempo than the development of any other field of his experience, he discussed nine possible causal factors.

Goldman was interested in the effects of a gap between the level of religious thinking and the level of thinking in particular subject areas. He theorized that a sizable gap would set the stage for a rejection, sooner or later, of religion as childish and simpleminded. He found that some adolescents who had rejected religion expressed a feeling of betrayal at having been left to continue literal and childish beliefs for so long. In short, the greater the gap between overall capacity for formal operational thinking and concrete or Fundamentalist religious teachings, the more Goldman expected a major rejection of those religious teachings. The present study reports on research assessing the determinants of levels of religious thinking and also the theory that a gap will produce rejection of religious training.

Research design and methods. In the spring of 1976 a representative sample of suburban Roman Catholic, Southern Baptist, and United Methodist churches were asked for a total list of tenth-graders who were sons and daughters of church members. Complete information was obtained from 152 Catholics, 151 Baptists, and 148 Methodists. First, two scores were used from the Thinking About the Bible test. Second, a question was asked about the difference between religious knowledge and other knowledge. Third, a Disapproval of Organized Religion Index was administered. Fourth and fifth were two items to be selected from a list by all respondents who said they could not relate to their present church.

Other tests included the Burney Logical Reasoning test and measures of those eight other variables that Goldman had considered likely to influence the level of religious thinking: (1) strongly held attitudes and beliefs, (2) religious interest or motivation, (3) attitudes toward peers, (4) attendance at church or sunday school, (5) type of religious education, (6) attitude of parents toward religion, (7) Bible reading and prayer habits, and (8) familiarity with religious material.

Data analysis and discussion. First, regarding determinants of religious thinking (whether it will be concrete or abstract), among Catholic youth amount of religious instruction and exposure to biblical materials have clear abstracting influences. Especially for those in private and religious schools, religious education appears to have had a strong effect. For Baptists religious education had the opposite effect: Doctrinal factors, peer influences, and devotional commitments are all associated with more concrete religious thinking, and they represent an influence that is so strong that cognitive capacity in general has no relationship with level of religious thinking. Among the Methodists the picture is less clear. Strongly held doctrinal beliefs are moderately associated with concrete thinking, but familiarity with biblical materials is moderately associated with abstract thinking.

Second, regarding consequences of religious thinking, while Goldman hypothesized that the larger the gap between religious and other kinds of learning, the more rejection of religion, the opposite was the case. For Baptists and Methodists, all correlations —smaller gaps between religious thinking and overall cognitive capacity—are associated with more rejection of doctrine and the church. The pattern is the same for public school Catholics, but not the same for private school Catholics whose education apparently has both encouraged more abstract religious thinking and also reduced the amount of criticism of the church.

Hoge and Petrillo conclude, then, that Goldman's theory about the gap between the level of religious thinking and other thinking is difficult to verify, and future researchers should use a variety of methods. Most evidence suggests that Goldman's view is wrong: More abstract religious thinking among these high school students is associated with more, not less religious rejection. Also, the case of the private school Catholics emphasizes that religious education of one type or another has considerable impact, and the Goldman hypothesis must be recast in more specific terms stating expected relationships *within* one or another system of religious education.

BASIC CONCLUSION: *Sophisticated Religious Cognitive Abilities Are More Likely to Be Associated with Rejection of Religion.*

Other aspects of Piaget's research help to explain the origins of religious thought in the child and the stages of religious development (Elkind, 1964, 1970). Researchers have explored the fit between cognitive need capacities and the major elements of institutional religion, that is, the ways in which children's religious thinking has reflected concrete rather than formal modes of intellectual operation. Sometimes the efforts have been designed to explore some aspect of Piaget's own work on religion, such as the effect of different types of religious upbringing on children's responses to questions involving physical causality or the effect of different types of family church membership on the child's church membership identity.

MORALITY AND COGNITIVE DEVELOPMENT. Further research on Piaget's morality studies show that children's moral judgments do not exist in a social or cultural vacuum; however spontaneous these judgments may be in their origins, they are very much subject to direct and indirect social influence, both in their rate of development and in the shape they take in adulthood. The available research shows plainly that the child's moral thought as it unfolds in Piagetian interviews is not all of a piece but more of a patchwork of diverse parts. The findings also suggest that while Piaget's analysis of the cognitive basis of moral judgment is well founded, his speculations about its affective side are on shaky ground (Lickona, 1979). Lawrence Kohlberg points out the problems in Piaget's much earlier research and has developed a more refined series of schemata. Kohlberg's served as the basis for the following, more specialized research.

HERBERT D. SALTZSTEIN AND SHARON OSGOOD. "The Development of Children's Reasoning About Group Interdependence and Obligation," *Journal of Psychology* 90 (1975): 147–55.

Introduction and hypotheses. Stages were designed to parallel Kohlberg's stages of moral reasoning and involved different levels of understanding of an individual's obligation to conform and his right to expect others to conform in an interdependent group. In this research the focus was on the development of obligation to groups.

Piaget and others have demonstrated that young children have great difficulty in taking the physical or social perspective of others. Piaget and Kohlberg, following G. H. Mead, have hypothesized that decentering or taking the perspectives of others is the central process by which moral reasoning develops. Recent research has helped confirm the hypothesis. This research suggests that the (moral) obligation to conform because of group interdependence might be weak or nonexistent in younger and morally immature children but might grow along with their evolving capacity to decenter and reason morally.

Research was designed to explore the question further by interviewing children about obligation to groups in interdependent situations when conformity would be in the interests of the group. The extent to which interdependence may serve as a moral justification for conformity to the group at different stages of development was of primary interest. The general hypothesis was that children's reasoning about the obligations arising from group interdependence develops in stages that parallel the stages of moral reasoning.

Research design and methods. The subjects were 40 children, 22 boys and 18 girls, from grades one, three, five, and eight in a socioeconomically diverse suburban school system. The subjects ranged in IQ from 93 to 144. IQ, parent education, and father's occupation were all obtained from school records after all the interviews had been completed and analyzed. Each child was individually interviewed for about thirty to forty-five minutes. The interviews were transcribed and coded without knowledge of the child's age. In the first part of the interview the child was shown a simple unassembled construction model (e.g. a battleship) and asked to imagine that he or she was working on a team with two friends of the same sex to complete the model. Initial questions were designed to see whether the subject literally understood the meaning of team competition (that is, the interdependent nature of the goal). The next series of questions was concerned with the best way to divide up the subtasks, which were described as gluing, putting the component pieces together, and painting the assembled model.

The coding categories were developed from extensive pretesting of a separate sample of about sixty children in another school and were inspired by, though not identical with, Kohlberg's first four moral reasoning stages. The following levels of understanding were used to code interviews for the four stages:

Stage 1. Influence was based on coercion by self over others or by others over self. ("It wouldn't be fair to ask him because he'd get madder and madder.")

Stage 2. There was no obligation to others and no legitimate expectations proceeding from other. ("It depends on how I felt—like if I didn't want to do it, I wouldn't do it.")

Stage 3. Obligation to the group was understood as being nice, being sympathetic, having good intentions, and maintaining good personal relationships for their own sake. ("You're not going to help the team if you're going to quit . . . we're all friends and like each other a lot and want to work together.")

Stage 4. Obligation to the group as a group was recognized and was based on the fact of interdependence and/or prior commitment to the group. ("They depend on me and now they're left with no one, so its only fair for me to continue.")

Data analysis and discussion. The data generally demonstrated that children's reasoning about conformity and obligation to interdependent groups develops in a way that seems to parallel their reasoning about strictly moral situations. Children's stage score did not relate significantly to IQ but was associated with father's occupation. Parental education (years in school, divided between at least some college for both parents, as against no college) and stage score were also positively correlated.

Stages of development involve a series of differentiations and integrations. In the development of social thought under investigation, the critical elements seem to be the concepts of obligation to others and expectations of others. The following is intended as a first approximation of a description of the developmental sequence. At first, obligation and expectation are not differentiated from coercion and thus have no distinctly social or moral character. As the child's thought moves to stage 2, obligation and expectation become differentiated but integrated, so that obligation is to oneself and expectation is factual but not legitimate. For example, "They can expect me to do it, but I don't have to if I don't want to". At stage 3, obligation to others and expectations from others begin to be coordinated but in an asymmetrical way. Expectation implies obligation, but obligations does not imply expectation. For example, "The others want you to do it, and you should do it because it's the nice thing, but they have no right to ask you to do it." At stage 4, obligation and expectation are fully coordinated and imply one another. For example, "They have a right to ask you to continue, and you should ... whether you like them or not."

The research confirms Kohlberg's theory of moral stages by inquiring into a specialized feature of socio-moral development.

BASIC CONCLUSION: *The Development of Reasoning About Socially Interdependent Obligations Parallels Moral Development.*

In the foregoing research, and in similar research, the study of religious belief and behavior is so much the study of development in the psychosocial context of Judeo-Christian society that it seems risky to make the results a basis for any universal theory of moral development. It is far easier to generalize across cultures about cognitive development. And there is, of course, the much broader issue of whether or not training is the primary cause of maturation: Just how important is training to children's moral development?

Research on Eriksonian concepts is seldom specifically religious. Take the examples of two early efforts to see if identity and intimacy with their religious concomitants develop across time in ways described by Erikson. One researcher was able to conclude that identity diffusion is a negative measure of personality development and of balanced religious ideology (Bronson, 1959). Another concluded that there are degrees of maturity in the development of intimacy and that isolation could be associated with specific defense mechanisms (Yufit, 1969). Some of Erikson's more recent ideas, however, have been applied to religion. (Capps, 1979b; Driedger, 1982.)

Social Psychology

The exploration of attitudes has been at the center of much of the religious research in social psychology. Reactions to people and situations provide obvious target data for the social psychologist. We have seen that research on attitudes is often collected under headings suggestive of religious phenomena other than attitudes. The term "dimensions" has come to be an important term, and the question then becomes whether religion is unidimensional or multidimensional (Dittes, 1969). Does it involve one basic attitude or a variety of attitudes? The question is discussed in the following research.

Morton B. King and Richard A. Hunt. "Measuring the Religious Variable: Replication," *Journal for the Scientific Study of Religion* 11 (1972): 24–51.

Introduction and hypotheses. Some sociologists have directed attention to the multidimensional aspects of religious belief, commitment, and practice. Researchers, however, have not developed (1) an empirical test of the multidimensional hypothesis itself, and (2) a systematic empirical search for usable dimensions using correlational techniques. King and Hunt then developed a questionnaire containing 132 items. Of these, 91 related to religious belief, knowledge, and practice; 27 to cognitive style variables; and 14 to a variety of personal information ranging from conditions of first joining the church (conversion, confirmation training, and so on) to such demographic data as age, sex, education, and income.

Research design and methods. Subjects were members of four Protestant denominations in the Dallas–Fort Worth metropolitan area. As in an earlier survey, inner-city and suburban congregations were purposively selected to include different socioeconomic levels and varied theological and liturgical styles. A systematic sample was drawn in each congregation of all members sixteen and over who were local residents.

Ten different scales were used in order to assess the responses. The Appendix lists the items for the ten religious scales believed to be of greatest potential interest to social scientists and church officials. Each is now discussed briefly in relation to the work of Allport, Glock, Lenski, and others, and the earlier work of King and Hunt.

The first scales shown are similar to dimensions discussed by Glock and Lenski:

1. *Creedal Assent* is similar to Glock's "ideological" and Lenski's "doctrinal orthodoxy." One difference is that the King–Hunt items attempted to avoid a literal-Fundamentalist bias. They were worded to encourage assent from a broad spectrum of believing Christians.

2. *Devotionalism* bears some similarity to Glock's definition of "experiential" but is most like Lenski's "devotionalism." The items deal with personal prayer, closeness to God, and communication with God.

3. There are three *Congregational Involvement* scales: *Church Attendance, Organizational Activity,* and *Financial Support.*

4. *Religious Knowledge* provides a way of measuring Glock's "intellectual" dimension.

The following scales are different in two ways. First, three of them are "composite" scales, containing one or more items present in one or more other scales. Second, they measure orientations to religion, at least in its institutionalized congregational form, rather than dimensions of religious behavior:

5. *Orientation.* A *Growth and Striving* scale appears to measure the opposite of an "I've-got-it-made" attitude. Rather, the high scorer expresses dissatisfaction with his current religious state and a feeling of need to learn, change, and grow. The *Extrinsic* scale measures an instrumental, selfish attitude toward religion.

6. The *Salience* scales are concerned with the importance of religion for *Behavior* and *Cognition.*

Interpretation and discussion. The methods enabled multiple dimensions of religious belief and practice to be identified by reasonably homogeneous scales. The scales, when correlated with each other and with measures of cognitive style variables, exhibited enough explanatory power to indicate potential usefulness.

The study has a number of limitations to be considered in evaluating its findings and conclusions. The authors point out a number of them. The study is culture-bound. It emphasizes, and is largely confined to, congregationally related aspects of institutional, mainline Protestant Christianity. The subjects are not a "sample" of any population. The end product is not a description of the four denominations but a set of scales to be tested on other populations. Also, questionnaire data of the kind used present problems of reliability and validity. Correlation methods are not inductive statistics. They do not usually test hypotheses. Decisions regarding the "existence" of dimensions and the utility of scales are personal judgments of the researchers. Such judgments are influenced by subjective considerations, by knowledge of the data and subjects, and by results of the quantitative analysis. The mathematical procedures used only put the data in forms that instruct the human judgments and partially objectify them.

Therefore, King and Hunt offer for use ten scales measuring selected aspects of religious behavior. The scales are not finished products with established reliability, validity, and norms for different populations. They are only ready for testing in use on a variety of populations and in questionnaires with other items. The proof of their value will be in repeated cautious use.

ITEMS FOR TEN RELIGIOUS SCALES

I. Creedal Assent

> 1. I believe that the world of God is revealed in the Scriptures.
> 2. I believe in God as a Heavenly Father who watches over me and to whom I am accountable.
> 3. I believe that God revealed himself to man in Jesus Christ.
> 4. I believe that Christ is a living reality.
> 5. I believe in eternal life.
> 6. I believe in salvation as release from sin and freedom for new life with God.
> 7. I believe honestly and wholeheartedly in the doctrines and teaching of the Church.

II. Devotionalism

> 1. How often do you pray privately in places other than at Church?
> 2. How often do you ask God to forgive your sin?
> 3. Private prayer is one of the most important and satisfying aspects of my religious experience.
> 4. When you have decisions to make in your everyday life, how often do you try to find out what God wants you to do?
> 5. I frequently feel very close to God in prayer, during public worship, or at important moments in my daily life.

III. Congregational Involvement

> A. Church Attendance
>
> > 1. How often have you taken Holy Communion (the Lord's Supper, the Eucharist) during the past year?
> > 2. During the last year, how many Sundays per month on the average have you gone to a worship service) (None—Three or more)
> > 3. If not prevented by unavoidable circumstances, I attend Church: (More than once a week—Less than once a month)
>
> B. Organizational Activity
>
> > 1. How would you rate your activity in this congregation? (Very active—Inactive)
> > 2. How often do you spend evenings in church meetings or in church work?
> > 3. I enjoy working in the activities of the Church.

4. Church activities (meeting, committee work, etc.) are a major source of satisfaction in my life.

5. I keep pretty well informed about my congregation and have some influence on its decisions.

6. List the church offices, committees, or jobs of any kind in which you served during the past 12 months.

C. Financial Support

1. Last year, approximately what percent of your income was contributed to the Church? (Answer in terms of your individual income or that of your family, whichever is appropriate.) (1% or less—10% or more)

2. I make financial contributions to church: (In regular, planned amounts—seldom or never)

3. During the last year, what was the average monthly contribution of your family to your local congregation? (Under $5—$50 and up)

4. In proportion to your income, do you consider that your contributions to the church are? (Generous—Small)

5. During the last year, how often have you made contributions to the church in addition to general budget and Sunday School? (Regularly—Never)

IV. Religious Knowledge

1. Which of the following were Old Testament prophets? (Deuteronomy; Ecclesiastes; Elijah; Isaiah; Jeremiah; Leviticus)

2. Which of the following books are included in the Four Gospels? (James; John; Mark; Matthew; Peter; Thomas)

3. Which of the following were among the Twelve Disciples of Christ? (Daniel; John; Judas; Paul; Peter; Samuel)

4. Which of the following acts were performed by Jesus Christ during His early ministry? (Resisting the temptations of Satan; Healing ten lepers; Leading His people against the priests of Baal; Parting the waters to cross the Red Sea; Overcoming Goliath; Turning water into wine)

5. Which of the following men were leaders of the Protestant Reformation? (Aquinas; Augustine; Calvin; Cranmer; Hegel; Luther)

6. Which of the following principles are supported by most Protestant denominations? (Bible as the Word of God; Separation of Church and State; Power of clergy to forgive sins; Final authority of the Church; Justification by faith; Justification by good works)

7. Which of the following books are in the Old Testament? (Acts; Amos; Gelatians; Hebrews; Hosea; Psalms)

8. Which of the following denominations in the United States have bishops? (Disciples; Episcopal; Lutheran; Methodist; Presbyterian; Roman Catholic)

V. Orientation to Religion

A. Growth and Striving

1. How often do you read literature about your faith (or church)? (Frequently—Never)
2. How often do you read the Bible?
3. I try hard to grow in understanding of what it means to live as a child of God.
4. When you have decisions to make in your everyday life, how often do you try to find out what God wants you to do?
5. The amount of time I spend trying to grow in understanding of my faith is: (Very much—Little or none)
6. I try hard to carry my religion over into all my other dealings in life.

B. Extrinsic

1. It is part of one's patriotic duty to worship in the church of his choice.
2. The church is most important as a place to formulate good social relationships.
3. The purpose of prayer is to secure a happy and peaceful life.
4. Church membership has helped me to meet the right kind of people.
5. What religion offers me most is comfort when sorrows and misfortune strike.
6. One reason for my being a church member is that such membership helps to establish a person in the community.
7. Religion helps to keep my life balanced and steady in exactly the same way as my citizenship, friendships, and other memberships do.

VI. Salience

A. Behavior

1. How often in the last year have you shared with another church member the problems and joys of trying to live a life of faith in God?
2. How often have you personally tried to convert someone to faith in God?
3. How often do you talk about religion with your friends, neighbors, or fellow workers?
4. When faced by decisions regarding social problems, how often do you seek guidance from statements and publications provided by the Church?

    5. How often do you read the Bible?

    6. How often do you talk with the pastor (or some other official) about some part of the worship service: for example, their sermon, scripture, choice of hymns, etc.?

    7. During the last year, how often have you visited someone in need, besides your own relatives?

B. Cognition

    1. My religious beliefs are what really live behind your whole approach to life.

    2. I try hard to grow in understanding of what it means to live as a child of God.

    3. Religion is especially important to me because it answers many questions about the meaning of life.

    4. I try hard to carry my religion over into all my other dealing in life.

    5. I frequently feel very close to God in prayer, during public worship, or at important moments in my daily life.

BASIC CONCLUSION: *Multiple Dimensions of Religious Belief and Practice Can Be Identified by Reasonably Homogeneous Scales.*

Evaluating the Reports

In spite of, and maybe because of, the obvious attempts to be precise, empirical psychology leaves us with a number of problems that will take many years to resolve if they are resolvable at all (Warren, 1977). First, very little of the research on religion is true experimental study. The ethics of the situation is such that researchers tend most often toward correlational studies of attitudes. Second, the nature of the samples taken is problematic: Use of volunteers (usually necessary in religious research) has always been a doubtful procedure, and so has the use of samplings of groups that change over the decades (students today are radically different from those of ten years ago, for example). Third, there is always the problem of controls: Since religion involves such diffuse experiences with so many interrelated variables, experimenters often seem to assume that any extraneous variables will be controlled by randomization. Fourth, only recently have experimental designs become sophisticated, allowing for the study of three, four, or more independent variables at once. Fifth, there is always the tendency to overgeneralize findings or to encourage readers to do so. Within the last few years, however, much of the research has tried to take these problems into full consideration.

A debate has been going on about the possibility of true experiments in the psychology of religion (Batson, 1977, 1979; Yeatts and Asher, 1979). Experimental research is fully controlled research whereby the psychologist is able to determine that a change in one variable really causes a change in another. In a true experiment the researchers must be able to change the level of one variable themselves and able to compare the group of experimental subjects with another comparable group of people who are not put through the experiment (the control group). They must be able to assign subjects at random to the experimental and control groups, selecting them from one common pool of participants, and must ensure that the groups are as equivalent as possible so that results will not be due to some third variable. As you can see, almost none of the research summarized in this chapter has been so controlled as to be an experiment.

Correlational studies are considerably different. Researchers examine naturally occurring change in one variable (changes not caused by the researcher) and measure the associated changes in a second variable. For example, one can examine the association of churchgoing with prejudice without manipulating the churchgoing at all.

The only solution offered thus far has been the use of the quasi-experiment.

Quasi-experimental designs stand halfway between the true experiment and the correlational study. In the quasi-experiment the psychologist can change the independent variable but cannot assign subjects randomly to groups.

A psychologist who has taken the lead in promoting quasi-experiments has prepared some possibly valuable designs for such research (Batson, 1977). A time-series design could be used to examine the relationship between religious experiences and either psychological antecedents or behavioral consequences. In such studies one can go beyond associational to fairly confident causal inferences. Another possible design is the pretest–posttest nonequivalent comparison group design. A study was conducted in which junior high school females on a church retreat divided themselves into two groups, believers in Jesus as Son of

God and nonbelievers. After an initial questionnaire measuring belief, everyone read a contrived news story supposedly proving Christianity to be hoax. While not all participants believed the article, about one-third indicated they did. Consistent with Festinger's (1957) theory of cognitive dissonance (but not with logic), those believers who indicated they accepted the article as true actually expressed more intense religious belief on a subsequent questionnaire. An increase was not observed for other groups. Yet another possible research design is a mixture of associational and experimental designs. With another researcher Batson tested the "Good Samaritan" response of a number of seminary students. They had some of the seminarians read the parable of the Good Samaritan and then sent them across the way to another building past a contrived dramatic setup: a somewhat sinister-looking stranger coughing and groaning in the doorway in a cold, windy alley. They manipulated two experimental variables, whether the subject passed through the alley in a hurry and whether he had just read the parable. With this type of research design hypotheses concerning the interaction of religious orientation with other psychological variables can be tested (Darley and Batson, 1973).

Given the difficulties of true experiments on people's personal religious experience—except in the area of education (Yeatts and Asher, 1977)—the quasi-experiment may be the goal for the time being. Perhaps we should simply get on with our empirical psychology, satisfied when we can set up a hypothesis and try it out. A noted British philosopher says, "One bright idea which is testable is worth a whole book of advice on how to make psychology scientific" (Peters, 1965, p. 762).

Therapeutic Approaches to Religious Problems

WHAT DO WE DO if someone has bizarre fantasies about Christ's crucifixion or has a hidden hatred of God that he is unwilling to admit? How about a more typical case of a middle-aged woman who cannot stabilize herself in life, or how about anyone who has extreme hatred for people of another race or religion—what do we do there? Youngsters who throw fits or are morose—might there be some religious reason? If there are group problems that seem to result from religious causes, is there any appropriate group therapy to help resolve them?

Today we can look at an enormous repertoire of therapy and guidance approaches and attempt to design what is appropriate for the lives of people. Descriptions and examples of therapy presented here coordinate well with earlier chapters, as you will see from the presentation of the "mad at God" syndrome, Seward Hiltner's Mrs. Merz, the conditioning of a prejudiced person, the developmental problems of Erikson's Sam, and the challenge of religious problems for family therapy. We hold that each of these therapies is appropriate for the particular religious problems presented. This is an eclectic approach, obviously, but it predominates in the therapy world today.

In a recent book on the eclectic approach to psychotherapy, a leading surveyer says:

> It can be noted that whereas the best known and most popular orientations such as psychoanalysis and its derivatives and behavior therapy have had a marked influence on developments within the field, it appears that a majority of practitioners do not follow any particular school exclusively, or limit themselves to the procedures of just one theoretical orientation. For example, in a recent survey of 855 clinical psychologists over half of them indicated that they were eclectics. Thus, while much of the published work and training in psychotherapy appears to be very much "school" oriented, the devoted adherents of these schools constitute less than a majority of those engaging in psychotherapy. [Garfield, 1980, p. 3]

Even when there is a deliberate choice of an orthodox psychotherapy, the reasons for choosing are usually something other than the efficacy of the approach in question. Many psychotherapists originally became Freudians, Skinnerians, and so on for reasons more personal then scientific. In the long run, too, individual orthodox therapists use varieties of other approaches in their work.

Based on job description rather than theoretical orientation, mental health practitioners can be divided up into several groups, although an individual may be a member of more than one group. Often it is a matter of emphasis whether someone calls himself or herself therapist, a clinical psychologist, or a counselor. The therapist concentrates almost exclusively on working with specific, often profound mental problems; the clinical psychologist also works directly with patients or clients but is involved in research also. Those who call themselves counselors concentrate on those who cannot "find themselves" or find a rewarding direction in life (Korchin, 1976; Tyler, 1961). Two specialized professions are psychiatrist and psychoanalyst. The psychiatrist is an M.D., and the psychoanalyst has received a certificate in Freudian therapy. Of the approaches that we show in this chapter, the conflict approach requires the competency of the therapist, and the fulfillment approach, the competency of the counselor. Clinical psychologists might be trained to follow whatever approach best coordinates with research interests or any other predilections. Clergy are more likely to be counselors—though more must be said about this at the end of the chapter.

Since the three basic approaches to personality are at the same time three approaches to psychotherapy, we take them individually. Space and order do not permit specific considerations of Jung's therapy—considerably different from Freud's—or Rollo May's therapy, which emphasizes interpretations that Rogers would not favor, nor can we provide a fuller summary of conditioning techniques. Of the therapies designed for children and groups we can give but examples.

Conflict Approach

The best-known therapy is the "conflict" reducing therapy of Sigmund Freud. Freud and his followers have written extensively about it, and some aspects of it have entered into the repertoire of popular knowledge through jokes, cartoons, and so on—the bearded, German-accented analyst, pad in hand, with the patient on the couch. In fact Freud's therapy, psychoanalysis in its pure form, is not that accessible to the general population and is not suitable for people who are severely disturbed. A psychoanalyst sees a very limited number of patients, because the sessions with each patient are long and frequent; the average number of patients per analyst is usually less than thirty, hence often one patient has to terminate treatment before another can be taken on. Psychoanalysis has been an intellectual influence far beyond the extremely limited number of patients involved, having inspired an extensive literature in philosophy and religious studies, and has had a widespread influence in that the diagnosis of severely disturbed mental patients (who never would be able to enter formal psychoanalysis) is often done in Freudian terms. Difficulties inherent in the profession have been considerably highlighted in recent years (Malcolm, 1981).

Elements of Freud's Therapy

Psychoanalysis is built on two elements: repression and transference. Repression is the dynamic resistance of the ego to ideas and emotions that threaten to come up from the unconscious mind, memories of deeds witnessed or accomplished, along with the emotional reaction to them (infancy and early childhood experiences being the primary data here). Repressed memories exert a dynamic pressure upon the resisting ego. Transference is the projection of the repressed personal images and emotions upon the analyst in the therapy session. When religious problems are the result of repressed experiences relating to earliest life in the family, psychoanalytic technique is perhaps most appropriate. The composition of the affectivity that is involved in bizarre and troubling forms of love or hatred of God can be the result of associations with the earliest experiences of mother and father, and the resultant sexual activity.

The clearest modern general explanation of Freudian therapeutic techniques is given by Karl Menninger, who considers Freud's theory of technique separately from his theories about the personality. He says that the theory came about from a happy accident, a discovery made by Freud in the course of several years of trial and error in trying to unravel the meaning of his patients' neurotic suffering. His theory as we have described it is thus more in the nature of a rationale, an explanation of what it is that the psychoanalyst does on the basis of clinical theory and an *ad hoc* rationalization of what the treatment accomplishes. This explanation makes use of a number of concepts employed in clinical theory, such as unconscious functioning, primary and secondary processes, regression, unconscious fantasy, the libidinal and aggressive qualities of interpersonal relations, the persistence of the past in the present and the tendency to repeat the past, and inter- and intro-systemic resistances. But the technique is not derivable from these concepts (Menninger and Holzman, 1973).

Menninger gives the elements of psychoanalytic technique as an initial contract involving regression (reaction of the patient to the treatment situation); transference and countertransference (special exchange between both therapist and patient); resistence (paradoxical reaction of the patient to the treatment situation); and interpretation (which is, of course, the special work of the analyst).

Transference and countertransference are at the heart of the psychoanalytic treatment situation. Here the patient transfers to the analyst the roles that problem figures have played in the patient's past. By so doing the patient can work through the problems that those figures once caused. Patients relive many phases and incidents in their lives in relation to a neutral figure to whom they ascribe many roles or "as-if" identities. Little details of identification—inflections of the voice and irrelevant coincidences such as the color of a necktie worn—always come to the fore. The patient takes advantage of subtle situations and even creates opportunities for some apparent actualization of a role. Gradually patients become aware that they have responded to the analyst as if he were mother or father or someone else, and when this is clearly understood, the former value of the myth is lost. Patients then correct their mistakes, accept reality, and move on to another phase or period of life. Near the end of the analysis the patient becomes a recovering patient talking to a soon-no-longer-necessary psychoanalyst, and the old fantasy assignments to the analyst tend to be abandoned.

Although transference is the principle dynamic by which a patient works through problems, the countertransference by the analyst is not desirable. Here the analyst as a human being reacts to frustrations and makes use of various personal defense measures, particularly identification and projection, sometimes denial and avoidance, or reaction formation and isolation. The analyst, too, undergoes temporary regression and temporarily misidentifies the patient. The patient has momentarily become mother, father, pupil, colleague, another patient, or even a projection of the analyst's own self. Here Menninger advises a balanced concern on the part of young analysts: they should identify transferences that cause problems, but over-concentration will only impair a proper therapeutic attitude (Menninger and Holzman, 1973, p. 180).

Some Examples

Freud himself diagnosed some of these connections in the autobiography of Daniel Paul Schreber, Senatsprasident in Dresden at the end of the nineteenth century. At the onset of Schreber's illness his ideas were severely hypochondriacal; later they took the form of visual and auditory illusions. He believed that he was dead and decomposing and that his body was being handled in all kinds of revolting ways. The culminating point of his delusional system was the belief that he had a mission to redeem the world by being transformed into a woman. In the meantime not only the sun, but trees and birds "bemiracled residues of former human souls," spoke to him in human accents, and miraculous things happened everywhere around him (Freud, 1950a, p. 17).

Freud says that the germ of Schreber's delusional system was the idea of being transformed into a woman. He proceeds to examine Schreber's theological-psychological system by considering the themes *nerves, state of bliss, the divine hierarchy,* and *attributes of God* in themselves and as part of Schreber's therapeutic relationship with Flechsig, his own doctor. Freud then concludes that in the case of Schreber we find ourselves once again on the familiar ground of the father complex.

The whole case was interpreted by Freud at a distance; he did not deal with Schreber personally but only read the autobiography and other accounts of Schreber. Even when Freud reports on cases that he worked with himself, the techniques he uses are not described in any detail because he describes his techniques in other essays specifically on the topic. Better to present here more ordinary case histories reported by contemporary theorists.

Because those who would be inclined to base their therapeutic analysis on Freud run the gamut from the most orthodox through the eclectics who choose from many different theories, I present two examples of problematic religious experiences that submit to Freudian interpretations and therapeutic practices. In the first case the orthodox Freudian therapist describes a problem of crucifixion fantasies that can be dealt with best and interpreted as representative of the "primal scene" (the parents' lovemaking witnessed by the baby) active in the unconscious years later (Edelheit, 1974).

An unmarried woman had suffered a nearly fatal illness at puberty. Phobic symptoms and hypochondriacal anxieties brought her into analysis at the age of 28. In the fourth year of analysis she reported the following dream: "A long rectangular stage projected out into an auditorium. There were three people—an actress, a director, and a designer. Later the actress seemed to be herself. An archway stood about two-thirds of the way downstage. The actress was instructed to stand beside the archway and then to pass slowly *beside* it upstage. She insisted that the only proper way was to pass directly *through* the archway, which seemed to be covered with a thin material, like a paper hoop—and this would be broken—'but it was the only right way.'"

On the previous evening she had had "stage fright" in anticipation of a date. Her associations turned to a visit with married friends in El Salvador several years before. It was Holy Week. For Good Friday the Indians had made carpets of coloured sawdust depicting the Stations of the Cross on the road to the church. The procession, in which figures of the Virgin and saints were carried, passed *beside* the carpets. The last figure in the procession was that of Christ bearing the cross. This was carried directly *through* the carpets, destroying them.

The therapist is being faithful to his patient's associations. In actuality the figure of the Virgin is carried over the carpet after the Christ figure has passed. In the patient's revision the two figures are condensed, perhaps representing a fusion of Madonna and Child.

Thus in her *associations* to the dream, the patient revealed her identification with Christ on his way to the crucifixion—and also the sado-masochistic view of sexual intercourse which accounted in large part for her many sexual avoidances. A number of primal scene references were contained in her further associations: On Easter Sunday she had rushed down to the Indian market to buy souvenirs. The booths were made of white cloth stretched between wooden posts. She bought some squares of fabric with the thought that they would make nice gift napkins. Later she noticed that they were decorated with pictures of animals mating (such "fertility cloths" are often sold at festival times). The Indians had been shooting off rockets throughout the night. She had had a strong urge, she said, to go to the market place during the night to watch, but ... she could not go to the room of her married friends to wake them and ask them to join her. She remarked on the heavy bamboo sticks that were carried aloft by the rockets: "It was a wonder nobody got hurt." [Edelheit, 1974, pp. 196-97]

To understand the relationship between these fantasies and the primal scene is the basic step toward "working through" them.

A second example illustrates the "mad at God" syndrome. The therapist here is Freudian only to the extent that he emphasizes the image of God that is in the mind (Stamey, 1971):

Mr. N. M., sixty-seven years old, was referred to our department because of depression and anxiety. His main symptoms were somatic, with complaints of epigastric distress and fluttering plus a dry burning sensation in the mouth; complete physical evaluation had been negative.

This man had no history of a past psychiatric disorder. He had long been an effective member of the community and had worked for a long period of time with the same company, retiring about one year before entering therapy. In conjunction with the retirement he had some difficulty over his social security pension in which he felt that he was unfairly treated, and he became upset about it. It was quite evident that this was simply the focus for his dissatisfaction in what he felt was poor treatment at the hands of the government after a long life of service. However, he had always been strongly oriented to an obsessive way of living, had never been able to freely show his feelings, particularly any angry feelings, and was unable to speak up to anyone for what he felt were his rights. He was a very avid member of church committees ... on the board of trustees of various charitable organizations, and the like. He continued to function fairly well and the trouble with his dry mouth and the fluttering of the abdomen were the only complaints at the moment.

On examination, he was a very obese man who related in a friendly fashion and showed no evidence of a thinking disorder. There was also no evidence of any organic disorder. His affect was primarily one of mild anxiety and slight depression with the need to control himself strictly at all times. He had a reasonably good relationship with his peer group, with his wife and family, and the community, although he had been a bit more irritable lately.

The patient did not have any serious psychiatric disorder but it was indeed felt that his somatic complaints were depressive equivalents and were related to his feeling that he had been unfairly handled by the Social Security Administration. [pp. 98–99]

The therapist had found that in religious people who have mild problems with irritability, anger, or guilt, any direct indictment of or anger against God is replaced by words such as "life" or "fate." He therefore agrees that patients with strong religious backgrounds are little able to express anger directly and turn it back onto themselves. When "God" is the problem, therapeutic approaches must be subtle. Patients must explore their dependency needs, get a better image of themselves, and develop the ability to stand on their own two feet. When God is the "loved enemy," the task is more difficult. Friends in religious social circles encourage people to snap out of depression but can hardly encourage a troubled person to give up "God." In fact, the request to have more faith increases depression about anger and other feelings. It has been suggested that patients be encouraged to express their anger directly, but the therapist here suggests that "God," more often than not, be replaced by a substitute target. Accordingly, he urged his patient to redirect anger against the government (Social Security Administration). The therapist was an orthodox Freudian to the extent that he was concerned with God-images, defenses, and the importance of transference, but he went his own way in the brevity of his therapy and the directness of his suggestions.

The therapist who has a thorough understanding of the teachings, even the theology, of a patient's religious tradition can help the patient become aware of the relativity of the God-image in the patient's imagination. Reviewing research on the God-image would be a further help to the therapist.

Usefulness

In therapy and counseling that are related to religious matters, then, we might suggest that the therapeutic approach designed for the personality in conflict be used when there is a relatively severe disturbance that is localized (too widespread, and we are talking of hospitalization, which involves much more than the handling of a religion-based neurosis or psychosis). When there is extreme conflict related to belief and behavior it quite often relates to family life and early training. This involves the formation of religious images of the divinity in particular, where much of the experience of parent and authority figures is closely bound up with the sense of God and the qualities of this God. Very severe conflict, depression, and religious anxieties have to do with mental images of a God and the ethics that this image seems to require. Relationship to parents is a significant factor in the building of a self-image, and here too there can be great conflict. Great hatred and/or great fear of the divinity, with consequent anxieties over these reactions, is often bound up with great hatred of self and its accompanying depressions. Doubts and guilt that considerably disrupt personal functioning are the prime subject matter for a conflict therapy that is basically Freudian.

Fulfillment Approach

The fulfillment theory therapies use a variety of techniques that resemble more or less the frequent one-to-one discussions of psychoanalysis. Allport himself is not remembered as a therapist, nor has he left any extended discussion on how therapy is to be conducted. Neither have Maslow and May. However, another humanistic psychologist, Carl Rogers, is known more for his therapy than anything else. Since the 1940s Rogers's client-centered therapy, often referred to as nondirective counseling, has had more influence than any other therapy. Rogers believes that the clients themselves contain within them the means for realizing their potential, so he tries to provide an atmosphere where they will gradually reveal themselves to themselves.

Elements of Rogers's Therapy

In one of his principal papers Rogers describes the changes that might take place in a client. Although the paper is entitled "A Process Conception of Therapy," he does not discourse on the philosophy of process so much as he describes the changes in people, giving stages of development and clear examples of each stage. He begins, "I would like to take you with me on a journey of exploration. The object of the trip, the goal of the search, is to try to learn something of the *process* of psychotherapy, or the *process* by which personality change takes place." Rogers wishes to avoid a description of "frozen moments" and somehow to convey the ongoing movement, but he must do so by simply repeating often enough that he is describing continuing behavior (he does, after all, talk of seven stages that are, in effect, "frozen moments") (Rogers, 1961, pp. 126–31).

In the first stage there is an unwillingness to communicate self, and communication is only about externals. No real problems are recognized at this stage. Feelings, personal meaning, and close and communicative relationships are construed as dangerous. "I think I'm practically healthy," says the client, and "it always seems a little bit nonsensical to talk about oneself except in times of dire necessity" (p. 132).

In the second stage expression begins to flow in regard to nonself topics; although a full range of self topics are discussed, they are still regarded as external to self. Contradictions may be expressed, but with little recognition of them as contradictions. Instead of saying, "I was depressed," the client says, "The symptom was—it was—just being very depressed," and he or she can say, "I want to know things, but I look at the same page for an hour" (p. 134).

Stage three is a freer flow of expression about the self as an object. One's own experiences, others' view of oneself, and personal experiences in the past are discussed. But there is very little acceptance of feelings, which are for the most part revealed as something shameful, bad, abnormal, and unacceptable in other ways. The client says, "And this feeling that came into me was just the feeling I remember as a kid." But feelings are slightly more differentiated, and there is a recognition of contradictions in experience. Personal constructs, though rigid, are recognized as personal constructs, not external facts: "I'm so afraid wherever affection is involved it just means submission. And this I hate, but I seem to equate the two, that if I am going to get affection, then it means that I must give in to what the other person wants to do" (pp. 135–36).

There is a gradual loosening of constructs and a freer flow of feelings that develop out of the clients' stage-three sense of being understood and accepted. Feelings are described as objects in the present, sometimes breaking through almost against the client's wishes, since there is still distrust and fear of feelings. The rigidities of one's personal ways of construing experience are recognized as rigid constructs, which may not be valid. Rogers reports a client as saying:

> It amuses me. Why? Oh, because it's a little stupid of me—and I feel a little tense about it, or a little embarrassed—and a little helpless. [His voice softens and he looks sad.] Humor has been my bulwark all my life; maybe it's a little out of place in trying to really look at myself. A curtain to pull down . . . I feel sort of

at a loss right now. Where was I? What was I saying? I lost my grip on something—that I've been holding myself up with. [p. 138]

In stage five feelings are expressed freely as in the present and as vaguely referable to someone or something immediate. There is an increasing ownership of self-feelings and a desire to be these, to be the "real me." These feelings are differentiated more clearly, contradictions are faced, and personal constructs are loosened. There is an increasing quality of acceptance of self-responsibility for the problems being faced, and clients are concerned as to how they have contributed to these problems. All this means that there are freer dialogues within the self, which may be verbalized in this way: "Something in me is saying, 'What more do I have to give up? You've taken so much from me already.' This is *me* talking to *me*—the *me* way back in there who talks to the *me* who runs the show. It's complaining now, saying, 'You're getting too close! Go away!'" (p. 142).

Rogers considers stage six to be crucial for the "breakthrough." A feeling that has been "stuck," or inhibited in its process quality, is experienced with immediacy now, so that the immediacy of experiencing and the feeling that constitutes its content are accepted. Feelings are no longer to be denied, feared, or struggled against. People just loosen up: Self as an object tends to disappear. Contradictions are fully recognized, and defensive constructs are no longer used. In this stage there are no longer "problems," external or internal. The client is living, subjectively, a phase of his or her problem. Rogers gives the following example of a client coming into stage six:

> I could even conceive of it as a possibility that I could have a kind of tender concern for me.... Still, how could *I* be tender, be concerned for *myself*, when they're one and the same thing? But yet I can *feel* it so clearly.... You know, like taking care of a child. You want to give it this and give it that.... I can kind of clearly see the purposes for somebody else.... but I can never see them for ... myself, that I could do this for me, you know. Is it possible that I can really want to take care of myself, and make that a major purpose of my life? That means I'd have to deal with the whole world as if I were guardian of the most cherished and most wanted possession, that this *I* was between this precious *me* that I wanted to take care of and the

whole world.... It's almost as if I *loved* myself—you know—that's strange—but it's true. [p. 146]

Stage seven occurs as much outside the therapeutic relationship as in it; it is an ongoing development of the breakthrough in stage six. There is a growing and continuing sense of acceptance ownership of the changing feelings, a basic trust in one's own process. Experiencing has almost completely lost its structure-bound aspects and becomes process-experiencing—that is, the situation is experienced and interpreted in its newness, not as the past. The self increasingly becomes simply the subjective and reflexive awareness of experiencing. The self is much less frequently a perceived object, and much more frequently something confidently felt in process. Personal constructs are tentatively reformulated, to be validated against further experience, but even then to be held loosely.

An Example: Pastoral Counseling

Rogers's views on personal progress and his counseling methods have become popular with religious counselors, because no great knowledge or experience of the complex pathologies is required. Without a full psychological education, it would seem, one can be of help to those in pain who are trying to integrate or give meaning to different aspects of their lives. Some of the fullest descriptions of counseling those with religious problems and goals have been written by Seward Hiltner, who worked with Rogers at the University of Chicago some years ago.

Hiltner's description of one woman who was counseled by one of his protégés is a good example of the application of Rogers's approach in a Christian church setting. Mrs. Esther Merz was attracted to church membership and the more specialized help available in counseling. In her first interview she told of frequent periods of depression, adding that she was finding no meaning in her existence. Other problems had to do with feelings of inadequacy relative to her older sister, her desires for a mature sexual relationship, regrets about her mother's emotional formality, and the problem of prayer (Hiltner and Colston, 1961).

Because of recurring depressions and her fear of them, Mrs.

Merz began counseling with intensity. She was attracted by the possibility of acquiring a religious faith, something she never really had before. She began to reflect seriously about religion and was able to approach, first of all, her own basic prejudice against the Jews (she had a strain of Jewishness in her family background). She began to own up to those feelings. Then she was able to discern other feelings, about family and sexual intimacies, although she still considered the feelings somewhat external to her. She began to see, though, that her feelings toward herself were especially complicated in those areas where she began to see the negative elements of her feeling toward her sister. Opening up about the way men had treated her in several relationships, she achieved a leveling off in which she genuinely appreciated some of the gains she had made in self-understanding.

Although she had probably attained what Rogers would call stage three, she still could not have felt fully understood and accepted, because she canceled several appointments. When she resumed counseling, she was able to continue reviewing her attitudes toward family members, her dead father, and her still-living mother. Her new-found religiousness was reviewed in light of these attitudes. But the "level" remained the same: Although she had some new insights into her life and had explored some new areas of thought and emotion, the way she looked at all this changed very little. Reflecting on herself she said this:

> I think some of my thinking has changed a little bit. I don't know whether it's a subtle thing because of some of the things that have happened. I seemed to have changed my thinking a little bit. Some things that happened about a week or so ago made me wonder about some of the things that I think I want most in life. And—ah—I'm beginning to think or wonder whether these are the things I really want after all. Such as marriage and children. All of a sudden—ah—it seems like for some reason this is becoming not so important all at once.... And it seems that some of the things that have happened—ah —perhaps things in the past I have blamed myself for—now it appears that I'm either wrong in blaming myself or I wasn't at fault.... If someone should ask me what I wanted most, or what I was unhappiest about—of course I would say that I wasn't married and I didn't have children. But—ah—so many things have happened that have put me in a position where I

just can't, and I turn my back on it. [Hiltner and Colston, 1961, pp. 83–84]

Hiltner contends that Mrs. Merz was more a success than a failure: "The counseling enabled her to reach a certain new level in considering herself, her relationships, and her whole situation, but did not force her to go beneath that. As it turned out, this new level will probably have enormous meaning in the rest of her life" (p. 90).

Why did Mrs. Merz not achieve higher stages in counseling? Hiltner interprets her as a very intelligent person, torn in her youthful years between a cold mother and a warm father who differed in their approach to religion. While very young she accepted her sister's self-estimate, and this caused her to judge herself harshly and negatively. Her marriages, one unsuccessful and the second successful but terminated by the early death of her husband, left her in such a state of anxiety that she sought psychiatric help. Desire to pull things together caused her to search for a faith that would be meaningful.

As she entered counseling, she was captive to her sister's standards and expectations, to the idea that a woman's life without children was not a full life, and to expectations of many other people. Early religious discussions in the family served a useful purpose in that they enabled her to see and focus her desires for fulfillment and for freedom.

Usefulness

We might suggest that the therapeutic approach to the personality seeking fulfillment be used when there is no real disturbance but rather a fragmentation of life, a listlessness, an inability to achieve self-appointed goals of one sort or another. Where there is pain but not bizarre behavior, where there is great dissatisfaction but not deep conflict, in other words, where there are issues involving the unification and direction of activities rather than the removal of an obvious disturbance, then the therapist might facilitate the reflection on goals and the options open for the attainment of these goals. Patients or counselees might be led to considerations of religious or ethical behavior relative to their understanding of life's values and to their sense of divine presence and power.

Conditioning Approach

Relationship to Other Therapies: The Example of Prejudice

At the moment, one of the most significant "religious" concerns of conditioning therapists is the problem of prejudice, the analysis of which we associate more with fulfillment theory. In fact, conditioning therapies focus on problems that are explained in other approaches to psychology, such as obsession, prejudices, and the like. Conditioning therapists have no interest in explaining obsessive behavior in people's lives but have every interest in conditioning them out of such behavior.

We digress briefly to contrast the interests of conflict and fulfillment theorists in the problem of prejudice. Freud wrote at some length about obsessive ritual practices, and Allport was a leader in research on prejudice. Conflict and fulfillment researchers have chosen to observe prejudice primarily through the study of the individual's attitudes and beliefs as revealed in oral reports. Attitudes are generally inferred from the verbal behavior of the individual. For example, if asked, "How do you feel about Jews?" an individual might say, "I hate Jews and Communists. Both groups amount the same thing. I'd like to throw them all in jail." Here the form and intensity of the words used and the relationships between those words indicate the characteristic attitudes of the person who utters them. Conflict and fulfillment researchers believe that people's attitudes direct their behavior toward things in a constant manner. For example, people with strong negative attitudes toward Jews and Communists would be expected to be attracted to a group that would go out and actually round up Jews and Communists and put them in jail, or at least vote for legislation that would authorize such behavior.

For conditioning therapists, however, consistency in verbal and motor behavior toward someone or something is a matter of reinforcement history.

The Example of Prejudice: Elements of Conditioning Therapy

So, to construct a therapy to lessen or eliminate prejudice, therapists first note the personal characteristics that function as stimuli of prejudiced behavior: (1) physical features—hair color, texture, and style, nose shape, hand shape, body build, skin color, and so on; (2) behavior—content of speech, mannerisms when making gestures, ritualized behavior, and special practices; (3) symbols—insignia used, ornaments worn, and names used. Some of these characteristics may be combined to form the exaggerated image of caricature we call a stereotype. Black Americans often are divided into the young revolutionary with the Afro haircut and the humble Uncle Tom with shambling gait and deference to whites.

Behaviorists believe that a program for the elimination of prejudice in society might well include the following procedures (Karen, 1974, pp. 276-77):

1. Those who have responsibility for a person, or the therapists, present "behavior suppression procedures" (punishment, interruption, connecting with results opposed to the ones desired) whenever the person deals with others and whenever he or she expresses dislike of or makes wrong or unsupported statements about minority groups, or gives evidence of avoidance, escape, or attack behavior.

2. Those responsible, or the therapists, present enhancement procedures (positive reinforcement) whenever the person deals with members of minority groups, expresses liking or affection for them, makes valid statements about race and ethnic background, and reaches out to these people positively or in friendship.

3. Appealing texts and pictures and other positive eliciting stimuli in relationship to racial or ethnic groups are placed in communications media. These "paired stimuli" are then presented to the exclusion of the opposite type of pairing.

4. Those who have frequent social dealings with the prejudiced person present themselves as models, showing positive emotional responses toward minority groups and verbalizing their appreciation of them. They make valid statements about minorities and approach them positively and freely.

5. Modifications are made in the environment to increase the contact, interaction, and cooperation of prejudiced people with members of racial and ethnic minorities. Efforts are made to lessen the likelihood of competition in these areas.

These conditioning activities are obviously appropriate to the conditioning therapy situation and everyday life. In therapy, more complex and intense manipulations might be introduced, and in society the range of possibilities for encouraging constructive behavior can be expanded. Gradually the prejudiced person can become open to a far wider world, because training to be open to differences within a country should train people to be understanding of other countries. Reinforcement of positive integrating activity can help build up the human family.

Usefulness

We might suggest that the conditioning approach be used where there is a persistent surface habit. Whether or not that habit is connected with conflicts or goals is often immaterial, though sometimes there is no way to extirpate a habit until connections with personal issues are found. Since within religious systems generally accepted as sane and sound in modern Western society there are a great number of beliefs and practices considered "superstitious" or weird, it may be that conditioning could lead to the extinction of the bizarre behavior. And when people are tormented by guilt or scruples, the malady might be reduced by the dicovery of the original reinforcements that caused it and the construction of reinforcement to render it extinct. If it was previously rewarding to flee a "temptation" (that really wasn't one but was felt to be a proximate occasion of sin by the scrupulous), conditions might be arranged wherein the strange pleasure that results from fleeing might somehow be generalized to include the pleasure of giving in.

Special Developmental Problems: An Example

Developmental psychologies as such do not usually provide therapeutic approaches, unless the means suggested for handling learning disabilities are considered therapeutic. However, it so happens that Erikson was one of the leading children's therapists years ago, and his experience served him well in his construction of the eight stages of man, with the discussion of "identity versus identity diffusion" and "intimacy versus isolation" presented within this construction. His therapy contains techniques widely different from orthodox Freudian therapy (especially as applied to children by Anna Freud), but Erikson does report on several of his own clinical experiences, one of which follows here (1950, pp. 25–38).

A small boy named Sam in a town in Northern California had violent seizures of an apparently epileptic nature. The first attack was five days after the death of his grandmother, and the other attacks occurred in the setting of the deaths of animals and insects. Gradually it became obvious that the attacks were due to some type of "psychic stimulus" connected with the death of the boy's grandmother.

The death of the grandmother was related in the child's mind to some teasing that he had done, which brought on the grandmother's final heart attack. Furthermore, his mother tried to pretend that his grandmother had not died but had gone on a long trip north to a large city; when a mysterious large box had been carried out of the house the mother had told him that his grandmother's books were in it.

Complications resulted from his being the only Jewish boy in a gentile neighborhood. His parents had to tell him not to hit other children, not to ask the ladies too many questions, and to treat the gentiles gently, contrary to what he had been taught in an earlier urban Jewish setting where he was called on to be tough and aggressive. Minor seizures came after any outbreaks of aggression on his part—he might throw a stone at a stranger, or he might say "God is a skunk" or "The whole world is full of skunks."

Erikson's therapy consisted in playing dominoes with the child and having him lose consistently, which caused some aggressive violence. Right after, when the child put the dominoes together in the form of an oblong box, Erikson said, "If you wanted to see the dots on your blocks, you would have to be inside the little box, like a dead person in a coffin.... This must mean that you are afraid you may have to die because you hit me." The child asked, "Must I?" And Erikson answered, "Of course not. But when they carried your grandmother away in the coffin you probably thought that you made her die and therefore had to die yourself. That's why you built those big boxes in your school, just as you built this little one today. In fact, you must have thought you were going to die every time you had one of those attacks" (pp. 29–30).

Gradually the child learned to control his aggression, especially the aggression that, for several reasons, he tended to direct against his mother. Eventually he would give her clear indications when he felt some kind of aggression coming on.

When Sam's problems became unsurmountable, his psychophysical constitution, his temperament, and his stage of development were all affected by his inability to tolerate restrictions on his locomotor freedom and aggressive self-expression. His needs for muscular and mental activity were not just physiological but were an important part of his total personality. He developed what might be called counterphobic defense mechanisms. When Sam was scared, he attacked, and when he saw that others were trying to avoid the communication of information in which he was interested he questioned them persistently. This way of acting was more suited to his first neighborhood, where tough was cute, but it became part of a process of "ego organization." This central process enables an individual to anticipate inner as well as outer dangers and to integrate personal endowment with social interaction. Erikson says that "it thus assures to the individual a sense of coherent individuation and identity: of being one's self, or being all right, and of being on the way to becoming what other people, at their kindest, take one to be." In his earliest environment Sam had become a clever teaser and a persistent questioner because these activities were helpful defenses in the face of danger. When they were no longer valued, his defensive system was in a sense put out of commission. He really had to provoke attacks for his systems to continue operation, and so Erikson believes that the "attack" came from a somatic source in the form of epilepsy-like seizures (p. 35).

There are obvious religious themes here that have to do with the cosmic problem of the meaning of death and the social problem of religious identity. Yet both are part of a peculiarly developmental problem, the construction of coherent individuality and identity. It is clear from cases like this that many different aspects of religion are operative in impeding or helping the overall personality development of human beings.

Social Psychology and Group Therapy

In social psychology, therapies concentrate on relationship deficiencies. On the attitudes level and the interaction level, there are corrections to be made in the lives of certain people if they are to live happily in society. But therapy takes place at the small-group interaction level.

The Development of Group Therapy

"Group dynamics" and "encounter groups" were so much discussed in the 1960s that the terms became clichés. Varieties of business executives, school staff members, and religious order members became part of intense group exchanges for an entire weekend at some specially chosen retreat. Groups designed to facilitate the personal liberation of individuals, to open them up to each other sexually, religiously, in any number of ways—such groups proliferated. People convinced of the importance of encounter groups prophesied the demise of the old one-to-one therapy relationship. Especially the Roman Catholic but also other Christian religious communities sought to make use of some of the experiences of these encounter groups, either by requesting the help of the trainers or by adapting whatever was written in the group psychology literature.

The encounter group movement started when a group of adult educators, public officials, and social scientists held a summer workshop at New Britain Teachers College to explore the use of small groups as a vehicle for personal and social change. The aims of the group were to train officials in intergroup relations agencies, to develop techniques in face-to-face groups, and to learn more about how they function. Most of the group leaders had come from MIT, where they had worked with Kurt Lewin, developer of the so-called field theory. Lewin constructed this theory to set the individual in a relevant environment or "life space." He had introduced new methods of observation in psychology that made it possible within the psychological laboratories to study volition and emotion. During the previous decade he had turned his interest to social problems. Taking the group as the unit of concern, he applied the concepts of direction, change, influence, and power to the whole group, talking about members as integrated parts of the group in the same way he had described parts of the personality as regions within the person. Workshops held on an ongoing basis affected many fields of applied social research and social science, and many professions. At the height of their popularity, training centers attracted thousands of people each month and became a multimillion-dollar business with monthly mass media descriptions of the more sensational aspects of center activities (Back, 1972).

Well before that time there were attempts to do therapy in groups, but these attempts did not have as unified and sensational a history. It was inevitable that a group therapy tradition would gradually assume the encounter group movement into its more broad and diffuse background. Encounter groups were generally composed of ambitious, often thriving professional people, while group therapy is a therapeutic approach to a much wider range of people and problems. By gathering those needing or desiring therapy into groups of various sizes, therapeutically helpful social values are encouraged: values as broad as altruism —simply helping other people—and as individual as the acquisition of a specialized behavior by observation of another patient with a similar problem constellation. Group therapy is based on the view that since people do not develop their problems on their own but in relation to other people, problems should be solved in relationship with others.

Some group therapies are designed to handle a special, pre-existing group structure, and the most important of those is family therapy. Such therapy deals with the inability of various members of the family to relate to one another and to those other areas of society that are reached through the family or as members of the family—school and church, for example.

An Example: Family Therapy and Religious Problems

If people's, especially children's, personalities are so much built up or torn down by those around them, then the experience of family is crucial, and personal improvement is related to good and bad relationships within the family. He or she is the identified patient, whom the family labels as "having problems" or "being the problem."

Salvador Minuchin, the leading comtemporary family therapist, says that "when a family labels one of its members 'the patient,' the identified patient's symptoms can be assumed to be a system-maintaining or a system-maintained device." The symptom in the child may be the expression of something that is wrong within the family system. Or it may have developed in the individual because of circumstances in outside life and then continued, encouraged, within the family system. In any case, when the family agrees that one member is the problem it probably means that "the symptom is being reinforced by the system" (Minuchin, 1974, p. 110).

New demands are constantly made upon the family by society and by the biological and psychological changes going on within the family. A family gets in trouble when it cannot adapt to these changes and meets all new challenges by unchanging, stereotyped methods. An ideal of group structure is absolutized, and the ways that the family members have for dealing with one another become rigid. By pointing out one person as the problem, other family members can safeguard the structures and transactional patterns they have absolutized.

The family therapist must help the patient and the family by assisting them all to deregulate, change, and gradually transform the family system. There are three important tasks for the therapists: They enter the family interchange in a position of leadership; they bring the underlying family structure to light and evaluate it; and they create circumstances that will allow the transformation of this structure.

If the therapy works, the expectations that determine the behavior of members are changed. This means that each individual member of the family experiences a different set of expectations, viewpoints, and behaviors from all the other members; the individual's own experience is thereby changed considerably. Such transformation is especially important for the so-called patient, who is freed from being in a deviant position. Minuchin puts it this way: "In family therapy, the transformation of structure is defined as changes in the position of family members vis-à-vis each other, with a consequent modification of their complementary demands." Transformation does not alter the composition of the family—they do not come up with new personalities, but they relate to one another differently (p. 111).

When the therapist enters the family, the family system becomes a therapeutic system with the therapist as leader. It is the therapist's responsibility to evaluate the family's problems in order to develop certain goals for them. The transformation of the family is accomplished by directing them toward these goals. Always it is the family that is the focus of therapy, though. The family is the setting and cause of the healing and growth of its members; the family, not the individual, is restructured. So the therapist has to ensure all along that the identity of the family as a unit undergoing therapy is firmly established.

What family therapists call restructuring operations are a series of more or less dramatic interventions that create movement toward the goals of the therapy. Such operations must be designed to allow for periods of consolidation and regrouping as the family changes. To give an example from Minuchin's text on family therapy:

> [I]n one family, conflict in the spouse subsystem is avoided by scapegoating a son. When the wife challenges her husband for not making more money, he directs his attention to the boy, correcting his behavior and thereby re-establishing his own threatened sense of competence. When the husband challenges the wife for being a sloppy housekeeper, she begins to talk about the child's misbehavior in school. The therapist joins the husband in a coalition against the wife, strongly supporting the demand for more order in the house. This technique results immediately in the emergence of spouse conflict which, with the therapist's help, is negotiated within the spouse subsystem, freeing the boy. [p. 149]

In this case the therapist causes the conflict between the husband and wife to emerge. With the therapist's help, the spouses work out a conflict that is basically between them, and the boy is freed from his scapegoat position. He is no longer the "patient."

Whenever religion plays a role in the family dynamics, the therapist must help the family to discern that role, because very often religion is a near absolute. That is the point at which we must find out if religion is stimulating or dulling, generous or self-seeking, too easy or too difficult, and on the whole healthy or sick. Is belief in some imagery (e.g. the mothering role of the Blessed Virgin Mary in Catholicism) or behavior in accordance with some specialized denominational tenets (no cosmetics in some branches of Pentecostalism) or some special activity (retreats, summer missionary activity) at the center of some kind of struggle within the family? If so, where does it come from and what relationship does it have to a family's presence within a larger community? Religion can be the means by which a parent manipulates a child or elevates the favorite child; conversely, it can be the means whereby a child or adolescent dramatically demonstrates rebellion against a variety of family strictures. However, religion, more than anything else, connects individual family members with a world outside the family. The shape that religion takes in the lives of individual family members is very much the result of previous experiences within the family—indeed, the very earliest experiences within the family. When "restructuring" the family, the power of religion as a manipulative tool or as a camouflage for real tensions and causes should be understood by the psychologist.

There are strategies useful to therapists and counselors working with strongly religious families (Larsen, 1978), assuming that the religious orientation, though not necessarily the therapist's own, is still broadly acceptable. To assess the religious influences in the family, the therapist should know what religious factors are important to each individual in each family: dimensions such as beliefs, rituals, and practices, and specific ideas or acts within these dimensions. At the same time one tries to get a feel for the strength, the instrumentality of each of these dimensions within the individual lives of family members, e.g. what weight attendance at church, as against personal kindness, has with the father, and why. The therapist must know how the religious values of the individual family members are affecting the total system. Obviously the therapists have their own ideas about the helpfulness or harmfulness of different religions and the dimensions within these religions, but it is equally obvious that therapists must work within limits set by the family's religious views if they are to have any credibility. They must mobilize those elements of the family's religious system that can be most helpful. If the therapist knows the family's religious views very well, he or she may find that what appears to be a harmful belief or practice may be a distortion of something good in the tradition. One therapist who has worked with very strict Christian families says that "the therapeutic strategy ... is to change religiously based values that may be incompatible with therapeutic objectives, but to reorder the value structure in a way that facilitates the goals of therapy without compromising the family faith" (Larsen, 1978, p. 266).

Often, too, the natural context of religious and social living has some of the helpful elements of family and other forms of group therapy (Herrenkohl, 1978; Oden, 1972), so the therapist may be able to suggest greater participation in some elements of church life. Clergy may suggest forms of church involvement that are especially appropriate to the families they are counseling.

Religion and the Therapies

Since the psychologies we have spoken of are modern European and American systems, it stands to reason that Christian and Jewish clergy are the most likely to make use of them. In fact, Hinduism and Buddhism are so "psychologically"oriented that the use within the traditions of anything other than experimental psychology would be a redundancy. On the other hand there have always been principles and procedures in the great world religions designed to transmit the religious tradition and to enable people to live well within it. From Vedic times Hinduism has had its distinct classes of gurus, some teachers plain and simple, and others mystics and ascetics of various types. From ordination rites believed to have been received from the Buddha we can discern the qualities of the pupil–instructor relationship (McNeil, 1977). In Christianity there has been a long history of therapy and guidance. One well-known historical study of Christian pastoral practice across the centuries divides the periods of Christian history into healing, sustaining, guiding, and reconciling (Clebsch and Jaeckle, 1964).

By studying the ways different therapists might deal with religion we are sidestepping the question of how religion in general or specific forms of religion help or hinder mental health. After all, Freud considered religion to be a universal obsessional neurosis, and Allport considered mature faith to be an important element of the well-developed personality. The compromise, of course, is to consider religious neurosis constructive (Boisen, 1971; Steere, 1969). Looking at statistics, we see that some Christian denominations have a higher percentage representation in American mental hospitals than others (Burgess and

Wagner, 1971). In fact—to speak only of American Christianity —any given denomination tends to help you in some ways and mess you up in others. The religious problems of psychiatric patients are quite varied (Burns and Aubrey, 1969). It appears that therapists give high marks to religious groups that promote the forms of personal development the therapist considers important. Conversely, religious groups look kindly on the forms of therapy that enhance the personal values that the religious group finds important (Loschen, 1974).

Humanistic therapists and mainline Protestants believe that the roles of therapists and clergy are either complementary or overlapping (Smith, 1974). At least the way the surveys are set up, the evidence is that religious faith helps improve some areas of the personality (Sharma, 1978) and that training in counseling assists in the personal growth of those practitioners who participate in such training (Geary, 1977).

The basic challenge remains choosing the right therapy for the right religious problem (Lovinger, 1979), and there are no developed suggestions beyond what we have put together in this chapter. After the fact it sometimes becomes very clear that a given therapy was not at all appropriate for a given set of personal and/or religious problems. For example, Freud tried to convince his patient Dora that her neurotic symptoms were the result of her sexual feelings, whereas she was living among adults who were deceitful and she should have been supported rather than accused of causing her own problems (Maddi, 1974). Nonreligious therapists frequently suspect religious therapists of letting their beliefs influence their therapy, but in one survey comparison there was not significant difference between religious and nonreligious therapists in amount, style, or content of therapist activities (Burns, 1972). It is possible to consider any kind of counseling to be "pastoral" counseling because of the caring and helping involved in a religious endeavor (Halmos, 1970).

While it is obvious that each type of therapy discussed in this chapter has been practiced by the clergy members or religious counselors, religious counseling in the American Christian context has emphasized nondirective counseling, with a strong attraction to depth psychology. One of the most popular writers on pastoral counseling suggests a number of approaches that would be usable by Christian clergy with basic training (seminary courses): He himself teaches elements of "depth pastoral counseling," "counseling on religious existential problems," and "family group therapy and transactional analysis" (Clinebell, 1966).

There are a number of pastors and therapists who have developed a way of discussing pathologies and developmental problems in Freudian and Jungian language. The religious problems concentrated upon are guilt and defenses (Uleyn, 1969), inner darkness or inner feminity (Hillman, 1967), and self-realization (Goldbrunner, 1966).

Those Christian counselors who have been trained for non-directive counseling have tended to develop styles of direction that stand on their own. Though their styles are very similar to Rogers's style, they carefully and consistently explain how they relate to their clients in their own distinct—liberal, clerical, Christian—setting (Johnson, 1967; Curran, 1969; Vanderpool, 1977). These varieties of specifically American Christian pastoral counseling have led to a new generation of pastoral theologians who interpret the human-religious meaning of these pastoral experiences within a sophisticated background in philosophy and social science (Browning, 1976; Capps, 1979; Oates, 1979, Oden, 1966).

To conclude, we return to a social-psychological explanation of the basic elements and setting of the various therapies. In this book the ultimate explanation has been social-psychological. This was as far as we could go in the interpretation of religion's role in people's lives: the dynamics of interaction with the consequent creation of attitudes. At the beginning of Part IV of this book we mentioned the possible ways that the therapy or guidance situation might be set up and the social context in which it is likely to take place.

We classified the different types of modern therapy and traditional guidance according to the elements of the system and of the setting, in order to understand what is going on psychologically and socially. But it is normative psychological (and sometimes religious) authority that *centers* both the dynamics of the system and the elements of the setting. The organization of the healing encounter, the beliefs about therapy, and the conduct and experiences of the participants, as well as the population career patterns, the ideologies and ethics of a given culture, and the background lives and personalities, are all pulled together, sometimes by psychological written authority (e.g. the works of Freud), sometimes by personal authority (e.g. the conditioner), and sometimes by the client's own personality (e.g. client-centered situation).

There are basically three types of normative psychological and religious authority:

First, transcendent authority–centered therapy and guidance, where references to some kind of book or set of standards or set of beliefs and behavior requirements is frequently made and where the person receiving therapy or guidance is expected to conform. Classical Freudian therapy is so dependent on the highly stylized views of Freud that we can say therapy is done in constant references to Freud's "scriptural" authority.

Second, therapist/guide–centered therapy and guidance, where the particular insights or procedures of the person providing the service are normative. Conditioning therapy, of course, is direct manipulation of the clients, who are conditioned to do whatever the therapist wants them to do. In all cases the idea is not so much to make use of an individual's thoughts and memories and turn them toward a set of norms exterior to the situation so much as to attempt to ensure adherence and conformity to the director's ideas and procedures.

Third, in person-centered therapy the individuals in therapy or guidance are simply given a setting in which to deal with themselves. This type of therapy and guidance did not become fully clear to us until recent decades, when the approach was so fully worked out by Carl Rogers. The idea was that you do not move the clients in any particular direction but simply provide an openness and response to their own reflections upon themselves. However, modern nondirective therapy presupposes a certain fundamental wholeness and capacity for self-regulating in the person. The expectation is that people, if everything goes right, can ultimately achieve a balance of physical and intellectual functioning, private and social living. Carl Rogers and others do have a general view of what constitutes the good person, the good society, and the good life. They expect that the interactions with therapists and with the "right" people in life will lead toward perfection on the individual, social, and cultural levels.

Periodically in this chapter, we have pointed out the usefulness of the therapies, but the ultimate value of these systems depends on how much they benefit the lives of people today. A once-and-for-all judgment on usefulness cannot be made, because whether we stand within or outside of a system our experience of it is incomplete. But we are free to judge however we want: to *choose* the religion, guidance system, and modern therapy that we believe most appropriate for ourselves and to *suggest* it for others; or to choose and suggest some combination of systems. Therapists should at least know how the ways of guidance can engender or sustain religious experience, and religious guides should make use of the therapies that are compatible with their traditions.

PART V

Conclusion

THROUGHOUT the book we have tried to present a repertoire of categories and explanations that account for the religious experience. The repertoire is not complete and cannot be completed, because every religious experience is unique, part of a unique life, which, in turn, is at the center of a unique set of social interactions. We have described the role of religion in some types of personality, subject to some common lines of development, and have identified some of the religious elements in social interaction, but we cannot really explain a religious experience or ongoing religious activity without refining away the general description and explanations until we have an original story.

Religion does not involve one unified activity like swimming or chess. Religion is manifold and can be understood only with knowledge of the religion to which an individual belongs, the style of that belonging, the shape of the individual's personality, and the type of personal development and social interaction that is part of that individual's life. Even further precision is called for in order to narrate a unique moment or a unique process in someone's religious life. The standard types, the commonalities, and the generalities that we have seen in the preceding chapters can only provide the backdrop for our own interpretation of the individual religious experience.

To conclude our study, we might summarize the theories that we have presented in this book and then relate them to the individual case of St. Augustine. Needless to say, the summary will serve only those who have familiarized themselves with the explanations and examples presented.

General Theories and Unique Lives

A Summary of Categories and Theories

RECALL THAT THOUGHTS and feelings are the basic elements of the religious experience. Following William James, we categorized a number of the components of religious cognitive activity. For James, there was a thought component to personality style— optimistic, pessimistic, and vacillating—although people's thoughts are generally considered to result from these different classes of feelings and temperaments. Mystical, devotional, and philosophical religious experiences themselves have a thought or cognitive component. Cognitive activity enables people to interpret their mystical perceptions; they mentally perceive, coordinate, and unify what is happening to them. On the devotional level people decide how to address the deity and how to interpret and describe this address. Philosophical reflection on religion is by definition intellectual activity, so all the logical and reflective processes involved there become part of a derived religious experience. Feelings are the basis of the personality styles listed by

James: Optimism, pessimism, and vacillation are categories of feelings or emotions. Mystical and devotional religion are composed primarily of feeling elements. Indescribable feeling, or felt meaning, characterizes mystical religion; poetic moments, dreamy states, nostalgia, and emotional memories can be included here, and feelings of self-surrender, a sense of transformation, joy, bodily lightness, peace, and happiness. The range of emotions proper to devotional religion is virtually identical with the ordinary range of emotions that humans experience in their relationships to one another. Philosophical religion is touched with emotion because of its aesthetic quality.

There can be considerable alteration of the normal range of perceptions. Researchers have examined the qualities of hallucinations and ecstasies at one end of the experience spectrum and deep meditative states at the other end. They say that when the energy-producing elements of the nervous system or the calming elements of the nervous system are operative people move either through excitement to ecstasy or through calmness to deep meditation. This is caused by a change in brain wave activity, eye movements, sensory–motor ratio (experience of intense sensations relative to the voluntary motor activity capable of verifying these sensations), apposition-to-proposition ratio (general feelings relative to clearly reasoned judgements), relationship of right hemisphere to left hemisphere, and subcortical to cortical activity. Given certain patterns of brain waves and eye movements and given certain ratios in brain activity, people will experience either ecstatic or meditative states of consciousness.

Using here one of the simplest and most studied of modern psychological concepts, attribution, we see that every psychological activity—from the most striking altered state through the most ordinary of perceptions—can have a religious meaning attributed to it. Today the study of brain waves and the relationship of cortical to subcortical activity provides an interpretation of the brain functions that cause mystical experience: When the level of the arousal is raised or lowered, the mental perception of the individual moves toward states that can be interpreted as ecstatic and visionary on one hand, or deeply meditative on the other. But whether the cognitive and emotions states are ordinary or "altered," the essential element is that there be a religious attribution. The perceptual, intellectual, linguistic, motor activities, and attitude formations or the alteration of cognitive powers and feeling tones must be attributed to a god, another world, or something classifiable within a culture as religious.

The cognitive components of all ordinary processes, functions, and relationships have received religious attributions. Whether these perceptions, functions, and relational attitudes are specifically intellectual or not, the mind always has to interpret a literal psychological or physical datum. If we take the metaphor of hearing the Word of God, we see that there is a perceptual process that is interpreted metaphorically. Then the metaphor affects the original perception. Vision, touch, positioning, smell and taste, pain, the selection of emotions, the generation and concentration of energies, and relations to others, things, and self must be interpreted cognitively. There are thought components to perceptual, emotional, linguistic, and relational activity. Concepts, images, and logic are the basis of cognitive activity. Emotional processes are responses to the supposed power, mystery, wrath, majesty, energy, admirability, and otherness of the deity. The response-feelings are creatureliness, awe, dread, humbleness, commitment, bliss, and nothingness. Linguistic functions are accompanied by feelings, especially when the language is expressive of erotic, pious, ecstatic, and fanatical sentiments. Psychomotor energy is controlled by rituals and interiorized norms and is liberated in physical refreshment and dream activities. It provides impetus for and is a result of emotional activity. The relationships to, or attitudes toward, persons and things are formed with and accompanied by emotions: reactions to family and social situation, time, space, nature, and art, and to the self-image formed in the light of religious teachings.

The role assumed for religion in personality theory and in developmental and social psychology is best described and explained not in terms of isolated thoughts and feelings, but in terms of two different aggregates of thoughts and feelings: faith and ethics. Freud and Jung on one hand, and Allport, Maslow, and May on the other, sorted out thoughts and feelings into images and intentions loosely pertaining to faith; they further sorted out thoughts and feelings into types of self-discovery and self-transcending consistency that represented the essence of ethical behavior. To understand faith, then, we must understand the origins of the images of God, religious community, the other world, and so on, by examining the infant's experience of parents (Freud) or the young person's experience of the basic persons in society—such as religious and authority figures—in relation to the internal images of such figures that they are born with (Jung). We must further understand the goals (Allport) and the key experiences (Maslow) that give people their most exalted and refined visions of themselves. Assimilating the anxieties and passions of life, people can reach out to one another, finding freedom in commitment (May). Ethics is constituted by a number of serious efforts. Self-discovery and self-realization, or consistency with the conscience and adequate response to both the freeing and driving goals and passions of one's life, constitute basic ethical efforts.

In developmental psychology we do not take a different approach to faith and ethics. Rather we try to discern the cognitive and emotional steps that are involved in faith and ethical development. The task of sorting out thoughts and feelings involved in the religious experience is more clearly done for us by Erikson and Piaget. Trust, autonomy, initiative, industry, identity, intimacy, generativity, and wisdom determine religious belief and behavior. As each of these developmental tasks is accomplished, a corresponding "religious" virtue is developed: hope, freedom, sense of purpose, moral dexterity, love, fidelity, care, and wisdom are well formed if the developmental tasks are accomplished. At the center of life, as it were, is the development of sexual identity and intimacy—with the accompanying understanding of others and willingness to communicate with them. This leads to fulfilling generativity and wisdom in adulthood and old age. All this involves felt meanings more than distinct cognitive efforts. Across the years the development of cognitive schemata to understand the meaning of individuality, spirit, and creation is at the center of faith. At the same time schemata for understanding the self and behavior appropriate to the self develop. Gradually, then, children develop schemata for thinking about their individuality in the world, the breath of life in things, and the way the elements of nature and people are created; they begin to make and follow rules, concern themselves with communicating truth, and develop a sense of justice and its dispensation. All of these stages of development involve positive progress in faith and morality. Erikson, Piaget, and others insist that the stages are absolute, while those of a more social-psychological orientation are concerned with human interaction, even from the earliest years.

Social psychology is really every kind of psychology, with a social emphasis. But we can isolate a number of human exchanges that determine the ways people's religious lives, and lives in general, evolve meaningfully. As social organisms, human beings instinctively seek a level of consistency and excitement. Religious experiences can maintain both consistency and excitement. Religious institutions are purveyors of meaning, novelty, and consolation. Private religion moves people to coordination and relationships with one another. When people experience cognitive dissonance because life does not correspond to their religious beliefs, religion is a negative, yet still vital, force in determining the modes of their social relationships. At a more complex level of social interaction the religious setting enables people to give performances that will determine their superiority or inferiority within a whole range of social categories. As part of a religious team, individuals will give performances that demand loyalty, discipline, and circumspection. But they do this as part of an attempt to create a social equilibrium: Individuals relate to other individuals as part of a common project of determining whose definitions of the situation will be honored. As an example illustrating the operation of all these social dynamics, recall the synagogue situation with the different members of the congregation playing a wide variety of formal and informal roles—during the service, around the synagogue, or in the surrounding community. The long-range results of interchange or the imagination of interchange are attitudes, which are mental relationships of a certain consistency that are expressed in behavior.

All these interpretations of life and religion are very general. They need to be verified, substantiated by research that includes the setting up artificial, experimental situations. Some kind of repetition of the situations that inspired the theories and interpretations is necessary. This kind of research has been carried out in empirical psychology. Researchers have tried to show that the God-image is formed in many ways, with the oedipal experience being of lesser importance. They have also tried to show that sudden religious conversions sometimes bring with them psychological problems that later must be regulated. They have tried to show that prejudice prevents people from passing to appropriate functioning because of indiscriminate thinking and that some types of religious practice help people to integrate their personalities. They have tried to correlate religious behavior and attitudes with an enormous range of other attitudes and practices.

Therapy and guidance represent the ultimate use of psychology in life, because here psychology is used not merely to analyze the personality but to facilitate the good life. We look, then, at the systems of therapy and their contexts to understand what therapies accomplish in human life, to see why the different therapeutic techniques work the way they do. Techniques of therapy and guidance are appropriate to the analysis and correction of religious aspects of personal life. Of course, those who would be therapists must decide what is appropriate for themselves and their work; those who enter therapy or ask for guidance must ultimately decide what is appropriate for them.

Interpretation of the Individual
Personality: The Case of St. Augustine

At this late stage in our study we cannot "prove" that every experience and every life is unique. Nor can we construct a thoroughgoing philosophical explanation of how an individual may be like every other individual and unlike every other individual at the same time. Let us assume that most of us believe that persons are in the last analysis unique, and let us proceed to a practical demonstration of how the conversion and the life of St. Augustine, the example we began with, can be examined in the light of our repertoire of psychological approaches with clear allowance for his uniqueness. My presentations of psychological categories and explanations would have to be verified and refined by appropriate Augustine scholars, but the suggestions and questions I give here are inspired by the psychologies presented—with their religious implications—in this book.

The Conversion of Augustine

To begin with, we want to know the relationship between Augustine's mother and father and the way he developed in relation to both of them. We know that he felt their power and their presence in his life from the way he wrote in *The Confessions* about their effect upon him. He felt that the influence of his father was harmful and that his mother should have been stricter, going against the ways of the father. Since his mother must have had a great effect on him because of her closeness to him across the years, we would like to know what were her own strivings as a Christian in the context of a family dominated by the paternal paganism. The image of the divine Father-figure did not seem to be so strong in Augustine's earlier life; later he did not address himself to God as a loving father but more as a loving spirit, in keeping with the philosophical heritage of the time of his conversion. We might ask to what extent the image of God was the image of his mother. One of his basic problems with his personal image of God was connected with the question, How can an all-powerful God permit evil? The search for goodness within himself did not enable him to rule out the sensual living that he wanted to avoid. Was his God-image as mild in the face of evil as his mother? As Augustine moved from adolescence through young manhood to adulthood he may have altered his projections of divine father-figure—with which he must be content and to which he must submit—to a divine figure with his mother's lovableness and lack of severity. This was not sufficient to overcome in his mind the evil presence, the evil cosmic "backdrop" onto which he would have projected this image.

Can we assume that neither the mother-image nor the father-image was strong enough for one to emerge? If the father-image was the one projected more naturally to begin with, it was strongly mixed with mother-image; but the mother-image did not take over. Neither, then, was sufficient to blot out the backdrop of the evil cosmos that the religious environment presented to him. Manichaeism was a religion that posited almost equal principles of good and evil, while neoplatonic intellectual inspiration gave people a desire to put off the requirements of the flesh. Not only was the fearsomeness of the universe pressing upon him, but a sense of the power of evil was an especially powerful image in his own world view. Given his human experience of mother and father, there was no powerful image of God to put before his mind's eye to blot out the evil and force of the universe. And all was unavailing in his attempts to ward off thoughts and impulses of sex.

Augustine was so philosophically sharp that he could not live with these contradictions the way many people throughout the ages could. It was important that he develop his understanding of a God who was not physically extended throughout the universe but was omnipresent because of his power. There was a short circuit in his God imagery, because he envisioned a God who could not ward off the powers of mystery and evil as they were presented to him by his religious thought environment. Augustine intellectualized a God who should have had more power, but how could he picture such a God when the earliest and most basic projections would probably have been of a vaguely bad father and a somewhat impotently good mother? It does not seem likely that a resolution to Augustine's problems of faith and behavior could have come from divinity-figure imagery in the years before his conversion. Once the Christian system began to make sense, his striving toward conversion was ineffective, because no single strong image presented itself attractively enough to draw forth all his energy. Integration and resolution had to come from somewhere else.

If we want to know how the integration of various aspects of Augustine's mental and emotional life came about, we should look to the opportunistic (survival or basic bodily) concerns. Augustine does give us details about his earliest sense of self in *The Confessions,* but these represent the later reflections of the middle-aged bishop, probably accurate in their way but to be interpreted in the light of his own experience. His sense of his own body and an overall sense of his intellectual and emotional self did not come together in a unified way at first. Certainly his opportunistic functioning in the sense of sexual needs did not allow him the freedom that the propriately functioning philosophical aspects of his personality seemed to be requiring. Not allowing ordinary bodily functions to be fulfilled to begin with, he then gradually constructed a self-image that included elements impossible to realize because of the resultant needs. His basic bodily sense and self-identity were kept from full development. Nor did he allow himself full ego-enhancement (healthy self-seeking) or ego-extensions (identifications with peoples and possessions). But the self-image, the combination of perceptions of present facts and projection of future goals, was the principal difficulty because of that hopeless aspiration toward an effectively bodiless purity, an aspiration that came from the religious and philosophical environment around him.

Yet the propriate functioning did finally bring Augustine close enough to a religious ideal so that the bodily functioning was integrated into an intellectualized or spiritualized unity. This ultimate integration can best be explained, then, by the power of the religious intention, by which a person actively moves toward a self-proposed goal. Augustine came to think that a goal of sexual abstinence and intellectual submission was valid and attainable. His desires for perfection were complex and future-oriented. In fact, the details of what finally happens in the personality are so complex, whether in Augustine or in any other convert, that we can say only that somehow the idea of the goal and the actual striving become one, producing a state of faith. Perhaps we might get to some kind of answer by reflecting on the possible cognitive schemata used by the youthful Augustine in developing a sense of the world.

Augustine's schemata to understand and express realism, animism, and artificialism might well have given him the sense of God as physically extended in the universe when he first began his personal and intellectual reflections. When his rhetorical and philosophical training were counterproductive in faith-building and morality, he went back to the earliest sense of the universe as an extension of himself and to understand how the universe is an extension of God. This would give him a God physically extended throughout the universe, a God who animates everything like some sort of fluid or electric power, and a God who makes everything after the manner of physical causality. His moral reasoning was most likely bound to these ways of thinking also, so that his senses of right and wrong, fair play and punishment would have had a materialistic quality to them. He seemed to leave behind any schemata that involved arbitrariness about rules. They had to come in an absolute way from a higher power, but they were not arbitrary; the works of his higher power reflected human fairness, coherence, and exchange. It would seem, though, that Augustine's sense of divine law was egocentric (where could he have gotten a sense of cooperation in the family and society of the era from which he came?); his view of divine law ultimately served the games he was playing. In the society where he lived survival was ultimately dependent upon war, just or otherwise, and his own personal survival and fulfillment were dependent upon a God who gave the strictest rules of sexual self-restraint and the feeling of bodily and intellectual "purity."

We can discern in a limited way the stages of his emotional development. If his mother's later attention was any indication of earlier concerns, then we must assume a nurturing attitude on her part. Augustine remembered her as a good and prayerful woman, so she must have inculcated a kind of trust from the beginning. Unless there were personal neuroses—and Augustine gives us no hints of them—we should assume that she calmed and reassured the infant personality. From what he describes of both his parents there may have been some kind of strain between them as regards the type of autonomy they would have encouraged in their young son. The father was described simply as someone who wanted Augustine to grow up and was happy to leave him alone, but we might ask if the mother was overprotective. If will power is the ability to choose the good presented, then there may have been something weak-willed about Augustine. Or there may have been a different kind of problem: the mother encouraging one kind of autonomy, the father another. The same problems would be present during those stages when initiative and industry were being developed. If he excelled in these areas—and we have every reason to suppose that he did—why did he feel such guilt about his moral actions as the years went on? If ever so many projects and personal activities were personally successful, so that we could say that in general initiative and industry were highly developed, why was religion (at the center of which was his problem with moral evil) an exception? Could it be that the moral and religious severity developed later on? I doubt it, and would suggest that there was some ideal of purity in his early life that was sensitized by his philosophical and personal encounters with the purity ideas of Manichaeism and Neoplatonism. Let us assume, too, that his adolescent identity was formed well enough; he seemed to love the woman he lived with very much, having no great sexual problems. The problems developed more fully later on.

All the developmental stages were lived quite well and quite positively, other than the obsession with intellectual and personal evil, especially sexual evil. If we look back over his life through his eyes, there seems to be an extraordinary emphasis on his mother, or the role of his mother. She could have had a strength that he himself did not realize, because, although he later felt that she did not stand up to the pagan father, she was the one to whom he joyfully returned when at last he conquered within himself the sensuality that had so displeased him and intellectually resolved the problem of evil somewhat to his satisfaction. The "pure" mother is, perhaps, a problem that should be examined further.

There are details of interaction, then, that a general discussion of developmental stages cannot get at. Not only were there subtleties in the relationship with his parents that led to Augustine's sense of control, but the relationship with the intellectual friends was something of importance. There were the companions in youthful misbehaving that he wrote about in a vivid description of stealing pears from a pear tree. There were the Manichaean associates, and we would do well to ask about their effect. It is obvious that older adolescents in particular, on those levels of society and in those civilizations where major developments are expected in adolescence, look for support from associates and companions, whom they join in behavior that gets away from the ordinary, often by relative extremes of licentiousness and dedication. Augustine did not tell us much about individual Manichaean associates, but more about those who were his companions a few years from the Manichaean period. He describes his philosopher companions, Alypius and Nebridius, in great detail. Although they were not as brilliant as he was, he praised them for their goodness; certainly he did not say anything about their intellects, but from what he says it is obvious that they did not have his intensity. And no one among them seems to have repeated or shared those fantastically dynamic moments that he went through at the moment of his conversion.

In later life he was always surrounded by a community. Contemporary scholars have taken pains to point out that many of his ideas were perfected in a community of intellectual exchange. He describes only his own intellectual development in *The Confessions,* so we cannot be absolutely sure what the contributions of the companions and colleagues were, because he developed a theological system that was his own. First as a priest and then as a bishop, Augustine was constantly in an interpretative frame of mind. This went on in spite of his extensive dealings with the common people of his day (often enough he referred to the responses of his listeners to the sermon, so one would think that there were veritable "Amen corners" in the churches where he preached).

To the interactions we attribute the changes of the bright and lusty young man, whose mother inculcated some kind of guilt while leaving his father free to encourage the independence and lustiness, and so begin a kind of divided self that could be resolved only by the dramatic conversion experience. The division might never have developed so fully had there not been a series of contracts in the companions of his youthful years: those with whom he stole, those with whom he reveled, those with whom he decried the power of evil, and those with whom he sought a pure philosophical goal. He must have had to present himself differently to those different groups; undoubtedly he had to vary his performances to fit his interpretation of their expectations. Ultimately the differing performances led him to such intense vacillation that only the unity-achieving performance of conversion enabled him to display himself to the world as Augustine the converted sinner, the spiritual teacher.

Our psychologies permit us very little greater detail than this, because they were fashioned for analysis of contemporaries. When Freud, Allport, Piaget, and others discussed psychological categories they assumed that these categories would be useful in an active psychological exchange, where a living therapist could observe or counsel a living patient. When we turn to history, things are different. The historian, naturally, works with the past. The data are different—not personally observed reactions but reactions recorded by others. And goals are different—not the reduction of various mental phenomena to a theory or standard but the exploration of a continuous series of events. Both historian and psychologist/therapist are eclectics, choosing concepts and terms from one another of the extant personality theories and testing a variety of possible terms for clarity in interpreting the evidence. At any given point in the work, however, the therapist has an infinitely greater amount of evidence at hand. Take the example of the psychoanalyst who day after day listens to associations and stories and observes a multitude of large and small reactions. He analyzes a person who sits there transmitting an infinite variety of data about himself or herself. But the historian has only a mass of writings or a mass of chronicles. He must adapt a number of psychological interpretations that were fashioned to understand personalities living and present to the interpreter.

You can see how our beginning interpretation of Augustine is, in fact, about as far as we can go psychologically. We would need him here in front of us in order to understand him further and to be sure that whatever psychological ideas we were using from our repertoire were really working.

Understanding the Religious Experience: Our Religious and Personal Limits

Even when we have the individuals right before us, we are seriously limited when we try to understand the religious experiences of others. We lack knowledge and personal experience of traditions other than our own, and we lack awareness of our own intellectual limits and cultural boundaries. They live within their boundaries; we live within ours.

Members of world religions other than those of our own culture must necessarily be different from us. Gods and goddesses have moved across the stage of history in innumerable forms, and the life story of each divinity is a summary of the dreams and sorrows, achievements and tragedies of some human group. Faith in the gods is the confidence of human beings that the universe does support their basic hopes and ideas. Great religious leaders, sometimes associated with and sometimes in place of the gods, have been equally important to people in their needs and aspirations, guiding them toward the gods or toward happiness with or without the gods. The great founder figures, Moses, Jesus, Muhammad, the Buddha, and Confucius, occupy a key position in the mental images and prayer lives of the many, many millions of adherents of the religions that they founded or organized. To understand religious experiences that are religiously or culturally different from our own we should know the images and stories of founder figures and gods that have been proposed to believers in sacred documents and recognized traditions. Then we should know how belief in founder/divinity figures influences a person's sense of self, and how the sense of self tends to promote a certain type of behavior or religious reaction.

In effect, we try to become aware of the limits to the possible range of psychological interpretations of the bona fide members of any given religion. For example, we should know that a Theravada Buddhist is not likely to have a view of God that is a projection of the father image. We should know that Hindus living within their own culture do not attempt to integrate aspects of their personality in the same way as Muslims, whose cultures in different areas of the world are usually quite unified. A nonbelieving Jew is more likely to identify with his or her "own kind" than a nonbelieving Christian. And so on.

Problems are even more specific than this, however. When studying the history of world religions, we generally organize our information around the significant texts that have come down to us and thereby assume we have a balanced view of how the religion looked and felt to its followers. But in fact we have to seek more information or do more guessing about the interaction between doctrines found in the texts and the thoughts and ideas of the religious devotees; more guessing, too, about the interaction between these religious thoughts and ideas and the general ordering of social and cultural life. A Catholic monk-professor at a French university is certainly more an experiencer of a Christianity close to biblical and other traditional texts than a South American peasant who has moved to one of the slums outside a large city. To explain the experience of founder/divinity figures and sense of self, we must see how members of a religion in different parts of the world, at least in one "sample" part of the world, behave as they respond to these normative notions.

In the last analysis we are limited by our own questions and concerns. Our questions are *our* questions. We ask them because of our personal concerns about life and religions, and these concerns are related to the society in which we were raised and our own unique experiences. Why do we want to know about religious experience and personality? What kind of personal and intellectual interest do we have in all of this? For some of us religion is strictly a matter of salvation; for others it is a fascinating study. And there are a number of approaches in between. But at least three kinds of personal and/or informational interest are invariably present. (Habermas, 1971).

A *technical* interest in religion is satisfied by the empirical and analytic aspects of our study. Those of us who preferred the chapter on research and the more empirically oriented work of

Piaget have, perhaps, this interest predominating. We have an interest in technical control over objectified processes of nature. Our goal is the production of technically exploitable knowledge, and so we concern ourselves with deducting lawlike hypotheses and statements about the correlation of observable events. We wish to understand in order to control life and the situation around us.

A practical and *interrelational* interest in religion is satisfied by historical and interpretative studies. Those of us who preferred the more historical aspects of our description of the development of psychology have, perhaps, this interest predominating. Here the validity of what we say does not depend upon the frame of reference of technical control. In these studies we start with our own world, our initial situation. We understand other people past and present to the extent that our own world becomes clarified. This type of knowledge is practical and effective to the extent that we arrive at an understanding of others and an understanding of ourselves. The historical and interpretive work by which we appropriate our own traditions and interpret foreign cultures is thus intersubjective. We communicate rather than control.

An *emancipatory*, or freeing, interest in religion is satisfied by the development of powers of self-reflection, reflection upon oneself as an individual and upon society as a whole. Lawlike information about the connections between people's minds and their psychological past, as well as the society around them, sets off a process of new and original reflection in the conciousness of those whom the laws are about—ourselves. This means that we can liberate ourselves from the very lawlike theories about mind and society that we are reflecting on. The ultimate goal, the ultimate interest, is autonomy and responsibility.

So our interests and concerns should lead us to a technical mastery of the psychological components of the religious experience, to an ability to communicate with others using religion as a starting point, and to achievement of personal freedom.

In sum, we are limited by the boundaries of our own culture and religion, and by the boundaries of the cultures and religions of others. We are further limited by the uniqueness of our own concerns and interests, which are generally speaking technical, practical, and emancipatory. But if there were no boundaries to our own experience of life and religion and no boundaries to the experience of life and religion of others, we would have no reason for studying the religious experiences of the "others." Technical, practical, and emancipatory interests motivate us to cross over the limiting boundaries of our own experience in the study of psychology of religion. But they have their own limitations built in, because knowledge depends on the personal interests that move us toward specific limiting goals.

This is the paradox, then, in life, in religion, and in the study we have just completed: Our limitations are our gifts and our gifts are our limitations. When we try to comprehend the infinite, we are at our most finite and our most sublime.

Bibliography

Given here are all references cited in the text, plus those for numerous other articles not specifically referred to. The latter were useful in the preparation of the book and are recommended for further reading and research.

AARONSON, BERNARD S. 1967. "Mystic and Schizophreniform States and the Experience of Depth," *Journal for the Scientific Study of Religion* 6:246-52.

ABELEY, PAUL, AND PIERRE DURBAN. 1969. "Attempt at a Psychosociological and Ethnological Study of a Region in France: The Occitanian Personality and Its Archtypes," *Annales medico-psychologiques* 1:713-26.

ACOCK, ALAN C., AND VERN L. BENGSTON. 1980. "Socialization and Attribution Processes: Actual Versus Perceived Similarity Among Parents and Youth," *Journal of Marriage and the Family* 42:501-15.

ADORNO, THEODORE W., et al. 1950. *The Authoritarian Personality.* New York: Harper & Row.

ALBRECH, STAN L.; BRUCE A. CHADWICK; AND DAVID S. ALCORN. 1977. "Religiosity and Deviance: Application of an Attitude–Behavior Contingent Consistency Model," *Journal for the Scientific Study of Religion* 16:263-74.

ALEXANDER, GARY T. 1979. "Psychological Foundations of William James's Theory of Religious Experience," *Journal of Religion* 59:421-34.

———. 1981. "William James, the Sick Soul, and the Negative Dimensions of Consciousness: A Partial Critique of Transpersonal Psychology," *Journal of the American Academy of Religion* 48:191–205.

ALKER, HENRY A., AND FRANK GAWIN. 1978. "On the Intrapsychic Specificity of Happiness," *Journal of Psychology* 96:205–10.

ALLEN, DONALD E.; REBECCA F. GUY; AND CHARLES K. EDGLEY. 1980. *Social Psychology as Social Process.* Belmont, Calif.: Wadsworth Publishing Co.

ALLEN, R. O., AND BERNARD SPILKA. 1967. "Committed and Consensual Religion: A Specification of Religion–Prejudice Relationships," *Journal for the Scientific Study of Religion* 6:191–206.

ALLISON, JOEL. 1969. "Religious Conversion: Regression and Progression in an Adolescent Experience," *Journal for the Scientific Study of Religion* 8:23–38.

ALLPORT, GORDON W. 1942. *The Use of Personal Documents in Psychological Science.* New York: Social Science Research Council.

———. 1943. "The Productive Paradoxes of William James," *Psychological Review* 50:95–120.

———. 1950. *The Individual and His Religion: A Psychological Interpretation.* New York: Macmillan.

———. 1955. *Becoming: Basic Considerations for a Psychology of Personality.* New Haven: Yale University Press.

ALLPORT, GORDON W., AND H. S. ODBERT. 1936. "Trait Names: A Psychological Study," *Psychological Monographs* 47, No. 211:1–171.

ALLPORT, GORDON W., AND J. MICHAEL ROSS. 1967. "Personal Religious Orientation and Prejudice," *Journal of Personality and Social Psychology* 5:432–43.

ALSTON, JON P. 1975. "Review of the Polls," *Journal for the Scientific Study of Religion* 14:165–68.

AMERICAN PSYCHOLOGICAL ASSOCIATION. 1969. *William James: Unfinished Business.* Washington, D.C.: American Psychological Association.

AMES, EDWARD SCRIBNER. 1910. *The Psychology of Religious Experience.* Boston: Houghton Mifflin.

ANAND, B. K.; G. S. CHHINA; AND BALDEV SINGH. 1969. "Some Aspects of Electroencephalographic Studies in Yogis." In *Altered States of Consciousness.* Edited by Charles T. Tart. Garden City, N.Y.: Doubleday.

ANDERSON, JAMES W. 1980. "William James's Depressive Period (1867–1872) and the Origins of his Creativity: A Psychobiographical Study." Dissertation, University of Chicago.

ANNIS, LAWRENCE V. 1976. "Emergency Helping and Religious Behavior," *Psychological Reports* 39:151-58.

ANTHONY, DICK, AND THOMAS ROBBINS. 1971. "Getting Straight with Meher Baba: A Study of Mysticism, Drug Rehabilitation and Post-adolescent Role Conflict," *Journal for the Scientific Study of Religion* 11:122-40.

APPLEBEE, ARTHUR N. 1978. *The Child's Concept of Story: Ages Two to Seventeen.* Chicago: University of Chicago Press.

ARGYLE, MICHAEL, AND BENJAMIN BEIT-HALLAHMI. 1975. *The Social Psychology of Religion.* Boston: Routledge & Kegan Paul.

AUSTIN, J. L. 1970. *Philosophical Papers.* Edited by J. O. Wisdom and J. W. Urmson. Second edition. New York: Oxford University Press.

AVENS, ROBERT. 1977. "The Image of the Devil in C. G. Jung's Psychology," *Journal of Religion & Health* 16:196-222.

BACHE, CHRISTOPHER M. 1981. "On the Emergence of Perinatal Symptoms in Buddhist Meditation," *Journal for the Scientific Study of Religion* 20:339-50.

BACK, KURT W. 1972. *Beyond Words: The Story of Sensitivity Training and the Encounter Movement.* New York: Russell Sage Foundation.

———. 1973. "Small Group Research and the Issues of Micro vs. Macro-Sociology: The Case of Demography," *Representative Research in Social Psychology* 4:83-92.

BAGOZZI, RICHARD P., AND ROBERT E. BURNKRANT. 1979. "Attitude Organization and the Attitude-Behavior Relationship," *Journal of Personality and Social Psychology* 37:913-29.

BAGWELL, H. ROBERTS. 1969. "The Abrupt Religious Conversion Experience," *Journal of Religion and Health* 8:359-74.

BAHR, HOWARD M.; LOIS FRANZ BARTEL; AND BRUCE A. CHADWICK. 1971. "Orthodoxy, Activism, and the Salience of Religion," *Journal for the Scientific Study of Religion* 10:69-75.

BAINBRIDGE, WILLIAM S., AND RODNEY STARK. 1981. "The 'Consciousness Reformation' Reconsidered," *Journal for the Scientific Study of Religion* 20:1-16.

BAKAN, DAVID. 1958. *Sigmund Freud and the Jewish Mystical Tradition.* Princeton, N.J.: Van Nostrand.

———. 1966. *The Duality of Human Existence.* Boston: Beacon Press.

BAKER, M., AND RICHARD GORSUCH. 1982. "Trait Anxiety and Intrinsic-Extrinsic Religiousness," *Journal for the Scientific Study of Religion* 21:119-22.

BALCH, ROBERT W., AND DAVID TAYLOR. 1977. "Seekers and Saucers: The Role of the Cultic Milieu in Joining a UFO Cult," *American Behavioral Scientist* 20:839–60.

BALES, ROBERT F., AND P. STEPHEN COHEN. 1979. *SYMLOG: A System for the Multiple Level Observation of Groups.* New York: Free Press.

BATSON, C. DANIEL. 1977. "Experimentation in Psychology of Religion: An Impossible Dream," *Journal for the Scientific Study of Religion* 16:413–18.

———. 1979. "Experimentation in Psychology of Religion: Living with or in a Dream?" *Journal for the Scientific Study of Religion* 18:90–93.

BATSON, C. DANIEL; STEPHEN J. NAIFEH; AND SUZANNE PATE. "Social Desirability, Religious Orientation, and Racial Prejudice," *Journal for the Scientific Study of Religion* 17:31–41.

BATSON, C. DANIEL, AND W. LARRY VENTIS. 1982. *The Religious Experience: A Social-Psychological Perspective.* New York: Oxford University Press.

BEIT-HALLAHMI, BENJAMIN. 1977. "Psychology of Religion, 1880–1930." In *Current Perspectives in the Psychology of Religion.* Edited by Newton Malony. Grand Rapids, Mich.: Eerdmans.

———. 1983. "Psychology and Religion," in *Psychology and its Allied Disciplines.* Edited by M. H. Bornstein. Hillsdale, N.J.: Lawrence Erlbaum Associates.

BEM, D. J. 1972. "Self-perception Theory." In *Advances in Experimental Social Psychology.* Edited by L. Berkowitz. Vol. 6. New York: Academic Press.

BEN-YAHUDA, NACHMAN. 1978–79. "Altered States of Consciousness: A Sociological Perspective," *Journal of Altered States of Consciousness* 4:345–56.

BENSON, PETER, AND BERNARD SPILKA. 1973. "God Images as a Function of Self-esteem and Locus of Control," *Journal for the Scientific Study of Religion* 12:297–310.

BERMAN, ALAN L. 1974. "Belief in Afterlife, Religion, Religiosity and Life-threatening Experiences," *Omega* 4:127–35.

BINSWANGER, LUDWIG. 1958a. "The Existential Analysis School of Thought." In *Existence.* Edited by Rollo May, Ernest Angel, and Henri F. Ellenberger. New York: Simon & Schuster.

———. 1958b. "The Case of Ilse." In *Existence.* Edited by Rollo May, Ernest Angel, and Henri F. Ellenberger. New York: Simon & Schuster.

BLANCHARD, KENDALL. 1975. "Changing Sex Roles and Protestantism

Among the Navajo Women in Ramah," *Journal for the Scientific Study of Religion* 14:43-50.

BLUMBERG, LEONARD. 1977. "The Ideology of a Therapeutic Social Movement: Alcoholics Anonymous," *Journal of Studies on Alcohol* 38:2122-43.

BOHRA, KAYYUM. 1979. "Social Perception of Ingroup and Outgroup Members in India," *Journal of Social Psychology* 108:9-12.

BOISEN, ANTON. 1971 (1936). *The Exploration of the Inner World: A Study of Mental Disorder and Religious Experience.* Philadelphia: University of Pennsylvania Press.

BORD, RICHARD J., AND JOSEPH E. FAULKNER. 1975. "Religiosity and Secular Attitudes: The Case of Catholic Pentecostals," *Journal for the Scientific Study of Religion* 14:257-70.

BORING, EDWIN G. 1950. *A History of Experimental Psychology.* Second edition. New York: Century.

BRISLIN, RICHARD W. 1968. "Contact as a Variable in Intergroup Interaction," *Journal of Social Psychology* 76:149-54.

BROMLEY, D. B. 1977. *Personality Description in Ordinary Language.* New York: John Wiley & Sons.

BROMLEY, DAVID G., AND ANSON D. SHUPE. 1979. *"Moonies" in America: Cult, Church, and Crusade.* Beverly Hills, Calif.: Sage Publications.

BRONSON, GORDON W. 1959. "Identity Diffusion in Late Adolescence," *Journal of Abnormal and Social Psychology* 59:414-17.

BROWDE, JOSEPH A. 1976. "Maturity: A Comparative Approach to Maslow, Rogers, Havighurst, and Erikson," *Character Potential* 7:181-88.

BROWN, L. B., editor. 1973. *Psychology of Religion.* Baltimore: Penguin Books.

BROWN, L. B., AND J.' P. FORGAS. "The Structure of Religion: A Multidimensional Scaling of Informal Elements," *Journal for the Scientific Study of Religion* 19:423-31.

BROWN, NORMAN O. 1959. *Life Against Death: The Psychoanalytical Meaning of History.* Middletown, Conn.: Wesleyan University Press.

BROWN, PETER. 1969. *Augustine of Hippo: A Biography.* Berkeley: University of California Press.

BROWNING, DON. 1975. "William James's Philosophy of the Person: the Concept of the Strenuous Life," *Zygon* 10:162-74.

———. 1976. *The Moral Context of Pastoral Care.* Philadelphia: Westminster Press.

——. 1979. "William James's Philosophy of Mysticism," *Journal of Religion* 59:56-70.

——. 1980. *Pluralism and Personality: William James and Some Contemporary Cultures of Psychology.* Lewisburg, Pa.: Bucknell University Press.

BULT, MARTIN. 1975. "Purpose in Life and Religious Orientation," *Journal of Psychology and Theology* 3:116-18.

BURGESS, JOHN H., AND RALPH LEE WAGNER. 1981. "Religion as a Factor in Extrustion to Public Mental Hospitals," *Journal for the Scientific Study of Religion* 10:237-40.

BURKE, JOSEPH F. 1978. "Mature Religious Behavior: A Psychological Perspective and Its Implications," *Journal of Religion and Health* 17:177-83.

BURNS, GEORGE W. 1972. "Religious Influences on Behavior of the Group Therapist," *Psychological Reports* 31:638.

BURNS, R. HUGH, AND DANIEL AUBREY. 1969. "A Factor Analytic Study of Religious Attitudes Among Psychiatric Patients and Normals," *Journal for the Scientific Study of Religion* 8:165.

BURRELL, DAVID. 1970. "Reading the Confessions of Augustine: An Exercise in Theological Understanding," *Journal of Religion* 50:327-51.

BUTTS, JUNE D. 1978. "Altered States of Consciousness," *Journal of the National Medical Association* 70:743-44.

CAPPS, DONALD. 1974. "Contemporary Psychology of Religion: Task of Theoretical Reconstruction," *Social Research* 41:61-83.

——. 1979a. *Pastoral Care: A Thematic Approach.* Philadelphia: Westminster.

——. 1979b. "Erikson's Theory of Religious Ritual: The Case of the Excommunication of Ann Hibbens," *Journal for the Scientific Study of Religion* 18:337-49.

——. 1980. "Research Models and Pedagogical Paradigms in Psychology of Religion," *Review of Religious Research* 21:218-27.

CAPPS, DONALD; PAUL RANSOHOFF; AND LEWIS RAMBO. 1976. "Publication Trends in Psychology of Religion to 1974," *Journal for the Scientific Study of Religion* 15:14-28.

CAREY, RAYMOND G. 1981. "Influence of Peers in Shaping Religious Behavior," *Journal for the Scientific Study of Religion* 10:157-59.

CARTER, JOHN D. 1977. "Secular and Sacred Models of Psychology and Religion," *Journal of Psychology and Theology* 5:197-208.

CHARTIER, MYRON R., AND LARRY A. GOEHNER. 1976. "A Study of the Relationship of Parent-Adolescent Communication, Self-Esteem, and God Image," *Journal of Psychology and Theology* 4:227-32.

CHATTERJI, PRITIBHUSHAN. 1975. "Jung's Approach to Religion," *Samiksa* 29:85–94.

CHILD, IRVIN L. 1973. *Humanistic Psychology and the Research Tradition: Their Several Virtues.* New York: John Wiley & Sons.

CHRISTOPHER, STEFAN, et al. 1971. "Social Deprivation and Religiosity," *Journal for the Scientific Study of Religion* 10:385–92.

CLARK, WALTER HOUSTON. 1958. *The Psychology of Religion: An Introduction to Religious Experience and Behaviour.* New York: Macmillan.

———. 1968. "The Psychology of the Religious Experience," *Psychology Today,* February, pp. 42 *ff.*

CLEBSCH, WILLIAM A., AND CHARLES R. JAECKLE. 1964. *Pastoral Care in Historical Perspective: An Essay with Exhibits.* New York: Harper & Row.

CLINEBELL, HOWARD J. 1966. *Basic Types of Pastoral Counseling.* Nashville: Abingdon.

COE, GEORGE ALBERT. 1916. *The Psychology of Religion.* Chicago: University of Chicago Press.

COHEN, RONALD J., AND FREDERICK J. SMITH. 1976. "Social Reinforced Obsessing: Etiology of a Disorder in a Christian Scientist," *Journal of Consulting and Clinical Psychology* 44:142–44.

CONN, WALTER, editor. 1978. *Conversion: Perspectives on Personal and Social Transformation.* New York: Alba House.

———. 1979. "Erikson Identity: Essay on the Psychological Foundations of Religious Ethics," *Zygon* 14:125–34.

COVELLO, EDWARD M. 1977–78. "Symbolization of Conscious States in the *I Ching:* A Quantitative Study," *Journal of Altered States of Consciousness* 3:111–29.

CRAIG, ROBERT. 1972. "An Analysis of the Psychology of Moral Development of Lawrence Kohlberg," *Counseling and Values* 17:10–17.

CRANDALL, JAMES E., AND ROGER D. RASMUSSEN. 1975. "Purpose in Life as Related to Specific Values," *Journal of Clinical Psychology* 31:482–85.

CROOG, SYDNEY H., AND SOL LEVINE. 1972. "Religious Identity and Response to Serious Illness: A Report on Heart Patients," *Social Science and Medicine* 6:17–32.

CURRAN, CHARLES A. 1969. *Religious Values in Counseling and Psychotherapy.* New York: Sheed & Ward.

CYGNAR, THOMAS E.; DONALD L. NOEL; AND CARDELL K. JACOBSON. 1977. "Religiosity and Prejudice: An Interdimensional Analysis," *Journal for the Scientific Study of Religion* 16:183–91.

Dalal, A. S., and T. X. Barber. 1969. "Yoga, 'Yoga Feats,' and Hypnosis in the Light of Empirical Research," *American Journal of Clinical Hypnosis* 11:155-66.

Dalmau, C. J. 1967. "Anthropocentric Aspects of Religion," *Psychoanalytic Review* 54:123-31.

Daly, Lawrence J. 1978. "Psychohistory and St. Augustine's Conversion Process: An Historiographical Critique," *Augustiniana* 28:231-54.

Dare, Christopher. 1969. "An Aspect of the Ego Psychology of Religion: A Comment on Dr. Guntrip's Paper," *British Journal of Medical Psychology* 42:335-40.

Darley, J. M., and C. D. Batson. 1973. "From Jerusalem to Jericho': A Study of Situational and Dispositional Variables in Helping Behavior." *Journal of Personality and Social Psychology* 27:100-08.

Davidson, James D. 1972. "Religious Belief as an Independent Variable," *Journal for the Scientific Study of Religion* 11:65-75.

Day, Larry C. 1975. "The Development of the God Concept: A Symbolic Interaction Approach," *Journal of Psychology and Theology* 3:172-78.

De, B., and M. P. Jaiswal. 1972. "Sex Differences in Value Patterns of Adolescent Students," *Indian Educational Review* 7:187-94.

Dearman, Marion. 1974. "Christ and Conformity: A Study of Pentecostal Values," *Journal for the Scientific Study of Religion* 13:437-53.

Deikman, Arthur J. 1969. "Deautomatization and the Mystic Experience." In *Altered States of Consciousness*. Edited by Charles T. Tart. Garden City, N.Y.: Doubleday.

———. 1982. *The Observing Self: Mysticism and Psychotherapy*. Boston: Beacon Press.

Demerath, N. J., and Richard M. Levinson. 1971. "Baiting the Dissident Hook: Effects of Bias on Measuring Religious Belief," *Sociometry* 34:346-59.

Deutch, Alexander. 1980. "Tenacity of Attachment to a Cult Leader: A Psychiatric Perspective," *American Journal of Psychiatry* 137:1569-73.

Dewhurst, Kenneth, and A. W. Beard. 1970. "Sudden Religious Conversions in Temporal Lobe Epilepsy," *British Journal of Psychiatry* 117:497-507.

Didato, Salvatore. 1967. "Influence of Value-strength on Perceptual Distortion," *Perceptual and Motor Skills* 24:330.

DICKINSON, GEORGE D. 1976. "Religious Practices of Adolescents in a Southern Community: 1964-1974," *Journal for the Scientific Study of Religion* 15:361-63.

DITTES, JAMES E. 1965. "Continuities Between Life and Thought of Augustine," *Journal for the Scientific Study of Religion* 5:284-89.

——. 1969. "Psychology of Religion." In *The Handbook of Social Psychology.* Edited by Gardner Lindzey and Elliot Aronson. Second edition. Volume Five: *Applied Social Psychology,* pp. 602-59. Reading, Mass.: Addison-Wesley.

——. 1973. "Beyond William James." In *Beyond the Classics: Essays in the Scientific Study of Religion.* Edited by Charles E. Glock and Phillip E. Hammond. New York: Harper & Row.

DIXIT, RAMESH C., AND DEO D. SHARMA. 1970. "Transformation of Social and Religious Values of Different Castes," *Psychologia: An International Journal of Psychology in the Orient* 13:117-19.

DOWNTON, JAMES V. 1980. "An Evolutionary Theory of Spiritual Conversion and Commitment: The Case of the Divine Light Mission," *Journal for the Scientific Study of Religion* 19:381-96.

DRAPELA, VICTOR J. 1969. "Personality Adjustment and Religious Growth," *Journal of Religion and Health* 8:87-97.

DREIFUSS, GUSTAV. 1972. "The Figures of Satan and Abraham: In the Legends on Genesis 22, the Akadah," *Journal of Analytical Psychology* 17:166-78.

DRIEDGER, LEO. 1982. "Individual Freedom vs. Community Control: An Adaptation of Erikson's Ontogeny of Ritualization," *Journal for the Scientific Study of Religion* 21:226-41.

DUDLEY, ROGER LOUIS. 1978. "Alienation from Religion in Adolescents from Fundamentalist Religious Homes," *Journal for the Scientific Study of Religion* 17:389-98.

DURKA, GLORIA, AND JOANMARIE SMITH. 1976. "Theory and Practice in Religion and Education: 1. Modeling in Religious Education," *Religious Education* 71:115-32.

DYKSTRA, CRAIG. 1980. "Moral Virtue or Social Reasoning," *Religious Education* 75:115-28.

EDELHEIT, HENRY. 1974. "Crucifixion Fantasies and Their Relation to the Primal Scene," *International Journal of Psychoanalysis* 55:193-99.

EDINGER, EDWARD. 1972. *Ego and Archetype: Individuation and the Religious Function of the Psyche.* Baltimore: Penguin.

EITZEN, LANDO. 1969. "Confrontation Action Psychotherapy with Religio-moral Values," *Journal of Pastoral Care* 23:26-35.

ELKIND, DAVID. 1964. "Piaget's Semi-clinical Interview and the Study of Spontaneous Religion," *Journal for the Scientific Study of Religion* 3:40–47.

———. 1970. "The Origins of Religion in the Child," *Review of Religious Research* 12:35–42.

———. 1978. *The Child's Reality: Three Developmental Themes.* New York: John Wiley.

ELLENBERGER, HENRI F. 1970. *The Discovery of the Unconscious: The History and Evolution of Dynamic Psychiatry.* New York: Basic Books.

ELLWOOD, ROBERT. 1973. *Religious and Spiritual Groups in Modern America.* Englewood Cliffs, N.J.: Prentice-Hall.

EMBREE, ROBERT A. 1970. "The Religious Association Scales as an 'Abilities' Measure of the Religious Factor in Personality," *Journal for the Scientific Study of Religion* 9:299–302.

———. 1973. "The Religious Association Scale: A Follow-up Association Study," *Journal for the Scientific Study of Religion* 12:223–26.

EMMET, DOROTHY. 1972. *Function, Purpose and Powers: Some Concepts in the Study of Individuals and Societies.* Philadelphia: Temple University Press.

ENNIS, PHILIP H. 1967. "Ecstasy and Everyday Life," *Journal for the Scientific Study of Religion* 6:40–48.

ERHARDT, ANKE A.; SUSAN E. INCE; AND HEINO F. MEYER-BALHBURG. 1981. "Career Aspiration and Gender Role Development in Young Girls," *Archives of Sexual Behavior* 10:281–99.

ERIKSON, ERIK H. 1950. *Childhood and Society.* New York: W. W. Norton.

———. 1962. *Young Man Luther.* New York: W. W. Norton.

———. 1964. *Insight and Responsibility: Lectures on the Ethical Implications of Psychoanalytic Insight.* New York: W. W. Norton.

———. 1968. *Identity, Youth, and Crisis.* New York: W. W. Norton.

———. 1969. *Gandhi's Truth.* New York: W. W. Norton.

———. 1975. *Life History and the Historical Moment.* New York: W. W. Norton.

———. 1977. *Toys and Reasons: Stages in the Ritualization of Experience.* New York: W. W. Norton.

———. 1982. *The Life Cycle Completed: A Review.* New York: W. W. Norton.

EZER, MELVIN. 1962. "The Effect of Religion upon Children's Responses to Questions Involving Physical Causality." In *The*

Causes of Behavior. Edited by J. F. Rosenblith and W. Allinsmith. Boston: Allyn & Bacon.

FAGOT, BEVERLY L. 1981. "Continuity and Change in Play Styles as a Function of Sex of Child," *International Journal of Behavioral Development* 4:37-43.

FARLEY, FRANK H.; AND DIONNE, MARY T. 1972. "Value Orientations of Sensation-seekers," *Perceptual and Motor Skills* 34:509-10.

FEHR, LAWRENCE A.; AND MARK E. HEINTZELMAN. 1977. "Personality and Attitude Correlates of Religiosity: A Source of Controversy;" *Journal of Psychology* 95:63-66.

FEHR, LAWRENCE A., AND LEIGHTON E. STAMPS. 1979. "The Mosher Guilt Scales: A Construct Validity Extension," *Journal of Personality Assessment* 43:257-60.

FEIFEL, HERMAN. 1974. "Religious Conviction and Fear of Death among the Healthy and Terminally Ill," *Journal for the Scientific Study of Religion* 13:353-60.

FESTINGER, LEON. 1957. *A Theory of Cognitive Dissonance.* Stanford, Calif.: Stanford University Press.

FESTINGER, LEON; HENRY W. RIECKEN; AND STANLEY SCHACHTER. 1956. *When Prophecy Fails.* Minneapolis: University of Minnesota Press.

FISCHER, ROLAND. 1971. "A Cartography of the Ecstatic and Meditative States," *Science* 174:897-904.

———. 1975. "A Cartography of Inner Space." In *Hallucinations: Behavior, Experience, and Theory.* Edited by R. K. Siegel and L. J. West. New York: John Wiley & Sons.

———. 1975-76. "A Dialog with Eccles, Ornstein and the Schwitzgebels," *Journal of Altered States of Consciousness* 2:267-73.

———. 1977-78a. "On Images and Pure Light: Integration of East and West, *Journal of Altered States of Consciousness* 3:205-12.

———. 1977-78b. "The Making of Reality," *Journal of Altered States of Consciousness* 3:371-89.

FISHER, SEYMOUR, AND ROGER P. GREENBERG. 1977. *The Scientific Credibility of Freud's Theories and Therapy.* New York: Basic Books.

FISKE, DONALD W. 1971. *Measuring the Concepts of Personality.* Chicago: Aldine.

———. 1978. *Strategies for Personality Research.* San Francisco: Jossey-Bass.

FISKE, DONALD W., AND SALVATORE R. MADDI, editors. 1961. *Functions of Varied Experience.* Homewood, Ill.: Dorsey Press.

Fowler, James W. 1981. *Stages of Faith; the Psychology of Human Development and the Quest for Meaning.* New York: Harper & Row.

Fox, William S., and Elton F. Jackson. 1973. "Protestant-Catholic Differences in Educational Achievement and Persistence in School," *Journal for the Scientific Study of Religion* 12:65-84.

Francis, Leslie. 1978. "The Psychology of Religion: Revived, Not Yet Reborn," *Bulletin of the British Psychological Society* 31:44-45.

———. 1979. "The Psychology of Religion: Beyond Revival," *Bulletin of the British Psychological Society* 32:141-42.

Frederiksen, P. 1978. "Augustine and His Analysts: The Possibility of a Psychohistory," *Soundings: An Interdisciplinary Journal* 61:206-27.

Freud, Sigmund. 1950a (1911). "Psycho-analytic Notes on an Auto-biographical Account of a Case of Paranoia." In *Complete Works.* Vol. 12. London: Hogarth Press.

———. 1950b (1913). *Totem and Taboo.* New York: W. W. Norton.

———. 1959a (1907). "Obsessive Acts and Religious Practices. *Collected Papers.* Vol. 2. Edited by James Strachey. New York: Basic Books.

———. 1959b (1928). "A Religious Experience." In *Collected Papers.* Volume 5. Edited by James Strachey. New York: Basic Books.

———. 1960 (1923). *The Ego and the Id.* Translated by Joan Riviere. New York: W. W. Norton.

———. 1961 (1927). *The Future of an Illusion.* Translated by James Strachey. W. W. Norton.

———. 1967 (1939). *Moses and Monotheism.* Translated by Katherine Jones. New York: Vintage Press.

Fromm, Erich. 1947. *Man for Himself: An Inquiry into the Psychology of Ethics.* New York: Fawcett.

———. 1956. *The Art of Loving.* New York: Harper & Row.

Fry, P. S., and R. Ghosh. 1980. "Attributional Differences in the Life Satisfactions of the Elderly: A Cross-cultural Comparison of Asian and United States Subjects," *International Journal of Psychology* 15:201-12.

Furman, Frieda Kerner. 1981. "Ritual as Social Mirror and Agent of Cultural Change: A Case Study in Synagogue Life," *Journal for the Scientific Study of Religion* 20:228-41.

Gadpaille, Warren J. 1978. "Psycho-sexual Developmental Tasks Imposed by Pathologically Delayed Childhood: A Cultural Dilemma," *Adolescent Psychiatry* 6:136-55.

GALANTER, MARC. 1980. "Psychological Induction into the Large Group: Findings from a Modern Religious Sect," *American Journal of Psychiatry* 137: 1574-79.

GALANTER, MARC, et al. 1979. "The 'Moonies': A Psychological Study of Conversion and Membership in a Contemporary Religious Sect," *American Journal of Psychiatry* 136:165-70.

GARFIELD, CHARLES A. 1975. "Consciousness Alteration and Fear of Death," *Journal of Transpersonal Psychology* 7:147-75.

GARFIELD, SOL L. 1980. *Psychotherapy: An Eclectic Approach.* New York: John Wiley.

GEARY, THOMAS F. 1977. "Personal Growth in CPE," *Journal of Pastoral Care* 31:12-17.

GELBOND, BLAIR. 1979. "Self-actualization and Unselfish Love," *Journal of Religious Humanism* 13:74-78.

GHOUGASSIAN, JOSEPH P. 1972. *Gordon Allport's Ontopsychology of the Person.* New York: Philosophical Library.

GIBBONS, DON, AND JAMES DE JARNETTE. 1972. "Hypnotic Susceptibility and Religious Experience," *Journal for the Scientific Study of Religion* 11:152-56.

GIBBS, HARRIETT W., AND JEANNE ACHTERBERG-LAWLIS. 1978. "Spiritual Values and Death Anxiety: Implications for Counseling with Terminal Cancer Patients," *Journal of Counseling Psychology* 25:563-69.

GINSBERG, HERBERT, AND SYLVIA OPPER. 1979. *Piaget's Theory of Intellectual Development.* Second edition. Englewood Cliffs, N.J.: Prentice-Hall.

GLADDING, SAMUEL T. 1977. "Psychological Anomie and Religious Identity in Two Adolescent Populations," *Psychological Reports* 41:419-24.

GLOCK, CHARLES Y. 1972. "Images of 'God,' Images of Man, and the Organization of Social Life," *Journal for the Scientific Study of Religion* 11:1-15.

GLOCK, CHARLES Y., AND RODNEY STARK. 1965. *Religion and Society in Tension.* Chicago: Rand McNally.

GLOCK, CHARLES Y., et al. 1975. *Adolescent Prejudice.* New York: Harper & Row.

GOBLE, FRANK G. 1970. *The Third Force: The Psychology of Abraham Maslow.* New York: Washington Square Press.

GODIN, ANDRÉ. 1965. *The Pastor as Counselor.* Translated by Bernard Phillips. New York: Holt, Rinehart & Winston.

———. 1972. "Religious Orthodoxy Studied by Social Psychologist," *Nouvelle Revue Theologique* 94:620-37.

Goffman, Erving. 1959. *The Presentation of Self in Everyday Life.* Garden City, N.Y.: Doubleday.

Goldbrunner, Josef. 1966. *Realization: Anthropology of Pastoral Care.* Notre Dame, Ind.: University of Notre Dame Press.

Goldenberg, Naomi R. 1979. "Archetypal Theory after Jung." *Spring* 199–220.

Goldman, Ronald J. 1964. *Religious Thinking from Childhood to Adolescence.* London: Routledge & Kegan Paul.

———. 1965. "The Application of Piaget's Schema of Operational Thinking to Religious Story Data by Means of the Guttman Scalogram," *British Journal of Psychology* 35:158–70.

Goldstein, L., and N. W. Stoltzfus. 1973. "Psychoactive Drug-induced Changes of Interhemispheric EEG Amplitude Relationships," *Agents and Actions* 3:124–32.

Goldstein, L.; N. W. Stoltzfus; and J. F. Gardocki. 1972. "Changes in Interhemispheric Amplitude Relationships in the EEG During Sleep," *Physiology and Behavior* 8:811–16.

Goleman, Daniel. 1978–79. "A Taxonomy of Meditation-specific Altered States," *Journal of Altered States of Consciousness* 4:203–13.

Goodman, Felicitas D. 1980. "Triggering of Altered States of Consciousness as Group Event: A New Case from Yucatan," *Confinia Psychiatrica* 23:26–34.

Gorlow, Leon, and Harold E. Schroeder. 1968. "Motives for Participating in the Religious Experience," *Journal for the Scientific Study of Religion* 7:241–51.

Gorman, Margaret. 1977. "Moral and Faith Development in Seventeen-year-old Students," *Religious Education* 72:491–504.

Gorsuch, Richard L. 1968. "The Conceptualization of God as Seen in Adjective Ratings," *Journal for the Scientific Study of Religion* 7:56–64.

———. 1982. "Practicality and Ethics of Experimental Research when Studying Religion," *Journal for the Scientific Study of Religion* 21:370–72.

Gorsuch, Richard L., and Daniel Aleshire. 1974. "Christian Faith and Ethnic Prejudice: A Review and Interpretation of Research," *Journal for the Scientific Study of Religion* 13:281–307.

Gorsuch, Richard L., and H. Newton Malony. 1976. *The Nature of Man: Social Psychological Perspectives. The Third John G. Finch Symposium on Psychology and Religion.* Springfield, Ill.: Thomas.

Gorsuch, Richard L., and Craig S. Smith. 1983. "Attributions of

Responsibility to God: An Interaction of Religious Beliefs and Outcomes,"*Journal for the Scientific Study of Religion* 22:340-52.

Gowan, J. C. 1978-79. "Altered States of Consciousness: A Taxonomy," *Journal of Altered States of Consciousness* 4:141-56.

Grattan, C. Hartley. 1962. *The Three Jameses: A Family of Minds.* With an introduction by Oscar Cargill. New York: New York University Press.

Greeley, Andrew. 1974. *Ecstasy: A Way of Knowing.* Englewood Cliffs, N.J.: Prentice-Hall.

Gray, David B. 1970. "Measuring Attitudes Toward the Church," *Journal for the Scientific Study of Religion* 9:293-97.

Gudeman, Howard E. 1966. "The Phenomenology of Delusions," *Review of Existential Psychology and Psychiatry* 6:196-210.

Habermas, Jurgen. 1971. *Knowledge and Human Interests.* Boston: Beacon Press.

Hadaway, Christopher Kirk. 1978. "Life Satisfaction and Religion: A Reanalysis," *Social Forces* 57:636-43.

Hadaway, C. Kirk, and Wade Clark Roof. 1979. "Those Who Stay Religious 'Nones' and Those Who Don't: A Research Note," *Journal for the Scientific Study of Religion* 18:194-200.

Hadden, Jeffrey K. 1963. "An Analysis of Some Factors Associated with Religion and Political Affiliation," *Journal for the Scientific Study of Religion* 2:209-16.

Hall, C. S.; and G. Lindzey. 1970. *Theories of Personality.* New York: Wiley.

Halmos, Paul. 1970. *The Faith of the Counselors: A Study in the Theory and Practice of Social Case Work and Psychotherapy.* New York: Schocken.

Hamon, Steven A. 1977. "Beyond Self-actualization: Comments on the Life and Death of Stephen the Martyr," *Journal of Psychology and Theology* 5:291-99.

Hanford, Jack Tyrus. 1975. "A Synoptic Approach: Resolving Problems in Empirical and Phenomenological Approaches to the Psychology of Religion 14:219-27.

Hare, A. Paul. 1976. *A Handbook of Small Group Research.* Second Edition. New York: Free Press.

Harrison, Michael L., and John K. Maniha. 1978. "Dynamics of Dissenting Movements Within Established Organizations: Two Cases and a Theoretical Interpretation," *Journal for the Scientific Study of Religion* 17:207-24.

HASSAN, M. K. 1975. "Religious Prejudice Among College Students: A Socio-pyschological Investigation," *Journal of Social and Economic Studies* 3:101-7.

HASTINGS, PHILIP K., AND DEAN R. HOGE. 1974. "Changes in Religion Among College Students, 1948-1974," *Journal for the Scientific Study of Religion* 15:237-49.

HAVENS, JOSEPH. 1964. "A Working Paper: Memo on the Religious Implications of the Consciousness-changing Drugs," *Journal for the Scientific Study of Religion* 3:216-26.

HAY, DAVID. 1979. "Religious Experience Amongst a Group of Postgraduate Students: A Qualitative Study," *Journal for the Scientific Study of Religion* 18:164-82.

HAY, DAVID, AND ANN MORISY. 1978. "Reports of Ecstatic, Paranormal, or Religious Experience in Great Britain and the United States: A Comparison of Trends," *Journal for the Scientific Study of Religion:* 17:255-68.

HEILMAN, SAMUEL. 1976. *Synagogue Life: A Study in Symbolic Interaction.* Chicago: University of Chicago Press.

HEIRICH, MAX. 1977. "Change of Heart: A Test of Some Widely Held Theories About Religious Conversion," *American Journal of Sociology* 83:653-80.

HELFAER, PHILIP M. 1972. *The Psychology of Religious Doubt.* Boston: Beacon Press.

HENDERSON, C. WILLIAM. 1975. *Awakening: Ways to Psychospiritual Growth.* Englewood Cliffs, N.J.: Prentice-Hall.

HERRENKOHL, ELLEN C. 1978. "Parallels in the Process of Achieving Personal Growth by Abusing Parents Through Participation in Group Therapy Programs or in Religious Groups," *Family Coordinator* 27:279-82.

HETHERINGTON, R. 1978. "Psychology of Religion," *Bulletin of the British Psychological Society* 31:299.

HILLERY, GEORGE A. 1969. "The Convent: Community, Prison, or Task Force?" *Journal for the Scientific Study of Religion* 8:140-51.

HILLMAN, JAMES. 1967. *Insearch: Psychology and Religion.* London: Hodder & Stoughton.

———. 1972. *The Myth of Analysis: Three Essays in Archetypal Psychology.* Evanston, Ill.: Northwestern University Press.

———. 1975. *Revisioning Psychology.* New York: Harper & Row.

HILTNER, SEWARD. 1963. "General Considerations on 'Method' in Research," *Journal for the Scientific Study of Religion* 2:204-8.

HILTNER, SEWARD, AND LOWELL G. COLSTON. 1961. *The Context of Pastoral Counselling.* New York: Abingdon.

HIMMELFARB, SAMUEL, AND MARTIN FISHBEIN. 1971. "Studies in the Perception of Ethnic Group Members: I. Attractiveness, Response Bias, and Anti-Semitism," *Journal of Social Psychology* 83:289-98.

HINES, DWIGHT E. 1977-78. "Olfaction and the Right Cerebral Hemisphere," *Journal of Altered States of Consciousness* 31:47-59.

HJELLE, LARRY A. 1975. "Relationship of a Measure of Self-actualization to Religious Participation," *Journal of Psychology* 89:179-82.

HOELTNER, JON W., AND RITA J. EPLEY. 1979. "Religious Correlates of Fear of Death," *Journal for the Scientific Study of Religion* 18:404-11.

HOGE, DEAN R. 1972. "A Validated Intrinsic Religious Motivation Scale," *Journal for the Scientific Study of Religion* 11: 369-76.

HOGE, DEAN R., AND GREGORY H. PETRILLO. 1978. "Development of Religious Thinking in Adolescence: A Test of Goldman's Theories," *Journal for the Scientific Study of Religion* 17:139-54.

HOMANS, PETER. 1970. *Theology After Freud: An Interpretative Inquiry.* Indianapolis: Bobbs-Merrill.

———. 1978. *Childhood and Selfhood: Essays on Tradition, Religion, and Modernity in the Psychology of Erik H. Erikson.* Lewisburg, Pa.: Bucknell University Press.

———. 1979. *Jung in Context: Modernity and the Making of a Psychology.* Chicago: University of Chicago Press.

HOOD, RALPH W. 1970. "Religious Orientation and the Report of Religious Experience," *Journal for the Scientific Study of Religion* 9:285-91.

———. 1971. "A Comparison of the Allport and Feagin Scoring Procedures for Intrinsic/Extrinsic Orientation," *Journal for the Scientific Study of Religion* 10:370-74.

———. 1973. "Religious Orientation and the Experience of Transcendence," *Journal for the Scientific Study of Religion* 12:441-48.

———. 1974. "Psychological Strength and the Report of Intense Religious Experience," *Journal for the Scientific Study of Religion* 13:65-71.

———. 1975. "The Construction and Preliminary Validation of a Measure of Reported Mystical Experience," *Journal for the Scientific Study of Religion* 14:29-41.

———. 1976. "Mystical Experience as Related to Present and Anticipated Church Participation," *Psychological Reports* 39:1127-36.

————. 1977. "Eliciting Mystical States of Consciousness with Semi-structured Nature Experiences," *Journal for the Scientific Study of Religion* 16:155-63.

————. 1978a. "Anticipatory Set and Setting: Stress Incongruities as Elicitors of Mystical Experience in Solitary Nature Situations," *Journal for the Scientific Study of Religion* 17:279-87.

————. 1978b. "The Usefulness of Indiscriminately Pro and Anti Categories of Religious Orientation," *Journal for the Scientific Study of Religion* 17:419-31.

Hood, Ralph W., and Ronald J. Morris. 1981. "Sensory Isolation and the Differential Elicitation of Religious Imagery in Intrinsic and Extrinsic Persons," *Journal for the Scientific Study of Religion* 20:261-73.

Hooper, Michael. 1976. "The Structure and Measurement of Social Identity," *Public Opinion Quarterly* 40:154-64.

Horowitz, Irving Louis, editor. 1978. *Science, Sin, and Scholarship: The Politics of Reverend Moon and the Unification Church.* Cambridge, Mass.: MIT Press.

Huber, John R., and Robin Steier. 1976. "Social Interest and Individuation: A Comparison of Jung and Adler," *Character Potential* 7:174-80.

Hunsberger, Bruce. 1976. "Background Denominations, Parental Emphasis, and the Religious Orientation of University Students," *Journal for the Scientific Study of Religion* 15:251-55.

————. 1979. "Sources of 'Psychology of Religion' Journal Articles: 1950-1974," *Journal for the Scientific Study of Religion* 18:82-85.

————. 1980. "Problems and Promise in the Psychology of Religion: An Emerging Social Psychology of Religion?" *Canadian Journal of Behvioral Science* 12:64-77.

Hunt, Richard A. 1968. "The Interpretation of the Religious Scale of the Allport-Vernon-Lindzey Study of Values," *Journal for the Scientific Study of Religion* 7:65-77.

Hynson, Lawrence. 1978-79. "Belief in Life After Death and Societal Integration," *Omega: Journal of Death and Dying* 9:13-18.

Isert, Louis. 1969. "Religious Education in the Light of Current Psychological Concepts of Development," *Catholic Educational Review* 66:656-63.

Jacobi, Jolande. 1973. *The Psychology of C. G. Jung.* Eighth edition. New Haven: Yale University Press.

Jacobson, George R.; Daniel P. Ritter; and Lynn Mueller. 1977. "Purpose in Life and Personal Values Among Adult Alcoholics," *Journal of Clinical Psychology* 33:314-16.

JACQUES, MARCELINE E.; EUGENE GAIER; AND DONALD C. LINKOWSKI. 1967. "Coping-Succumbing Attitudes Toward Physical and Mental Disabilities," *Journal of Social Psychology* 71:295-307.

JAHODA, GUSTAV. 1970. "Supernatural Beliefs and Changing Cognitive Structures Among Ghanaian University Students," *Journal of Cross-cultural Psychology* 1:115-30.

JAMES, WILLIAM. 1961 (1902). *The Varieties of Religious Experience.* New York: Collier Books.

——. 1962 (1892). *Psychology: Briefer Course.* Forward by Gardner Murphy. New York: Collier-Macmillan.

——. 1977- . *The Writings of William James: A Comprehensive Edition, Including an Annotated Bibliography, Updated Through 1977.* Edited with an intro. by John J. McDermott. Cambridge, Harvard University Press.

JOHNSON, PAUL E. 1967. *Person and Counselor.* Nashville: Abingdon.

JONES, ERNEST. 1961. *The Life and Work of Sigmund Freud.* Edited and abridged by Lionel Trilling. New York: Basic Books.

JUNG, CARL G. 1961. *Memories, Dreams, Reflections.* Recorded and edited by Aniela Jaffe. Translated by Richard and Clara Winston. New York: Vintage Books.

——. 1972 (1935, 1943). *Two Essays on Analytic Psychology.* Translated by R. F. C. Hull. Second edition. Princeton, N.J.: Princeton University Press.

——. 1974 (1921). *Psychological Types.* In *Collected Works.* Vol. 6. Princeton, N.J.: Princeton University Press.

JUNI, SAMUEL, AND ARTHUR FRENZ. 1981. "Psychosexual Fixation and Perceptual Defense," *Perceptual and Motor Skills* 52:83-89.

KAHOE, RICHARD D. 1974. "Personality and Achievement Correlates of Intrinsic and Extrinsic Religious Orientations." *Journal of Personality and Social Psychology* 29:812-18.

——. 1977. Intrinsic Religion and Authoritarianism: A Differentiated Relationship." *Journal for the Scientific Study of Religion* 16:179-82.

KAHOE, RICHARD D., AND REBECCA FOX DUNN. 1975. "The Fear of Death and Religious Attitudes and Behavior," *Journal for the Scientific Study of Religion* 14:379-82.

KALISH, RICHARD A., AND DAVID K. REYNOLDS. 1973. "Phenomenological Reality and Post-death Contact," *Journal for the Scientific Study of Religion* 12: 209-21.

KARAMATSU, AKIRA, AND TOMIO HIRAE. 1969. "An Electroencephalographic Study on the Zen Meditation." In *Altered States of Con-*

sciousness. Edited by Charles T. Tart. Garden City, N.Y.: Double-day.

KAREN, ROBERT L. 1974. *An Introduction to Behavior Therapy and Its Applications.* New York: Harper & Row.

KAYSER, BRIAN D. 1975. "Religious Identification, Sex, and Income Expectation: A Panel Study of Catholic and Non-Catholic High School Students," *Journal for the Scientific Study of Religion* 14:357-66.

KELLY, GEORGE A. 1955. *The Psychology of Personal Constructs.* 2 volumes. New York: W. W. Norton.

KHAN, M. MASUD. 1972. "The Finding and Becoming of Self," *International Journal of Psychoanalytic Psychotherapy* 1:97-111.

KHATAMI, MANOOCHEHR. 1978. "Creativity and Altered States of Consciousness," *Psychiatric Annals* 8:57-64.

KILDAHL, J. P. 1972. *The Psychology of Speaking in Tongues.* New York: Harper & Row.

KILMANN, RALPH H., AND VERN TAYLOR. 1974. "A Contingency Approach to Laboratory Learning: Psychological Types Versus Experiential Norms," *Human Relations* 17:891-909.

KING, MORTON B., AND RICHARD A. HUNT. 1972. "Measuring the Religious Variable: Replication," *Journal for the Scientific Study of Religion* 11:24-51.

———. 1975. "Measuring the Religious Variable: National Replication" *Journal for the Scientific Study of Religion* 14:13-22.

KING, STANLEY H., AND DANIEL H. FUNKENSTEIN. 1957. "Religious Practice and Cardio-vascular Reactions During Stress," *Journal of Abnormal and Social Psychology* 55:135-37.

KITAGAWA, JOSEPH. 1959. "The History of Religions in America." In *The History of Religions: Essays in Methodology.* Edited by Mircea Eliade and Joseph Kitagawa. Chicago: University of Chicago Press.

KLAUSNER, SAMUEL Z. 1964. "Methods of Data Collection in the Study of Religion," *Journal for the Scientific Study of Religion* 3:193-203.

———. 1970. "Scientific and Humanistic Study of Religion," *Journal for the Scientific Study of Religion* 9:100-106.

KOHLBERG, LAWRENCE. 1964. "Development of Moral Character and Moral Ideology. In *Review of Child Development Research.* Vol. 1. Edited by Martin L. Hoffman and Lois Wladis Hoffman. New York: Russell Sage Foundation.

———. 1976. "Critical Issues in the Study of Moral Development and Behavior." In *Moral Development and Behavior: Theory,*

Research and Social Issues. Edited by Thomas Lickona. New York: Holt, Rinehard & Winston.

———. 1981. *The Philosophy of Moral Development: Moral States and the Idea of Justice—Essays in Moral Development.* Vol. I. New York: Harper & Row.

KORCHIN, SHELDON J. 1976. *Modern Clinical Psychology: Principles of Intervention in the Clinic or Community.* New York: Basic Books.

KOSA, JOHN. 1961. "Religious Participation, Religious Knowledge, and Scholastic Aptitude: An Empirical Study," *Journal for the Scientific Study of Religion* 1:88–97.

KRIPPNER, STANLEY, AND RICHARD DAVIDSON. 1974. "Paranormal Events Occurring During Chemically Induced Psychedelic Experience and Their Implications for Religion," *Journal of Altered States of Consciousness* 1:175–84.

LARSEN, JOHN A. 1978. "Dysfunction in the Evangelical Family: Treatment Considerations," *Family Coordinator* 27:261–67.

———. 1979. "Self-actualization as Related to Frequency, Range, and Pattern of Religious Experience," *Journal of Psychology and Theology* 7:39–47.

LARSEN, LARRY, AND ROBERT KNAPP. 1964. "Sex Differences and Symbolic Conception of the Deity," *Journal of Projective Techniques* 28:303–6.

LASKI, MARGHANITA. 1961. *Ecstasy: A Study of Some Secular and Religious Experiences.* London: Cresset Press.

LAWRENCE, P. J. 1965. "Children's Thinking about Religion—A Study of Concrete Operational Thinking," *Religious Education* 60:111–16.

LEBRA, T. S. 1974. "The Interactional Perspective of Suffering and Curing in a Japanese Cult," *Journal of Social Psychiatry* 20:281–86.

LEE, ROBERT, AND FRED P. PIERCY. 1974. "Church Attendance and Self-actualization," *Journal of Social Psychiatry* 20:281–86.

LEFEVER, HARRY G. 1977. "The Religion of the Poor: Escape or Creative Force?" *Journal for the Scientific Study of Religion* 16:225–36.

LESH, TERRY V. 1970. "Zen and Psychotherapy: Partially Annotated Bibliography," *Journal of Humanistic Psychology* 10:75–83.

LEUBA, J. H. 1912. *A Psychological Study of Religion.* New York: Macmillan.

———. 1926. *The Psychology of Religious Mysticism.* New York: Harcourt, Brace & World.

LEWIN, MIRIAM. 1979. *Understanding Psychological Research*. New York: John Wiley.

LEWIS, MICHAEL. 1979. "The Self as a Developmental Concept," *Human Development* 22:416-19.

LICKONA, THOMAS, editor. 1979. *Moral Development and Behavior: Theory, Research, and Social Issues*. New York: Holt, Rinehart, & Winston.

LILLY, JOHN C. 1975. *Simulations of God: The Science of Belief*. New York: Simon & Schuster.

LINDENTHAL, JACOB J., et al. 1970. "Mental Status and Religious Behavior," *Journal for the Scientific Study of Religion* 9:143-49.

LINDSKOOG, DONALD, AND ROGER E. KIRK. 1975. "Some Life-history and Attitudinal Correlates of Self-actualization Among Evangelical Seminary Students," *Journal for the Scientific Study of Religion* 14:51-55.

LIVESLEY, W. J., AND D. W. BROMLEY. 1973. *Person Perception in Childhood and Adolescence*. London: John Wiley.

LOFLAND, JOHN, AND NORMAN SKONOVD. 1981. "Conversion Motifs," *Journal for the Scientific Study of Religion* 20:373-85.

LOMBILLO, JOSE R. 1973. "The Soldier Saint . . . a Psychological Analysis of the Conversion of Ignatius of Loyola," *Psychiatric Quarterly* 47:386-418.

LONG, DIANE; DAVID ELKIND; AND BERNARD SPILKA. 1967. "The Child's Conception of Prayer," *Journal for the Scientific Study of Religion* 6:101-9.

LOSCHEN, E. L. 1974. "Psychiatry and Religion: A Variable History," *Journal of Religion and Health* 13:137-41.

LOVEKIN, ADAMS, AND H. NEWTON MALONY. 1977. "Religious Glossolalia: A Longitudinal Study of Personality Changes," *Journal for the Scientific Study of Religion* 17:383-93.

LOVINGER, ROBERT J. 1979. "Therapeutic Strategies with Religious Resistances," *Psychotherapy: Theory, Research, and Practice* 16:419-27.

LOWRY, RICHARD J. 1973. *A. H. Maslow: An Intellectual Portrait*. Monterey, Calif.: Brooks/Cole.

LUDWIG, DAVID J. 1969. "Measurement of Religion as a Perceptual Set," *Journal for the Scientific Study of Religion* 8:319-21.

MCCONAHAY, JOHN B., AND JOSEPH C. HOUGH. 1973. "Love and Guilt-oriented Dimensions of Christian Belief," *Journal for the Scientific Study of Religion* 12:53-64.

MCCONNELL, THEODORE A. 1969. "Gordon Allport and the Quest for Selfhood," *Journal of Religion and Health* 8:375-81.

McNeil, John T. 1977. *A History of the Cure of Souls.* New York: Harper & Row.

McPhail, Clark. 1972. "Religious Self-designating Behaviors," *Journal for the Scientific Study of Religion* 11:262–70.

Maddi, Salvatore R. 1972. *Personality Theories: A Comparative Analysis.* Revised edition. Homewood, Ill.: Dorsey Press.

———. 1974. "The Victimization of Dora," *Psychology Today,* August, pp. 90 ff.

Maddi, Salvatore, and Paul T. Costa. 1972. *Humanism in Personology: Allport, Maslow, and Murray.* Chicago: Aldine-Atherton.

Maier, Henry W. 1969. *Three Theories of Development: The Contribution of Erik H. Erikson, Jean Piaget, and Robert W. Sears, and Their Application.* New York: Harper & Row.

Malcolm, Janet. 1981. *Psychoanalysis, the Impossible Profession.* New York: Knopf.

Malony, H. Newton. 1976. "New Methods in Psychology of Religion," *Journal of Psychology and Theology* 4:141–51.

———. editor. 1977. *Current Perspectives in the Psychology of Religion.* Grand Rapids, Mich.: William B. Eerdmans.

Maranell, Gary M. 1974. *Responses to Religion: Studies in the Social Psychology of Religious Belief.* Lawrence: University Press of Kansas.

Marcuse, Herbert. 1962. *Eros and Civilization: A Philosophical Inquiry into Freud.* New York: Vintage Books.

Margolis, Robert D., and Kirk W. Elifson. 1979. "A Typology of Religious Experience," *Journal for the Scientific Study of Religion* 18:61–67.

Marlowe, Mike. 1981. "Boyhood Sex-role Development: Implications for Counseling and School Practices," *Personnel & Guidance Journal* 60:210–14.

Marty, Martin E. 1976. *A Nation of Behavers.* Chicago: University of Chicago Press.

Maslow, Abraham. 1968a. *Toward a Psychology of Being.* New York: D. Van Nostrand.

———. 1968b. "A Conversation with Abraham Maslow," *Psychology Today,* February, pp. 38 ff.

———. 1970. *Religion, Values, and Peak Experiences.* New York: Viking Press.

Mathiessen, F. O. 1947. *The James Family, Including Selections from the Writings of Henry James, Senior, William, Henry, and Alice James.* New York: Alfred Knopf.

MAUPIN, EDWARD W. 1969. "On Meditation." In *Altered States of Consciousness*. Edited by Charles T. Tart. Garden City, N.Y.: Doubleday.

MAY, ROLLO. 1950. *The Meaning of Anxiety*. New York: Ronald Press.

———. 1953. *Man's Search for Himself*. New York: W. W. Norton.

———. 1958. "Contributions of Existential Psychotherapy." In *Existence*. Edited by Rollo May, Ernest Angel, and Henri F. Ellenberger. New York: Simon & Schuster.

———. 1960. "The Significance of Symbols," *Symbolism in Religion and Literature*. New York: George Braziller.

———. 1969. *Love and Will*. W. W. Norton.

———. 1972. *Power and Innocence*. W. W. Norton.

———. 1973. *Paulus: Reminiscences of a Friendship*. Harper & Row.

———. 1975. *The Courage to Create*. New York: W. W. Norton.

MAYKOVICH, MINAKO K. 1977. "The Difficulties of a Minority Researcher in Minority Communities," *Journal of Social Issues* 33:108–19.

MEAD, GEORGE H. 1962 (1934). *Mind, Self, and Society from the Standpoint of a Social Behaviorist*. Chicago: University of Chicago Press.

MEADOW, MARY J. 1979. "Symposium: The Spiritual and/Versus the Transpersonal," *Catalog of Selected Documents in Psychology*, 9:77–78.

MENNINGER, KARL A., AND PHILIP S. HOLZMAN. 1973. *Theory of Psychoanalytic Technique*. Second edition. New York: Basic Books.

MIDDLETON, RUSSELL. 1973. "Do Christian Beliefs Cause Anti-Semitism?" *American Sociological Review* 38:33–52.

MILES, T. R. 1979. "Psychological Research and Religious Truth," *Bulletin of the British Psychological Society* 32:204–5.

MILLER, JUSTIN. 1981. "Cultural and Class Values in Family Process," *Journal of Marital and Family Therapy* 9:467–73.

MINUCHIN, SALVADOR. 1974. *Families and Family Therapy*. Cambridge: Harvard University Press.

MOBERG, DAVID O. 1970. "Theological Position and Institutional Characteristics of Protestant Congregations: An Exploratory Study," *Journal for the Scientific Study of Religion* 9:53–58.

MONCRIEFF, J. R. 1978. "Psychology of Religion," *Bulletin of the British Psychological Society* 31:237.

MORRIS, HAROLD C., AND LYNN M. MORRIS. 1978. "Power and Purpose: Correlated to Conversion," *Psychology* 15:15–22.

MORRIS, J. E. 1980. "Humanistic Psychology and Religion: Steps Toward Reconciliation," *Journal of Religion and Health* 19:92-102.

MOSIER, RICHARD D. 1968-69. "Symbolic Logic and Psychological Symbolism," *Psychoanalytic Review* 55:646-54.

MUNNS, MEREDITH. 1972. "The Values of Adolescents Compared with Parents and Peers," *Adolescence* 7:519-24.

MURPHY, GARDNER, AND LOIS B. MURPHY, editors. 1968. *Asian Psychology.* New York: Basic Books.

MURRAY, C. 1978. "The Moral and Religious Beliefs of Catholic Adolescents: Scale Developments and Structure," *Journal for the Scientific Study of Religion* 17:439-47.

MUTTAGI, P. K. 1975. "Social Distance Among Religious and Linguistic Communities," *Indian Journal of Social Work* 36:159-71.

NARANJA, C., AND R. ORNSTEIN. 1976. *On the Psychology of Meditation.* New York: Viking.

NELSON, HART M. 1981. "Gender Differences in the Effects of Parental Discord on Preadolescent Religiousness," *Journal for the Scientific Study of Religion* 20:109-18.

NELSON, HART M., et al. 1976. "A Test of Yinger's Measure of Nondoctrinal Religion: Implications for Invisible Religion as a Belief System," *Journal for the Scientific Study of Religion* 15:263-67.

NELSON, JOHN J., AND HARRY H. HILLER. 1981. "Norms of Verbalization and the Decision Making Process in Religious Organizations," *Journal for the Scientific Study of Religion* 20:173-80.

NELSON, L. D., AND RUSSELL R. DYNES. 1976. "The Impact of Devotionalism and Attendance on Ordinary and Emergency Helping Behavior," *Journal for the Scientific Study of Religion* 15:47-59.

NELSON, MARVIN. 1971. "The Concept of God and Feelings Toward Parents," *Journal of Individual Psychology* 27:46-49.

NESS, ROBERT C., AND RONALD M. WINTROB. 1980. "The Emotional Impact of Fundamentalist Religious Participation: An Empirical Study of Intragroup Variation," *American Journal of Orthopsychiatry* 50:302-15.

NICHOLI, ARMAND M. 1974. "A New Dimension of the Youth Culture," *American Journal of Psychiatry* 131:396-401.

NURBAKHSHS, DJAVAD. 1978. "Sufism and Pschoanalysis: I. and II.," *International Journal of Social Psychiatry* 24:204-19.

NYE, ROBERT D. 1981. *Three Psychologies: Perspectives from Freud, Skinner, and Rogers.* Second edition. Monterey, Cal.: Brooks/Cole.

OAKLAND, JAMES A. 1977. "The Introjected and the Intrinsic in Psychology and Christianity," *Journal of Psychology and Theology* 5:91–94.

OATES, WAYNE E. 1979. *New Dimensions in Pastoral Care.* Philadelphia: Fortress Press.

ODEN, THOMAS C. 1966. *Kerygma and Counseling: Toward a Covenant Ontology for Secular Psychotherapy.* Philadelphia: Westminster Press.

——. 1972. "The New Pietism," *Journal of Humanistic Psychologist* 12:24–41.

ORLOWSKI, CHAD D. 1979. "Linguistic Dimension of Religious Measurement," *Journal for the Scientific Study of Religion* 18:306–11.

OSARCHUK, MICHAEL, AND SHERMAN J. TATZ. 1973. "Effect of Induced Fear of Death on Belief in Afterlife," *Journal of Personality and Social Psychology* 27:256–60.

OWENS, CLAIRE M. 1975. "Self-realization: Induced and Spontaneous," *Journal of Altered States of Consciousness* 2:59–73.

PAIVIO, ALLAN, AND RAY STEEVES. 1967. "Relations Between Personal Values and Imagery and Meaningfulness of Value Words," *Perceptual and Motor Skills* 24:337–38.

PALMA, ROBERT J. 1978. "The Prospects for a Normative Psychology of Religion: G. W. Allport as a Paradigm," *Journal of Psychology and Theology* 6:119–22.

PARGAMENT, KENNETH L.; ROBERT E. STEELE; AND FORREST B. TYLER. 1979. "Religious Participation, Religious Motivation and Individual Psychosocial Competence," *Journal for the Scientific Study of Religion* 18:412–19.

PARKER, JAMES H. 1968. "The Interaction of Negroes and Whites in an Integrated Church Setting," *Social Forces* 46:359–66.

PAXTON, ANNE L., AND EDWARD J. TURNER. 1978. "Self-actualization and Sexual Permissiveness, Satisfaction, Prudishness, and Drive Among Female Undergraduates," *Journal of Sex Research* 14:65–80.

PEARMAN, FRED C. 1975. "Catholic Scaled Values According to the Allport, Vernon and Lindzey Study of Values in Relation to the 1970 National High School Norms: Grades 10–12," *Adolescence* 10:499–506.

PETERS, R. S., editor. 1965. *Brett's History of Psychology.* Cambridge, Mass.: MIT Press.

PIAGET, JEAN. 1962 (1946). *Play, Dreams, and Imitation in Childhood.*

Translated by C. Gattegno and F. M. Hodgson. New York: W. W. Norton.

———. 1965 (1932). *The Moral Judgment of the Child.* Translated by Marjorie Gabain. New York: Free Press.

———. 1972 (1926). *The Child's Conception of the World.* Translated by Joan and Andrew Tomlinson. Totowa, N.J.: Littlefield, Adams.

PIKER, STEVEN. 1973. "Comments on the Integration of Religion," *Ethos* 1:298–320.

PIROJNIKOFF, LEO A.; ILANA HADAR; AND AVNER HADAR. 1971. "Dogmatism and Social Distance: A Cross-cultural Study," *Journal of Social Psychology* 85:187–93.

PORTER, JUDITH R., AND ALEXA A. ALBERT. 1977. "Subculture or Assimilation? A Cross-cultural Analysis of Religion and Women's Role," *Journal for the Scientific Study of Religion* 16:345–59.

PROUDFOOD, WAYNE, AND PHILIP SHAVER. 1975. "Attribution Theory and the Psychology of Religion," *Journal for the Scientific Study of Religion* 14:317–30.

PRUYSER, PAUL W. 1968. *A Dynamic Psychology of Religion.* New York: Harper & Row.

QUERY, JOY, AND MERIEL STEINES. 1974. "Disillusionment, Health Status and Age: A Study of Value Differences of Midwestern Women," *International Journal of Aging and Human Development* 5:245–56.

RAGAN, C.; H. N. MALONY; AND B. BEIT-HALLAHMI. 1980. "Psychologists and Religion: Professional Factors and Personal Belief," *Review of Religious Research* 21:208–17.

RAMBO, LEWIS R. 1982. "Current Research on Religious Conversion," *Religious Studies Review* 8:146–58.

RANDALL, TOM M., AND MARCEL DESROSIERS. 1980. "Measurement of Supernatural Belief: Sex Differences and Locus of Control," *Journal of Personality Assessment* 44:493–98.

RAPPAPORT, EDWARD. 1978. "The Effects of Dogmatism and Anxiety on Religious Identification," *Journal of Social Psychology* 104:141–42.

RASCHKE, VERNON. 1973. "Dogmatism and Committed and Consensual Religiosity," *Journal for the Scientific Study of Religion* 12:339–44.

REDFEARN, J. W. 1977. "The Self and Individuation," *Journal of Analytical Psychology* 22:125–41.

REEVES, CLEMENT. 1977. *The Psychology of Rollo May.* San Francisco: Jossey-Bass.

RICHARDSON, JAMES T. 1973. "Psychological Interpretations of Glossolalia: A Reexamination of Research," *Journal for the Scientific Study of Religion* 12:199-207.

RICHARDSON, JAMES T., AND MARY STEWART. 1977. "Conversion Process Models and the Jesus Movement," *American Behavioral Scientist* 20:819-38.

RICHEK, HERBERT G., AND BRAXTON REID. 1971. "Religious Authoritarianism and Psychopathology in College Students," *Psychiatric Quarterly* 45:363-71.

RICOEUR, PAUL. 1970. *Freud and Philosophy: An Essay on Interpretation.* Translated by Denis Savage. New Haven: Yale University Press.

RIEFF, PHILIP. 1961. *The Mind of a Moralist.* Garden City, N.Y.: Doubleday.

———. 1968. *The Triumph of the Therapeutic: Uses of Faith after Freud.* New York: Harper & Row.

RITZERMA, ROBERT J. 1979. "Attribution to Supernatural Causation: An Important Component of Religious Commitment?" *Journal of Psychology and Theology* 7:286-93.

RIZZUTO, ANA-MARIA. 1979. *The Birth of the Living God: A Psychoanalytic Study.* Chicago: University of Chicago Press.

ROBBINS, THOMAS, et al. 1976. "The Last Civil Religion: Reverend Moon and the Unification Church," *Sociological Analysis* 37:111-25.

ROBINSON, JOHN P., AND PHILIP SHAVER. 1973. *Measures of Social Psychological Attitudes.* Ann Arbor, Mich.: Institute for Social Research.

ROCK, ANDREW. 1967. *Introduction to William James: An Essay and Selected Texts.* Bloomington: Indiana University Press.

RODDY, JOAN M., et al. 1981. "Modification of Stereotypic Sex-typing in Young Children," *Journal of Genetic Psychology* 139:109-18.

ROGERS, CARL R. 1961. *On Becoming a Person: A Therapist's View of Psychotherapy.* Boston: Houghton Mifflin.

ROGERS, MARTHA L. 1975. "A Fundamentalist Church as an Autonomous Community and Its Relationship to the Larger Community," *Journal of Psychology and Theology* 3:210-15.

ROSEGRANT, JOHN. 1976. "The Impact of Set and Setting on Religious Experience in Nature," *Journal for the Scientific Study of Religion* 15:301-10.

ROSEN, AARON, AND KAREN BERRY. 1978. "Attribution of Responsibility for Marital Sexual Dysfunction and Traditionalism," *Journal of Social Service Research* 1:287-97.

ROSENZWEIG, LINDA W. 1977. "Toward Universal Justice: Some Implications of Lawrence Kohlberg's Research for Jewish Education," *Religious Education* 72:606–15.

ROTHENBERG, ALBERT. 1978–79. "Translogical Secondary Process Cognition in Creativity," *Journal of Altered States of Consciousness* 4:171–87.

RULE, BRENDON G.; HUGH HALEY; AND JAMES MCCORMICK. 1971. "Anti-Semitism, Distraction, and Physical Aggression," *Canadian Journal of Behavioral Science* 3:174–82.

RULLA, LUIGI M., AND SALVATORE R. MADDI. 1972. "Personality and the Catholic Religious Vocation, II: Self and Conflict in Male Entrants," *Journal of Personality* 40: 564–87.

RUSSELL, GERALD M., AND DALE O. JORGENSON. 1978. "Religious Group Membership, Locus of Control, and Dogmatism," *Psychological Reports* 42:1099–1102.

RYLE, GILBERT. 1949. *The Concept of Mind.* New York: Barnes & Noble.

SACKS, HOWARD L. 1979. "The Effect of Spiritual Exercises on the Integration of Self-system," *Journal for the Scientific Study of Religion* 18:46–50.

ST. CLAIR, SALLY, AND H. D. DAY. 1979. "Ego Identity Status and Values Among High School Females," *Journal of Youth and Adolescence* 8:317–26.

SALANCIK, GERALD, AND MARY CONWAY. 1975. "Attitude Inferences from Salient and Relevant Cognitive Content About Behavior," *Journal of Personality and Social Psychology* 32:829–40.

SALES, STEPHEN M. 1972. "Economic Threat as a Determinant of Conversion Rates in Authoritarian Churches," *Journal of Personality and Social Psychology* 23:420–28.

SALZMAN, LEON. 1953. "The Psychology of Religious and Ideological Conversion," *Psychiatry* 16:177–87.

SALZSTEIN, HERBERT D., AND SHARON OSGOOD. 1975. "The Development of Children's Reasoning About Group Interdependence and Obligation," *Journal of Psychology* 90:147–55.

SAMS, JANICE. 1975. "The Ghetto Child and Moral Development," *Religious Education* 70:636–48.

SANADA, TAKAKI, AND EDWARD NORBECK. 1975. "Prophecy Continues to Fail: A Japanese Sect," *Journal of Cross-cultural Psychology* 6:331–45.

SCHACHTER, S., AND J. E. SINGER. 1962. "Cognitive, Social, and Physiological Determinants of Emotional States," *Psychological Review* 69:379–99.

SCHEIDT, FREDRICK J. 1974. "Deviance, Power, and the Occult: A Field Study," *Journal of Psychology* 87:21-28.

SCHLEIFER, MICHAEL, AND VIRGINIA L. DOUGLAS. 1973. "Effects of Training on the Moral Judgment of Young Children," *Journal of Personality and Social Psychology* 28:62-68.

SCHNEIDERMAN, LEO. 1967. "Psychological Notes on the Nature of Mystical Experience," *Journal for the Scientific Study of Religion* 6:91-100.

SCHWARTZ, DAVID J. 1969. "The Reality of Illusion and the Illusion of Reality," *Science Teacher* 29-31.

SCHWEIKER, WILLIAM F. 1969. "Religion as a Superordinate Meaning System and Socio-psychological Integration," *Journal for the Scientific Study of Religion* 8:300-307.

SCIORTINO, RIO. 1970. "Allport-Vernon-Lindzey Study of Values: I. Factor Structure for a Combined Sample of Male and Female College Students," *Psychological Reports* 27:955-58.

SCOBIE, GEOFFREY E. W. 1975. *Psychology of Religion.* London: B. T. Batsford.

———. 1977a. "The Psychology of Religion: A Religious Revival?" *Bulletin of the British Psychological Society* 30:142-44.

———. 1977b. "Psychology of Religious and Political Attitudes," *Bulletin of the British Psychological Society* 30:184.

SCOTT, WILLIAM A., AND JOHN ROHRBAUGH. 1975. "Conceptions of Harmful Groups: Some Correlates of Group Descriptions in Three Cultures," *Journal of Personality and Social Psychology* 31:992-1003.

SCROGGS, JAMES R., AND WILLIAM G. T. DOUGLAS. 1976. "Issues in the Psychology of Religious Conversion," *Journal of Religion and Health* 6:206-16.

SEGAL, JONATHAN. 1981. "Age of Infants and Parental Sex-role Perceptions, *Journal of Psychology* 107:267-72.

SHANDS, HARLEY. 1976. "Myth of Illness: On the Function of Consensus," *Contemporary Psychoanalysis* 12:61-75.

SHANKER, PREM; LYNN CLARK; AND HARI ASTHANA. 1979. "Value Profiles and Value Contraditions in Canadian, East Indian and West Indian Studies," *Psychologia: An International Journal of Psychology in the Orient* 22:189-194.

SHARMA, SAVITRI. 1978. "A Comparison of Neurotic and Normal Individuals on Certain Important Variables: Faith in Religion as a Successful Method of Counseling," *Indian Journal of Psychometry and Education* 9:40-46.

SHARMA, K. N., AND G. P. TIWARI. 1973. "Value as a Function of Regression and Sex," *Journal of Psychological Researches* 17:19-21.

SHAVER, PHILIP; MICHAEL LENAUER; AND SUSAN LADD. 1980. "Religiousness, Conversion, and Subjective Well-being; The 'Healthy-minded' Religion of Modern American Women," *American Journal of Psychiatry* 137:1563-68.

SHINER, LARRY. 1967. "The Concept of Secularization in Empirical Research," *Journal for the Scientific Study of Religion* 6:207-20.

SHRAUGER, J. SIDNEY, AND RONALD E. SILVERMAN. 1971. "The Relationship of Religious Background and Participation to Locus of Control," *Journal for the Scientific Study of Religion* 10:11-16.

SHEILS, DEAN, AND PHILIP BERG. 1977. "A Research Note on Sociological Variables Related to Belief in Psychic Phenomena," *Wisconsin Sociologist* 14:24-31.

SIEGEL, R. K., AND L. J. WEST. 1975. *Hallucinations: Behavior, Experience, and Theory.* New York: John Wiley & Sons.

SIMONDS, ROBERT B. 1977. "Conversion or Addiction: Consequences of Joining a Jesus Movement Group," *American Behavioral Scientist* 20:909-24.

SIMMONS, HENRY C. 1976. "Theory and Practice in Religion and Education," *Religious Education* 71:132-42.

SINGER, JUNE. 1972. *The Boundaries of the Soul.* New York: Doubleday.

SKINNER, B. F. 1971. *Beyond Freedom and Dignity.* New York: Vintage Books.

———. 1976. *About Behaviorism.* New York: Vintage Books.

SLATER, PHILIP E. 1966. *Microcosm: Structural, Psychological, and Religious Evolution in Groups.* New York: John Wiley.

SMART, NINIAN. 1976. *The Religious Experience of Mankind.* Second edition. New York: Scribner's.

SMITH, DONALD E. 1974. "The Next Decade of Dialogue: Religion and Health," *Journal of Religion and Health* 13:161-79.

SMITH, WILFRED CANTWELL. 1959. "Comparative Religion: Whither—and Why?" In *The History of Religions: Essays in Methodology.* Edited by Mircea Eliade and Joseph Kitagawa. Chicago: University of Chicago Press.

SOBOSAN, JEFFREY G. 1975. "Kierkegaard and Jung on the Self," *Journal of Psychology and Theology* 3:31-35.

———. 1977. "Self-fulfillment, Asceticism, and the Function of Authority," *Journal of Religion and Health.* 16:333-40.

SPANOS, NICHOLAS P., AND ERIN C. HEWITT. 1979. "Glossolalia: A Test of the 'Trance' and Psychopathology Hypotheses," *Journal of Abnormal Psychology* 88:427-34.

SPELLMAN, CHARLES M., GLEN D. BASKETT; AND DONN BYRNE. 1971. "Manifest Anxiety as a Contributing Factor in Religious Conversion," *Journal of Consulting and Clinical Psychology* 36:245-47.

SPILKA, BERNARD, AND MICHAEL MULLIN. 1977. "Personal Religion and Psychological Schemata: A Research Approach to a Theological Psychology of Religion," *Character Potential* 8:57-66.

SPILKA, BERNARD, AND GREG SCHMIDT. 1983. "General Attribution Theory for the Psychology of Religion: The Influence of Event-Character on Attributions to God." *Journal for the Scientific Study of Religion* 22:326-39.

SPIRO, MELFORD E., AND ROY G. D'ANDRADE. 1958. "A Cross-cultural Study of Some Supernatural Beliefs," *American Anthropologist* 60:456-66.

STACKHOUSE, MAX L. 1966. "Technical Data and Ethical Norms: Some Theoretical Considerations," *Journal for the Scientific Study of Religion* 5:191-203.

STAMEY, HARRY C. 1971. "The 'Mad at God' Syndrome," *American Journal of Psychotherapy* 25:93-101.

STANLEY, GORDON. 1965. "Personality and Attitude Correlates of Religious Conversion," *Journal for the Scientific Study of Religion* 4:60-63.

STANLEY, GORDON; W. K. BARTLETT; AND TERRI MOYLE. 1978. "Some Characteristics of Charismatic Experience: Glossolalia in Australia," *Journal for the Scientific Study of Religion* 17:269-77.

STANTON, MICHAEL. 1976. "The Assessment of Moral Judgments: Cultural and Cognitive Considerations," *Religious Education* 71:610-71.

STARBUCK, EDWIN DILLER. 1899. *The Psychology of Religion: An Empirical Study of the Growth of Religious Consciousness.* New York: Charles Scribner's Sons.

STARK, MICHAEL J., AND MICHAEL C. WASHBURN. 1977. "Beyond the Norm: A Speculative Model of Self-realization," *Journal of Religion and Health* 16:58-68.

STARR, PAUL D. 1978. "Ethnic Categories and Identification in Lebanon," *Urban Life* 7:111-42.

STAUFFER, ROBERT E. 1973. "Church Members' Ignorance of Doctrinal Pluralism: A Probable Source of Church Cohesion," *Journal for the Scientific Study of Religion* 12:345-48.

STEERE, DAVID A. 1969. "Anton Boisen: Figure of the Future," *Journal of Religion and Health* 8:359-74.

STEPHAN, KAREN H., AND G. EDWARD STEPHAN. 1973. "Religion and the Survival of Utopian Communities," *Journal for the Scientific Study of Religion* 12:89-100.

STONES, CHRISTOPHER R. 1980. "A Jesus Community in South Africa: Self-actualization or Need for Security?" *Psychological Reports* 46:287-90.

STOUDENMIRE, JOHN. 1971. "On the Relationship Between Religious Beliefs and Emotion," *Journal for the Scientific Study of Religion* 10:254.

———. 1976. "Situation Ethics and Transactional Analysis," *Journal of Religion and Health* 15:297-300.

STRICKLAND, BONNIE R., AND SCOTT SHAFFER. 1971. "I-E, I-E, & F," *Journal for the Scientific Study of Religion* 10:366-369.

STRICKLAND, BONNIE R., AND SALLIE CONE WEDDELL. 1972. "Religious Orientation, Racial Prejudice, and Dogmatism: A Study of Baptists and Unitarians," *Journal for the Scientific Study of Religion* 11:395-99.

STROMMEN, MERTON P., editor. 1971. *Research on Religious Development: A Comprehensive Handbook.* New York: Hawthorn Books.

STRUNK, ORLO, editor. 1959. *The Psychology of Religion: Historical and Interpretative Readings.* New York: Abingdon Press.

STRUNK, ORLO. 1967. "Self-anchoring Scaling for Study of Perceptions of Religious Maturity," *Perceptual and Motor Skills* 25:471-72.

———. 1970. "Humanistic Religious Psychology: A New Chapter in the Psychology of Religion," *Journal of Pastoral Care* 24:90-97.

SULLOWAY, FRANK. 1979. *Freud, Biologist of the Mind: Beyond the Psychoanalytic Legend.* New York: Basic Books.

SWARTZ, PAUL. 1969. "Fourth Force Psychology: A Humanist Disclaimer," *Psychological Record* 19:557-59.

SWINDELL, DOROTHY H., AND LUCIANO L'ABATE. 1970. "Religiosity, Dogmatism, and Repression-Sensitization," *Journal for the Scientific Study of Religion* 9:289-97.

SZAFRAN, ROBERT. 1976. "The Distribution of Influence in Religious Organizations," *Journal for the Scientific Study of Religion* 15:339-49.

TAMAYO, ALVARO, AND LEANDRE DESJARDINS. 1976. "Belief Systems and Conceptual Images of Parents and God," *Journal of Psychology* 92:131-40.

TART, CHARLES T., editor. 1969. *Altered States of Consciousness.* New York: Doubleday.

———. 1975a. *Transpersonal Psychologies.* New York: Harper Row.

———. 1975b. "The Systems Approach to Consciousness." In *Consciousness, Brain, States of Awareness and Mysticism.* Edited by Daniel Goleman and Richard J. Davidson. New York: Harper & Row.

TAPPEINER, DANIEL A. 1977. "A Psychological Paradigm for the Interpretation of the Charismatic Phenomenon of Prophecy," *Journal of Psychology and Theology* 5:23-29.

TATE, EUGENE D., AND GERALD R. MILLER. 1971. "Differences in Value Systems of Persons with Varying Religious Orientations," *Journal for the Scientific Study of Religion* 10:357-65.

TAYLOR, EUGENE L. 1978. "Psychology of Religion and Asian Studies: The William James Legacy," *Journal of Transpersonal Psychology* 10:67-79.

TEELE, JAMES E. 1967. "Correlates of Voluntary Social Participation," *Genetic Psychology Monographs* 76:165-204.

TERRY, ROGER L. 1971. "Dependence, Nurturance and Monotheism: A Cross-cultural Study," *Journal of Social Psychology* 84:175-81.

THOMAS, L. EUGENE, AND PAMELA E. COOPER. 1978. "Measurement and Incidence of Mystical Experiences: An Exploratory Study, *Journal for the Scientific Study of Religion* 17:433-38.

THOMPSON, ANDREW D. 1974. "Open-mindedness and Indiscriminate Antireligious Orientation," *Journal for the Scientific Study of Religion* 13:471-77.

THOMSON, ROBERT. 1968. *The Pelican History of Psychology.* Baltimore: Penguin Books.

THOULESS, ROBERT H. 1956 (1924). *An Introduction to the Psychology of Religion.* Second edition. Cambridge: At the University Press.

TISDALE, JOHN R., editor. 1980. *The Growing Edges in the Psychology of Religion.* Chicago: Nelson-Hall.

TIWARI, CHAUHAN, AND GOVIND TIWARI. 1977. "Moral Judgment as a Function of Sex and Value-orientations," *Journal of Psychological Researches* 21:97-101.

TOULMIN, STEPHEN F. 1969. "Concepts and the Explanation of Human Behavior." In *Human Action: Conceptual and Empirical Issues.* Edited by Theodore Mischel. New York: Academic Press.

———. 1972. "Reasons and Causes." In *Explanation in the Behavioral Sciences.* Edited by R. Borger and F. Cioffi. Cambridge: At the University Press.

TROSMAN, HARRY. 1977. "After the Waste Land: Psychological Factors in the Religious Conversion of T. S. Eliot," *International Review of Psychoanalysis* 4:295–304.

TURNER, PAUL R. 1979. "Religious Conversion and Community Development," *Journal for the Scientific Study of Religion* 18:252–60.

TWEMLOW, S. W., AND W. T. BOWEN. 1977. "Sociocultural Predictors of Self-actualization in EEG-Biofeedback-Treated Alcoholics," *Psychological Reports* 40:591–98.

TYLER, LEONA. 1961. *The Work of the Counselor.* New York: Appleton-Century-Crofts.

ULEYN, ARNOLD. 1969. *Is It I, Lord? Pastoral Psychology and the Recognition of Guilt.* Translated by Mary Ilford. New York: Holt, Rinehart & Winston.

UNDERWOOD, RALPH L. 1975. "Cultural and Religious Implications of the Organismic Model in Psychology: A Reinterpretation of Abraham L. Maslow." Ph.D. Dissertation, University of Chicago.

UNGERLEIDER, J. THOMAS, AND DAVID K. WELLISCH. 1979. "Coercive Persuasion (Brainwashing), Religious Cults, and Deprogramming," *American Journal of Psychiatry* 136:279–82.

USUI, WAYNE, M.; TZUEN-JEN LEI; AND EDGAR W. BUTLER. 1977. "Patterns of Social Participation of Rural and Urban Migrants to an Urban Area," *Sociology and Social Research* 61:337–49.

VAN DER MEER, F. 1965. *Augustine the Bishop: Church and Society at the Dawn of the Middle Ages.* Translated by Brian Battershaw and G. R. Lamb. New York: Harper & Row.

VAN HERIK, JUDITH. 1982. *Freud on Femininity and Faith.* Berkeley: University of California Press.

VANDERPOOL, HAROLD Y. 1980. "Religion and Medicine: A Theoretical Overview," *Journal of Religion and Health* 19:9–17.

VANDERPOOL, JAMES A. 1977. *Person to Person: A Handbook of Christian Counseling.* Garden City, N.Y.: Doubleday.

VERGOTE, ANTOINE. 1969. *The Religious Man: A Psychological Study of Religious Attitudes.* Dayton, Ohio: Pflaum.

VERGOTE, ANTOINE, AND ALVARO TAMAYO. 1981. *The Parental Figures and the Representation of God: A Psychological and Cross-cultural Study.* New York: Mouton.

VERGOTE, ANTOINE, et al. 1969. "Concept of God and Parental Images," *Journal for the Scientific Study of Religion* 8:79–87.

VERNON, GLENN M. 1966. "Communication Between Theologians and Social Scientists in Research," *Review of Religious Research* 7:93–101.

————. 1974. "Dying as a Social-symbolic Process," *Humanitas* 10:21–32.

VINE, IAN. 1978. "Facts and Values in the Psychology of Religion," *Bulletin of the British Psychological Society* 31:414–17.

VRGA, DJURO J., AND FRANK FAHEY. 1971. "Political Ideology and Religious Factionalism," *Journal for the Scientific Study of Religion* 10:111–13.

VYGOTSKY, L. S. 1978. *Mind and Society: The Development of Higher Psychological Processes.* Edited by Michael Cole et al. Cambridge: Harvard University Press.

WALLACE, RUTH A. 1975. "A Model of Change of Religious Affiliation," *Journal for the Scientific Study of Religion* 14:345–55.

WALLIN, PAUL, AND ALEXANDER L. CLARK. 1964. "Religiosity, Sexual Gratification, and Marital Satisfaction in the Middle Years of Marriage," *Social Forces* 42:303–9.

WARD, COLLEEN A., AND MICHAEL BEAUBRUN. 1980. "Psychodynamics of Demon Possession," *Journal for the Scientific Study of Religion* 19:201–7.

————. 1979. "Trance Induction and Hallucination in Spiritualism: Baptist Mourning," *Journal of Psychological Anthropology* 2:479–88.

WARNER, REX, translator. 1963. *The Confessions of St. Augustine.* New York: Mentor Books.

WARREN, NEIL C. 1977. "Empirical Studies in the Psychology of Religion: An Assessment of the Period 1960–1970." In *Current Perspectives in the Psychology of Religion.* Edited by H. Newton Malony. Grand Rapids, Mich.: William B. Eerdmans.

WEARING, A. J., AND L. B. BROWN. 1972. "The Dimensionality of Religion," *British Journal of Social and Clinical Psychology* 11:143–48.

WEBER, CARLO A. 1970. *Pastoral Psychology: New Trends in Theory and Practice* New York: Sheed & Ward.

WEINER, ALAN S. 1977. "Cognitive and Social-emotional Development in Adolescence," *Journal of Pediatric Psychology* 2:87–92.

WESTENDORP, FLOYD. 1975. "The Value of Freud's Illusion," *Journal of Psychology and Theology* 3:82–89.

WHITE, JOHN, editor. 1972. *The Highest State of Consciousness.* New York: Anchor Books.

WHITEHEAD, PAUL C. 1970. "Religious Affiliation and Use of Drugs Among Adolescent Students," *Journal for the Scientific Study of Religion* 9:152–54.

WHITMONT, EDWARD C. 1969. *The Symbolic Quest: Basic Concepts of Analytical Psychology.* New York: Putnam's.

WILLIAMS, CYRIL G. 1981. *Tongues of the Spirit: A Study of Pentecostal Glossolalia and Related Phenomenon.* Cardiff: University of Wales Press.

WILLIAMS, ROBERT L. 1967. "Psychological Efficacy of Religiosity in Late Adolescence," *Psychological Reports* 20:926.

WILSON, JOHN. 1978. *Religion in American Society: the Effective Presence.* Englewood Cliffs, N.J.: Prentice-Hall.

WILSON, WARNER, AND HOWARD L. MILLER. 1968. "Fear, Anxiety, and Religiousness," *Journal for the Scientific Study of Religion* 7:111.

WIMBERLY, RONALD C., et al. 1975. "Conversion in a Billy Graham Crusade: Spontaneous Event or Ritual Performance?" *Sociological Quarterly* 16:162-70.

WINQUIST, CHARLES, AND DAVID WINZENZ. 1977. "Scientific Models and Symbolic Meanings in Altered States of Consciousness," *Journal of Drug Issues* 7:237-46.

WINTER, GIBSON. 1963. "Methodological Reflection on the 'Religious factor'," *Journal for the Scientific Study of Religion* 2:53-63.

WOLMAN, BENJAMIN B. 1967. "The Socio-psycho-somatic Theory of Schizophrenia," *Psychotherapy and Psychosomatics* 15:373-87.

WRITER, ALLAN W., AND ANNE MEHLER. 1971. "Assimilation of New Members in a Large and Small Church," *Journal of Applied Psychology* 52:151-56.

WUNDT, WILHELM. 1904 (1874). *Principles of Physiological Psychology.* New York: Macmillan.

WUTHNOW, ROBERT. 1981. "Two Traditions in the Study of Religion." *Journal for the Scientific Study of Religion* 20:16-32.

WUTHNOW, ROBERT; KEVIN CHRISTIANO; AND JOHN KUZLOWSKI. 1980. "Religion and Bereavement: A Conceptual Framework," *Journal for the Scientific Study of Religion* 19:408-22.

YABRUDI, PHILIP F., AND LUTFY N. DIAB. 1978. "The Effects of Similarity–Dissimilarity, Religion, and Topic Importance on Interpersonal Attraction Among Lebanese University Students," *Journal of Social Psychology* 106:167-71.

YALOM, IRVING D. 1975. *The Theory and Practice of Group Psychotherapy.* New York: Basic Books.

YEATTS, JOHN P., AND WILLIAM ASHER. 1979. "Can We Afford Not to Do True Experiments in the Psychology of Religion? A Reply to Batson," *Journal for the Scientific Study of Religion* 18:86-89.

YINGER, J. MILTON. 1970. *The Scientific Study of Religion.* New York: Macmillan.

YUFIT, ROBERT L. 1969. "Variations of Intimacy and Isolation," *Journal of Projective Techniques and Personality Assessment* 33:49–58.

ZABLOCKI, BENJAMIN. 1980. *Alienation and Charisma: A Study of Contemporary American Communes.* New York: Free Press.

Index